ED WOOD and the Lost LUGOSI Screenplays

Gary D. Rhodes

Designed by Michael Kronenberg

Printed in the United States

Published by BearManor Media
P. O. Box 71426
Albany, Georgia 31708
books@benohmart.com

Library of Congress Cataloguing-in-Publication Data
Rhodes, Gary D.
Ed Wood and the Lost Lugosi Screenplays / Gary D. Rhodes
p.cm.
ISBN 1-59393-920-5

1. Wood, Ed, 1924-1978.   2. Lugosi, Bela, 1882-1956.   I. Rhodes, Gary D.   II. Weaver, Tom.   III. Title.
PN1997.E33 A44

Editor's Note: Some images chosen for this book are of an imperfect quality, but they are reproduced herein due to their rarity and their importance to the narrative.

Dedicated

to

Buddy Barnett

and

Michael Copner

Table of Contents

Foreword

By Leo Eaton

When Gary Rhodes contacted me to ask if he might use something I wrote many years ago about Ed Wood Jr. as the foreword for this book, I thought how surprised but delighted Ed would have been to see the strange and quirky immortality he has achieved so long after his death. When Tim Burton's movie *Ed Wood* was released in 1994, people were suddenly talking about this cult director who had

a fetish for angora, sometimes wore miniskirts in public and had been called the "worst director of all time" for such epics as *Glen or Glenda, Plan 9 from Outer Space* and *Bride of the Monster.*

It was only after the movie came out that I began to wonder if this was the same man I'd worked with in Los Angeles more than two decades earlier. Over the years I'd often told stories of "this old drunk" who wore miniskirts and angora sweaters and said he'd worked with Bela Lugosi. But it was just party-chatter and I never even remembered his name. Only when the *Ed Wood* movie came out did I wonder: "Could this be the same guy?"

Sarah Jessica Parker and Johnny Depp in Tim Burton's *Ed Wood* (1994).

After I tracked down Rudolph Grey's book *Nightmare of Ecstasy: The Life and Art of Edward Wood Jr.*, I was amazed to see the time we worked together at an "adult" publishing house called Pendulum so well documented. My period at Pendulum (I think its official business name at the time was Calga Publishers, although many of the magazines came out under the Pendulum title) was one of those strange periods one falls into when young and wandering the world.

I'd left the UK in 1969 for Mexico and lived there until my money ran out, then hitch-hiked to Los Angeles in 1970 flat broke with just a couple of phone numbers for people I'd met in Mexico. One was a writer who wrote books for Bernie Bloom, the owner of Pendulum Publishing. Knowing I needed a job, my friend introduced us. Bernie asked if I knew how to edit magazines (I didn't but of course said I did) and he hired me. For a green kid new to America, working for Pendulum was like Alice having falling down the rabbit hole.

Ed Wood was one of four writers Bernie employed at that time to write copy for the range of adult magazines Pendulum put out each month. Ed was at least twenty years older than the rest of us; a big gap when one's in one's twenties. We "young Turks" (as we called ourselves) saw Pendulum as only a stepping stone to fame and fortune as "real" writers but Ed seemed to be there for the duration. I find it strange to realize he was only in his mid-forties at the time, although the booze was already taking its toll. He had a reputation for being a mean drunk but I remember him as kind and gentle. He'd always help out when one of the younger writers was stuck on a story or article.

There were many different magazine titles in use at that time; the soft-core and hard-core pornographic magazines coming under different names. The four of us had a range of writing duties, creating the "case studies" that went with the picture layouts as well as one or more articles and a piece of fiction per magazine. Since nobody cared (readers bought the magazines for the pictures), we'd have fun with them. I was into sci-fi at the time so I wrote a lot of straight sci-fi short stories; totally out of keeping with the magazines but nobody ever complained.

We writers were off on one side of the West Pico building, down a corridor cut off from the rest of the building by an electric lock. Pendulum was set up just like a factory. We all had time cards and we were required to punch in and out every day. Bernie Bloom said that he hired his writers to write. If he was paying for eight hours, that's how long he expected us to write. We young Turks would be out of our cells (the windowless offices where the writers lived) in the corridor, playing "push-pins" (our version of darts) when we'd hear the "click" of the electric lock and immediately scurry back to our electric typewriters and start banging away. Often it was Bernie, ushering some visitor through with the sweeping explanation, "These are my writers." Heaven help us if he didn't hear all four typewriters clattering away in unison on such occasions.

I'd been told police raids were a regular occurrence but I remember only one during my time at Pendulum. Coming in the main entrance from Pico Boulevard, there was a small vestibule with a window-hatch through which one could talk to the receptionist. A door with an electric lock closing off the rest of the building could only be opened when the receptionist tripped the switch. On the police raid

Edward D. Wood, Jr.
(Courtesy of George Chastain)

I experienced, they refused to wait until the receptionist opened the door, instead climbing in through the hatch and scaring everyone in the front office. We all kept our heads down in the back and tried to ignore the shouting and banging.

What do I remember most about Ed Wood? The tragedy is, not nearly enough. Yes, he sometimes wore mini-skirts around the office and he often wore his trademark angora sweaters. He was certainly the first transvestite I'd ever met. But we never took him seriously. We liked him well enough but he was a figure of fun, just a washed-up old drunk. While he talked about the movies he'd made, and about working with Bela Lugosi, I'm ashamed to say I didn't really believe him. Youth can be very cruel.

Ed seldom joined us out in the corridor for our push-pin tournaments; he'd just write away in his tiny windowless office. I suspect he disapproved of the lack of seriousness with which we took our job. He certainly dis-

Ed Wood in the 1970s with author Richard Bojarski. *(Courtesy of Roger Hurlburt)*

approved of our attitude towards the books that Bernie expected us to write outside office hours. In addition to the princely sum of $200 a week I was paid as a Pendulum staff writer, we were all encouraged to write a book a month in our spare time, for which we were paid an additional $800-$1000. While the books could be fiction, what Bernie really wanted was pseudo-scientific factual books that could be illustrated with hard-core pictures.

We used pseudonyms on all the books and magazines and it's been said that Dr. T. K. Peters was one of Ed Wood's. But this poor man really existed. Pendulum had bought a serious, boring and excruciatingly long scientific study of sexuality from Dr. T. K. Peters. It was an unpublished manuscript that the doctor had probably labored on for years without finding a buyer (he was a Kinsey-style researcher). I hate to think what he was paid – probably peanuts – but he was very old (semi-senile was the word around the office) and he'd let it go without realizing what use would be made of it. The manuscript gave Bernie a sort of "semi-legitimacy" for the books and magazine articles and we were all encouraged to make use of it whenever and wherever possible. Adding Dr. Peters' name as co-writer added a spurious legitimacy.

While we liked the extra money from writing the books, none of us (except maybe Ed) liked the idea of spending our free time writing them, especially since people only bought them for the pictures. Before I joined Pendulum, the younger writers had developed a unique short-cut, dipping into the files for magazine articles that had been written a year or more before, collecting seven or eight together, then rewriting the first paragraph of each to fit a new generic title. Such a "new" manuscript was then sent straight down to typesetting. I think the record for 'writing' a 'new' non-fiction book was an hour. Eight hundred bucks is certainly good money for an hour's work! Ed used to disapprove strongly and always wrote his manuscripts completely, although he too culled heavily from the T. K. Peters material. Apparently the scam was discovered some months after I'd left Pendulum and at least one of my fellow writers was fired.

Because I'd been in the British film industry before coming to America, Ed clearly found me more of a kindred spirit than my other colleagues, once even taking me shopping with him. He needed a new bra and what surprised me most was that the sales girl was totally unfazed as he tried on a variety of different colors and

Artwork by Stephen B. Whatley. *(Courtesy of Stephen B. Whatley)*

shapes. I guess Los Angeles sales girls in 1970 were far more used to transvestites than I was.

We tended not to socialize much outside the office, although the four of us went to lunch several days a week (there was a little dive just up the road on Pico that had the best Spanish hot dogs I've ever tasted) and sometimes met for a drink in the evening. But before I left Los Angeles to return to Mexico (working at Pendulum had restocked my depleted finances), Ed invited me home for dinner. I remember little about the evening except my surprise that Kathy, his wife, was so nice and normal.

I left Pendulum and for many years afterwards the old guy who wore miniskirts and angora sweaters and made films with Bela Lugosi was a cocktail-party story, even though I couldn't remember his name. After Tim Burton's film was released, everyone knew his name and I find myself regretting all those wasted opportunities. I wish I'd been kinder, wish I'd spent more time with him, wish I'd asked the questions that, in hindsight, we would all like to ask Ed Wood Jr. I'm reminded of a quote from a Hollywood producer in the introduction to Rudolph Grey's book, *Nightmare of Ecstasy*: "The really funny thing is that here is this alcoholic, this old bum that I really liked, and all the time I never knew that he was something special."

The increasing array of articles and books that have come out since Tim Burton's film twenty years ago are revealing even more about Ed's work and times, and increasing numbers of people around the world are discovering his unique way of being "something special." I hope you enjoy *Ed Wood and the Lost Lugosi Screenplays* as another insight into a remarkable man whose constant optimism about everything he wrote and filmed, no matter how ill-founded, made even disaster triumphant. I am grateful to have known him and been his friend, if only for a short while.

Unfinished Symphonies

The Vampire's Tomb and The Ghoul Goes West

A Non-Production Background

By Gary D. Rhodes

The Amazing Criswell, self-proclaimed Nostradamus of the twentieth century, became famous in the 1950s and '60s thanks to his broadcasts on radio and television. Decades later, he is best known for having appeared in a trio of Edward D. Wood, Jr. movies: *Plan 9 from Outer Space* (1958), *Night of the Ghouls* (1958) and *Orgy of the Dead* (1965).

Criswell predicted many things: A "dude-and-nude" ranch would open somewhere in the Midwest in 1966; corpses would be compressed into cubes rather than being buried in 1976 due to a real estate shortage; flying saucers would land on the White House lawn on May 6, 1991; the world as we know it would end on August 18, 1999.

None of these predictions came to pass. Nor did most of Criswell's other divinations, many of them equally or more outlandish. Criswell focused on the future, because – as he famously heralded over and over again – "that is where you and I are going to spend the rest of our lives, whether we want to or not." At least in public, Criswell was not interested in the past, including his past mistakes.

What if these events had occurred? Cowboys might be saddle-sore, cemeteries might be bankrupt, and the aliens who relocated to 1600 Pennsylvania Avenue would not have partied like it was 1999 when the world ended.

The lure of the "What If" can be strong, particularly if we oscillate away from Criswell to other, more important subjects. What if JFK had not been assassinated? What if there had been no war in Vietnam? What if the Water-gate break-in hadn't taken place? The world would be different, extremely different. It isn't, but *what if* it was?

Film history percolates with fascinating examples of this type, one after the other. What if Irving Thalberg had not died at the young age of 37? What if *Citizen Kane* had been a hit movie on its original 1941 release? What if Ronald Reagan had starred in *Casablanca* (1942) instead of Humphrey Bogart?

The same can be said of the horror movie. What if *Nosferatu* (1922) had not been banned due to copyright infringement? What if *Frankenstein* had been made into a 1927 film with Lon Chaney, as was announced in the trade press? What if Bela Lugosi had played the Monster in *Frankenstein* (1931) instead of Boris Karloff?

Scientists and logicians refer to such thinking as counterfactual, and rightly so, because here is a world potentially as strange as that which Criswell predicted, one that tries to bring into sharp relief events that never took place. Here is a speculative enterprise, one that operates outside of serious historiographical research and its methodologies. After all, that which did not happen did not happen.

"Can you prove that it didn't happen?" Criswell notably asked at the end of *Plan 9 from Outer Space*, a film some viewers have dubbed the worst movie ever made. But the question is not without merit. Sometimes that which did not happen *did* happen, if only to a limited extent.

Consider Ed Wood's unmade projects for an aging and financially strapped Bela Lugosi in the period between circa 1952 and 1956. There were many of them, perhaps even more than historians have uncovered. Two have reached legendary proportions: *The Vampire's Tomb* and *The Ghoul Goes West* (aka *The Phantom Ghoul*). Such films would not only have provided much-needed income for Lugosi, but also the potential for a comeback. Likewise, they could have transformed Wood into a mainstream writer-director, one who might have worked on major movies, or at least reputable B-movies. But they were never produced. They didn't happen.

Except that they did, at least insofar as scripts that were written and rewritten, scripts that still survive and that are reproduced in this volume. And then there is the fact that these scripts became the basis of all manner of get-togethers with would-be investors and consultations with the intended cast members.

But more than just typed pages and now-forgotten meetings, *The Vampire's Tomb* and *The Ghoul Goes West* became something real, even if ethereal. For a period of time, the two projects represented hope to various persons involved, including Ed Wood and Bela Lugosi. Rather than being counterfactual fantasy, these two proj-

ects did exist, and do survive in various respects, not only in their scripts, but also in press accounts of the 1950s and in the memories of those involved.

Meaningfully or not, we can ponder such "What If"s as the effect these two scripts might have had on the lives of the participants had they been translated onto the silver screen. But more importantly, we should consider that – much as unfinished symphonies exist, even if in an incomplete form — unmade films also exist, even if not captured on celluloid, and their stories deserve to be heard, even if just in the auditoria of our minds.

Doppelgängers

As different as the two men were, Ed Wood and Bela Lugosi were both in desperate need of work in 1952. With Wood's youthful charm and good looks, a film career might have seemed assured. And then there was the aging charm and good looks of Bela Lugosi, who had made one major comeback into the Hollywood spotlight (in the late '30s) after a period of inactivity. He was angling for another in 1952.

As noted in the *Los Angeles Times* in December 1951, "[H]orror movies have been scarce of late, unless you broaden the term 'horror.'" At roughly the same time, Lugosi returned from a disastrous tour of *Dracula–The Vampire Play* in Great Britain and Northern Ireland. At one performance, only three ticket-buyers appeared. Lugosi later wrote his friend Lyman Brown, "the 8 month job in England certainly took the skids from under me. I never want to go through a spell like that again."

Lugosi's career had been on the downswing since 1945, but until leaving for England in 1951, he had managed to stay consistently busy with live appearances, vaudeville sketches, nightclub acts and spook shows. Though he starred in only two movies during those years, he did play in summer stock every season from 1947 through 1950. After the British tour, all of this kind of work in America dried up.

His only new movie after returning from England was for Jack Broder Productions: *White Woman of the Lost Jungle*, which was retitled *Bela Lugosi Meets the Gorilla Man* and then, finally, *Bela Lugosi Meets a Brooklyn Gorilla* (1952). Co-starring Duke Mitchell and Sammy Petrillo – a comedy team that imitated Dean Martin and Jerry Lewis – the film seemed cheaper and more ridiculous than just about any Lugosi had made up until that point. Audience

SPACEWAY
SCIENCE FICTION

35c
FEB. '55

CRISWELL PREDICTS ON OUTER SPACE
A. E. VAN VOGT ON DIANETICS

Criswell Predicts on the cover of a February 1955 magazine.
(Courtesy of George Chastain)

response varied, with *Boxoffice* publishing the following reports:

> Did about as much business as a new Bowery Boys show. Billed it with a Rex Allen.
> — Rochester, Pennsylvania, December 13, 1952

> This was a cute sleeper. Despite a basketball game and a church festival, we did well. Played this up in advance and got the whole town arguing whether or not "Sammy" was Jerry Lewis. They liked it.
> — Riversville, West Virginia, June 13, 1953

> This is one of the poorest we have played in ages. ... No sense to the picture at all. Record walk-out crowd. Pleased only those with low intelligence.
> — Spring Valley, Illinois, February 13, 1954

When asked about the movie in 1952, Lugosi said that it would be good publicity, given that his name was in the title. His prediction proved no more accurate than most of Criswell's. No film work followed.

More than anything else, Lugosi's major competition was himself. It would be easy to examine his sparse filmography in the late '40s and early '50s and presume that he was absent from the screen, but that conclusion would be quite mistaken. Between 1947 and 1952, old Lugosi movies were re-released in large numbers, meaning that Lugosi the Actor was on the screen with much regularity, even if Lugosi the Man wasn't reaping any financial rewards as a result.

These Lugosi revivals were hardly unique in the period. As the *New York Times* wrote on February 16, 1947, the trend of reissuing old films was on the rise, Lugosi's *Dracula* (1931) being but one of many. A survey conducted in New York concluded that, of 211 features being screened on a recent date, a surprising 125 were revivals.

The success of such reissues brought even more of the same in 1948. In February of that year, *The Hollywood*

Reporter announced that 130 re-releases were scheduled, the "greatest number of repeats for a single year's program in motion picture distribution history." The practice continued in 1949, despite warnings from some in the industry that reissues would cause more problems than they solved.

Jack Broder, producer of *Bela Lugosi Meets a Brooklyn Gorilla*, was responsible for many of the Lugosi reissues. He was president of Realart Pictures, which Universal formed to re-release their old films. And, thanks to other companies, Lugosi's Monogram films of the war era also

Advertisement published in the *Evening Times* (Cumberland, Maryland) on October 26, 1951.

Advertisement published in the *Nashua Telegraph* (Nashua, New Hampshire) on April 12, 1951.

returned to the screen. The following breakdown provides a partial list of the Lugosi films screened in the postwar era:

1947: *Dracula* (1931), *The Black Cat* (1934), *Phantom Ship* (1937, aka *The Mystery of the Mary Celeste*, 1935), *The Human Monster* (aka *The Dark Eyes of London*, 1939), *Black Friday* (1940), *The Devil Bat* (1940), *The Black Cat* (1941), *Bowery at Midnight* (1942), *The Corpse Vanishes* (1942), *Ghosts on the Loose* (1943), *The Ape Man* (1943), *Return of the Ape Man* (1944), *Voodoo Man* (1944).

1948: *Dracula, White Zombie* (1932), *Son of Fran-*

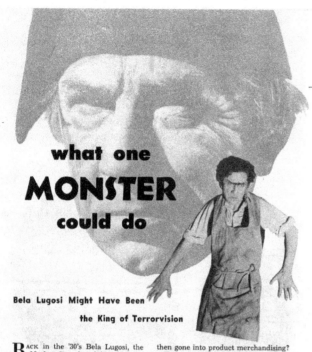

what one MONSTER could do

Bela Lugosi Might Have Been the King of Terrorvision

BACK in the '30's Bela Lugosi, the Marlon Brando of his day (he worked in a ripped straitjacket), made more horror pictures than a near-sighted Boy Scout with a water-logged Brownie.

Epics with names like *The Bride of Dracula Meets Frankenstein's Chiropodist, The Ghouls of Goolie-Goolie,* and *Professor Zorch's Invisible Meat-Cleaver* kept audiences from coast to coast on the edge of their seats. Which is why today so many houses suffer from Orchestra Sag.

Had Mr. Lugosi foreseen television and bought up his movies as Bill (Hopalong) Boyd did, he too would be making a fortune. The rental rights would be stupendous. But what if Lugosi had packaged all his pictures into a series like *Hopalong Cassidy* and

then gone into product merchandising? He might have called the series *This Is Your Death.* It could have featured Leeralong Lugosi, his wonder-monster Rigor, his trained dragon Mortis, and his blood-sucking sweetheart, Corpuscle Kate.

Just think of the merchandise tie-ins some smart business manager could have arranged for him! Such as:

Lugosi Cigarettes: One puff and poof!

Lugosi-Cola: More blood to the ounce.

Lugosi Sports Jackets: Hand stitched —that is, with the hands left on.

Lugosi Coffee: It lets you sleep . . . forever.

Lugosi Liniment: Guaranteed to rub you the wrong way—out.

And think of all the sponsors Bela

A-6

could have interested in his series. Tombstone makers . . . your local iodine bottler . . . rope manufacturers . . . agents for haunted houses.

Monsters of both sexes would feel they had a program they could write to.

Mental torture, now so popular in divorce cases, would become a thing of the past, and good old physical torture would come into its own again.

In fact, Lugosi might even be doing a live television show today. It would be telecast from the Vampire State building. Title? How about *Bride and Goon?* Or what do you suggest?—HERB RIKLES.

* * *

BELA LUGOSI, butt of the spoofing above, was born in Lugos, Hungary, October 29, 1884, the son of a baron. Bela attended high school and the Academy of Theatrical Art in Budapest.

At 20, he played Romeo in Shakespeare's love drama, then went on to establish himself as one of the Continent's better actors. He came to New York in 1921 and acted in four plays, gaining stature with each. His fifth role was that of the Count in Bram Stoker's chiller, *Dracula.*

Lugosi went on to star in the film version of that play. His name has conjured up things macabre ever since. He made a fortune playing bogey men but lost it when the market on menace crashed, albeit temporarily.

After three years, during which he worked a total of eight weeks, he got a new lease on his career. The manager of a tiny Hollywood movie house wanted him to appear in person at a revival showing of *Dracula.* Lugosi accepted and packed the house at each performance.

Other similar offers poured in, and then a call came from Universal for him to play in *Son of Frankenstein. The Wolf Man* and *The Return of the Vampire* are but two of the many horror movies in which he's appeared since his "comeback."

Lugosi is 6-feet-1 and weighs 178 pounds. He has blue eyes and his hair, once dark brown, is now grey. He has a son, Bela George, 15. Lugosi was recently divorced from his wife after a 20-year marriage. He makes his home in Hollywood.

A-7

From *TV Guide* of August 1953.

kenstein (1939), *Black Friday, The Devil Bat, The Wolf Man* (1941), *The Black Cat* (1941), *The Ghost of Frankenstein* (1942), *The Ape Man, Ghosts on the Loose, Return of the Ape Man, Voodoo Man, The Body Snatcher* (1945).

1949: *Dracula, Murders in the Rue Morgue* (1932), *White Zombie, The Raven* (1935), *The Invisible Ray* (1936), *Son of Frankenstein, The Black Cat* (1941), *Invisible Ghost* (1941), *Spooks Run Wild* (1941), *Black Dragons* (1942), *Bowery at Midnight, The Corpse Vanishes, The Ghost of Frankenstein, The Ape Man, Frankenstein Meets the Wolf Man* (1943), *Ghosts on the Loose, Voodoo Man, The Body Snatcher, Scared to Death* (1947).

1950: *Murders in the Rue Morgue, White Zombie, The Mysterious Mr. Wong* (1935), *The Raven, The Invisible*

Ray, The Gorilla (1939), *Son of Frankenstein, Black Friday, The Devil Bat, The Black Cat* (1941), *Invisible Ghost, Spooks Run Wild, The Wolf Man, Black Dragons, Bowery at Midnight, The Corpse Vanishes, The Ghost of Frankenstein, Night Monster* (1942), *The Ape Man, Frankenstein Meets the Wolf Man, Ghosts on the Loose, Return of the Ape Man, Voodoo Man, Zombies on Broadway* (1945), *Scared to Death.*

1951: *Murders in the Rue Morgue, White Zombie, The Death Kiss* (1933), *The Mysterious Mr. Wong, The Raven, The Invisible Ray, Son of Frankenstein, The Human Monster, Black Friday, The Devil Bat, The Black Cat* (1941), *Invisible Ghost, Spooks Run Wild, The Wolf Man, Black Dragons, Bowery at Midnight, The Corpse Vanishes, The Ghost of Frankenstein, Night Monster, The Ape Man, Frankenstein Meets the Wolf Man, Ghosts on the Loose, The Return of the Vampire*

(1943), *Return of the Ape Man, Voodoo Man, The Body Snatcher, Scared to Death.*

Ironically, given that Lugosi had such difficulty finding new roles, newspaper ads for some of these films often gave him better billing than he received in them on-screen. In fact, Lugosi appeared on theater screens so regularly during those years that his name was even used at times in publicity for old horror movies in which he did *not* appear, including *Bride of Frankenstein* (1935), *Son of Dracula* (1943), *House of Frankenstein* (1944) and *House of Dracula* (1945).

These reissues continued in 1952, the year in which Lugosi first met Ed Wood. Adjacent to a theater manager report on *Bela Lugosi Meets a Brooklyn Gorilla* in December 1952, *Boxoffice* published one that described response to a double feature of *Dracula* (1931) and *Frankenstein* (1931): "These will do as much business as a weak 'A' picture and cost a lot less." And for Lugosi, the sting of England continued. In December 1952, Jack Broder acquired distribution rights to Lugosi's old British-made film *The Dark Eyes of London* for reissue through Realart.

Not surprisingly, given their numbers, audience response to at least some of these films was strong. After screening *The Body Snatcher* (1945) in 1954, a happy theater manager in Tarboro, North Carolina, wrote to *Boxoffice* claiming, "If this old one won't scare them, they're unscareable!" But strong ticket sales hardly helped Lugosi's hopes for a comeback.

Indeed, these re-releases plagued Lugosi until the time of his death. Consider Boston in December 1955. *Dracula* appeared on-screen, as did a double feature of *Murders in the Rue Morgue* (1932) and *The Mummy* (1932, a film that did not feature Lugosi), as well as a double feature of *The Black Cat* (1941) and *House of Horrors* (1946, another non-Lugosi film), all during the same month. Then, in Los Angeles in January 1956, a Los Angeles theater in scheduled a "Horrorama Week" of 14 old movies, five of them starring Lugosi.

That's to say nothing of the regularity with which his films appeared on television starting in the late '40s and throughout the '50s. Initially, these were his B-movies, specifically his work for Monogram, PRC, Imperial-Cameo and Victory. But in 1954, Fox's *The Black Camel* (1931) – a Charlie Chan mystery with Lugosi – was first broadcast. That same year, RKO released three of his movies to TV: *Zombies on Broadway* (1945), *The Body Snatcher* (1945), and *Genius at Work* (1946).

Even *Bela Lugosi Meets a Brooklyn Gorilla* was made available for TV broadcast in 1953, while it could still be rented from film exchanges for theatrical screenings. By May 1954, New York's WCBS had played the movie. (The Screen Actors Guild was hardly pleased, given that it was produced after 1948 and none of the actors had been paid for it to be broadcast on TV.)

Lugosi on the large *and* small screens was ubiquitous, so much so that *TV Guide* in 1953 published a two-page article about how unfortunate it was that Lugosi did not retain the rights to his many films then making late-night TV reappearances.

All of these reasons likely made Lugosi happy to meet Edward D. Wood Jr. Wood didn't want to project old Lugosi films. He wanted to make new Lugosi films, one after another. He wanted to help Lugosi's career, and by extension he wanted to help his own.

Angora Pictures

Ed Wood remains infamous, but Alex Gordon is little known outside of a coterie of devoted horror film buffs. Alex and his brother Richard grew up as horror film fans in England during the '30s; in 1948, soon after their migration to America, they went out of their way to meet Bela Lugosi. By 1952, Alex was vice-president of Renown Pictures of America.

In February of that year, he went to Hollywood for a four-week stay to negotiate some deals for Renown. But his month-long trip became a permanent relocation. By June 1952, Gordon was executive producer on a Western that eventually became *The Lawless Rider* (1954). Its cast

Angora's Six New Horrors

NEW YORK—Six horror melodramas are to be produced by Alexander Gordon, president of Angora Pictures, in association with Edward D. Wood jr. The first will be "The Atomic Monster," starring Bela Lugosi, with Helen Gilbert in the feminine lead. Production is due to begin July 20. It will be followed by "Doctor Voodoo," based on stories about a black magic sex cult. All six screenplays have been written by Gordon and Wood.

From *Boxoffice* of July 5, 1952.

Edward D. Wood, Jr.

included Bud Osborne, who would later play "Mac" in *Bride of the Monster* (1956). Gordon also met Ed Wood. The two became friends, roommates and collaborators on several projects intended for Lugosi.

In his *Fangoria* magazine column "The Pit and the Pen," Alex remembered:

> One night in the early '50s, Eddie [Wood], Bela Lugosi and I sat in Lugosi's tiny one-room apartment on Hollywood's Carlton Way. ... Now Bela sat in front of the life-size oil painting showing him in an early stage role and lit a cigar. 'We may have some good news, Bela,' I told him. 'Eddie and I have three scripts for you, and I'm meeting with [financier] Eliot Hyman next week to try and set them up.'
>
> [My] brother, producer Richard Gordon...pitched Hyman for me to produce a duo of low-budget horror films with Lugosi as star. Eddie and I had come

up with *Doctor Voodoo, The Vampire's Tomb* and *The Phantom Ghoul.*

Gordon added that *Doctor Voodoo* was "designed" to pair Lugosi and Boris Karloff. He also said that he "found Eddie easy to collaborate with, but hard to pin down at the typewriter. He had charm and an eye for the girls, and it was no easy job to get those pages out of him."

A July 5, 1952, article in the industry trade *Boxoffice* paired Lugosi and Wood's names for the very first time:

> Six horror melodramas are to be produced by Alexander Gordon, president of Angora Pictures, in association with Edward D. Wood Jr. The first will be *The Atomic Monster* starring Bela Lugosi, with Helen Gilbert in the feminine lead. Production is due to begin July 20. ...All six screenplays have been written by Gordon and Wood.

Whether or not Gordon realized it at the time, Wood was a transvestite, his favorite fabric being angora, hence the name of their new company.

On July 8, 1952, Erskine Johnson's syndicated column told newspaper readers something akin to *Boxoffice*'s announcement: "A new cycle of horror movies, as Lon Chaney predicted, is about to hit the sound stages. Alex Gordon, an independent producer, will star Bela Lugosi and Helen Gilbert in *An* [sic] *Atomic Monster*. Gordon's also planning *Doctor Voodoo, The Vampire's Tomb* and *The Zombie's Curse*."

Where did Angora Pictures hope to get its money? In May 1952, the press announced that producer George Minter intended to reteam Lugosi with Boris Karloff in two films in England. Gordon and Minter knew one another, and so Minter may have been the first person that Gordon and Wood approached for backing.

At any rate, Alex most definitely approached Allied Artists with the projects. He later told historian Tom Weaver:

> I had written a script, before I came out to Hollywood, called *The Atomic Monster*, which I intended for Boris Karloff, and a second script, which I thought Bela Lugosi might do. One day I said to Sam Arkoff, 'Let's see if we can set these two pictures up.' So we went to Allied Artists; this was

Alex Gordon (right) with actor Frank Lackteen.

1953. We went there, and who would be there but of course Steve Broidy, and Broidy said, 'Let me read the scripts. The idea of a Karloff and a Lugosi film, after all this time, is not a bad idea.'

He probably had Ben Schwalb read the scripts, but anyway, he called us back in again, and he said, 'I tell you what: I think that the second picture needs somebody in addition to Bela Lugosi. How 'bout Lon Chaney Jr.?' I said, 'All right, so one picture with Boris Karloff and one with Lugosi and Lon Chaney Jr.?' and he said yes. 'But,' he said, 'your credits are not good enough for you to produce the pictures. You have to get somebody to be like an executive producer, to physically produce 'em, and you can be associate producer.'

So, who would I get to help me rewrite the scripts but Eddie Wood. He wasn't going to be associated with the production, but we were rewriting these two scripts together.

Here Gordon's memory seems at odds with the "Angora Pictures" story published in *Boxoffice* in 1952, which clearly indicates Wood would have been involved in the production phase; that, or at a given point in 1953,

Gordon tried to move ahead without him.

At any rate, Gordon continued this version of the story by recalling that Lugosi and Chaney readily agreed to appear, and that Karloff – pending some script rewrites – was amenable as well. But new problems emerged:

Broidy said, 'Well, y'know, I've been thinking this over. I think I would prefer to have one picture with all three of 'em in it, rather than two separate pictures.' I said, 'Oh my God, that's gonna be really tough for me. Karloff already agreed to do this low-budget script, but now he and Lugosi together again, and Chaney … it's rather awkward.' He said, 'Well, that's what you need to do. And don't forget, you gotta get an executive producer.'

Gordon said that the one script to go forward would have been *The Atomic Monster*, which eventually became *Bride of the Monster*.

Remembering his return visit to Karloff, informing him that Broidy would only okay a single film teaming all three stars, Gordon said:

Karloff sort of became very thoughtful, and he said, 'Well, they really want me and Bela together again…' And I said, 'Yes, Boris. I don't know how you feel

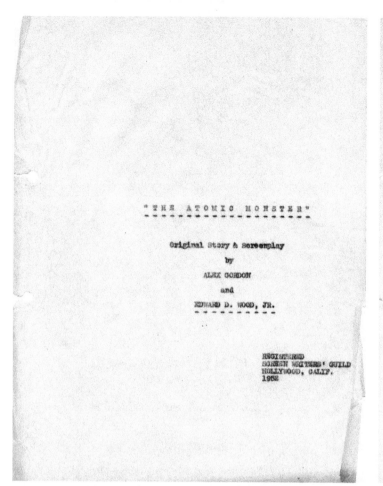

"THE ATOMIC MONSTER"

Original Story & Screenplay
by
ALEX GORDON
and
EDWARD D. WOOD, JR.

REGISTERED
SCREEN WRITERS' GUILD
HOLLYWOOD, CALIF.
1952

"THE ATOMIC MONSTER"

CAST OF CHARACTERS

1. DOCTOR ERIC VORNOFF –
   distinguished scientist,
   now outlawed and hunted........ Mr. BORIS KARLOFF

2. POLICE LIEUT. DICK CRAIG –
   young detective, the hero .....

3. JANET GRAYSON – beautiful blonde
   newspaper reporter, heroine ... HELEN GILBERT

4. INSPECTOR TOM ROBBINS – tough but
   friendly, Dick's boss ....

5. PROFESSOR STROWSKI – bearded
   scientist from a foreign power.

6. LOBO – mute giant, Vornoff's slave .

7. TILLIE – young brunette newspaper
   morgue attendant ....

8. JAKE, a hunter in the jungle ....

9. MAC, another hunter, his companion .

10. MARTIN – Dick's police assistant ...

11. SERGEANT CASEY, jovial Irishman ....

12. NEWSPAPER BOY (bit part) ....

13. POLICE DRIVER (silent bit) ....

NOTE: See descriptions in story of various characters.
JANET should have long blonde hair at all times.
STROWSKI should have a small beard.
LOBO is a mute half-naked giant with bald head.

Title page from an early script draft of *The Atomic Monster*. *(Courtesy of Bambi Everson)*

Early cast list for *The Atomic Monster*, with Boris Karloff proposed as Dr. Eric Vornoff. *(Courtesy of Bambi Everson)*

about it, but…that's the only basis on which he will go.' And he said, 'Well, all right. Bela and I have always worked well together. I'm willing to do it.'

Gordon detected a slight hesitation on Karloff's part, followed by Karloff's admission that he felt "sorry for Bela," that "he could really use the money; he just hasn't done much lately." By contrast, Gordon recalled the financially strapped Lugosi immediately approving the change of plans. "There was no animosity" on either side, Gordon underscored.

With the actors on board for Broidy's one-picture plan, Gordon then attempted to locate a producer. He told Tom Weaver:

So through [Richard Gordon], we approached Hal Roach, who expressed a little interest but then really didn't want to get into any horror stuff, and was sort of semi-retired and hard of hearing and all of that.

[Then Richard] said, well, he could get Eliot Hyman.

Eliot Hyman was the head of Seven Arts Pictures… He said he wouldn't physically be there [on the set], but he would have a representative, but he would put his name on it if that's what Allied Artists insisted [on]. But at the very last moment, although Hyman actually met with Broidy and Broidy agreed to this, Hyman backed out.

So then I had to have Ford Beebe rework the scripts. We thought Ford Beebe, who had a good record in low-budget pictures and horror films, would be like the producer-director and I could be the executive producer. Beebe wrote the scripts, and then Broidy cancelled the whole deal, never paid Ford Beebe anything, which I thought was a disgrace. I certainly didn't have the money to pay him. It was 7500 bucks per script, and that whole thing collapsed.

It is difficult to pinpoint exactly when this turn of events transpired. Presumably it was 1953, but what does seem clear is that Gordon's involvement in these projects began to lessen as Wood increasingly took the reins.

Steve Broidy of Allied Artists, pictured here with an unidentified child.

Un-Allied Artists

A handful of unmade Lugosi projects of the '50s did not involve Ed Wood or Alex Gordon. For example, in 1953, producer J. Arthur Rank intended to make *The Return of the White Zombie* with Lugosi. It never moved into production.

Then in January 1954, Hedda Hopper's column announced, "Double horror! Bela Lugosi and Sonny Tufts co-star in the same picture, *Oui, Oui, Paree*, and in a TV series, *Robinson Crusoe on Mars*." One month later, the press reported that Lugosi would appear in a "Bowery Kids pic," which became – without Lugosi's involvement – *The Bowery Boys Meet the Monsters* (1954).

But Wood's projects remain the best known. Not only was *The Vampire's Tomb* mentioned in Erskine Johnson's 1952 newspaper article, but the surviving copy herein also claims that it was registered with the Screen Writers Guild in 1951. Literary agent and horror movie collector Forrest J Ackerman knew Lugosi from 1953 to 1956. He later recalled:

During the three years before Bela's death, I met Ed Wood and became his literary agent. I recall one luncheon in Hollywood at a little eatery that doesn't exist any more – I think it was called the Nickodell – and there Ed Wood and Criswell … perhaps Dolores Fuller and Conrad Brooks, and perhaps a couple other of Wood's coterie (except Bela) discussed various Wood projects, one of which was

to be a vampire film – I believe *Tomb of the Vampire*. I suggested Bela would be welcome to use my pun name, Dr. Acula. Ed thought the idea was great….

Here is a clear indication that – even if the first draft of *The Vampire's Tomb* was written in 1951 – its character name for Lugosi changed as a result of Ackerman's suggestion. (As an aside, it is worth noting that "Dr. Dracula" had been a villain in a 1941 issue of *Silver Streak Comics*.)

By mid-1953, the same year that he completed *Glen or Glenda* starring Lugosi, Wood began pushing *The Ghoul Goes West* under the title *The Phantom Ghoul*, a project that he hoped would also feature Lon Chaney Jr. in the role of a dude ranch foreman. On July 20, 1953, Wood wrote Lugosi about the project:

As you have surmised, during the over two years in which we have been close friends, I have been trying to come up with a story which would deserve your fine talent. I think now I have that story in a thing called *The Phantom Ghoul*, which I plan to start in 3/D Wide Screen production within the next few weeks.

I know in our many get-to-gethers [sic] and telephone conversations during the last few weeks I

Forrest J Ackerman and Bela Lugosi. *(Courtesy of Ronald V. Borst and Hollywood Movie Posters)*

A page from Dr. Dracula's appearance in _Silver Streak Comics_ 17 (1941).

You Asked for It, hosted by Art Baker. The episode aired on the West Coast on July 27 and then on the East Coast on August 9:

> **Lugosi:** There are a few things coming up. The first is a three-dimensional motion picture called *The Phantom Ghoul*. And the second is a television series, which will be produced by Ted Allan and called *Dr. Acula*.
>
> **Baker:** *Dracula*?
>
> **Lugosi:** For Heaven's sake, no! Just Dr. Acula. [*Laughs*]
>
> **Baker:** I see.

The mention of *Dr. Acula* not only suggests that Wood was also planning a TV series using the same character name that he incorporated into *The Vampire's Tomb* (if not, indeed, the very same character), but it also suggests that the meeting with Ackerman likely occurred sometime during the first half of 1953, if not earlier.

Alex Gordon wrote that Samuel Z. Arkoff "liked the idea of *The Phantom Ghoul*, but Lugosi was having health problems and it seemed impossible to get insurance on him." Exactly when Arkoff expressed interest is unknown, though Gordon's use of the *Phantom Ghoul* title (as opposed to *The Ghoul Goes West*) could mean this anecdote dates to 1953.

Nevertheless, Wood forged ahead with his plans, submitting his script to the Production Code Administration for review. On October 6, 1953, Joseph I. Breen of the PCA responded to him:

> We have read the script, received here October 2, 1953, for your proposed production *The Phantom Ghoul*, and are pleased to tell you that this basic story seems acceptable under the requirements of the Production Code. However, we call your attention to the following details:
>
> At the outset, we direct your particular attention to the need for the greatest possible care in the selection and photographing of the costumes and dresses for your women. The Production Code

have not mentioned this story to you. ...Briefly, *The Phantom Ghoul* is a modern western horror film and should receive great praise from both Western and horror fans.

I enclose the script for *The Phantom Ghoul* and hope you will enjoy the role of Professor Smoke as much as I enjoyed writing the character strictly for you.

The question remains open as to whether Wood did write it specifically for Lugosi. Perhaps, though the title page of the script reproduced herein claims that Wood had registered it in 1951, thus predating Wood's first meeting with Lugosi.

At any rate, in the summer of 1953, Lugosi mentioned two different Wood projects on the television program

Lon Chaney, Jr., possible co-star of *The Phantom Ghoul*. (Courtesy of George Chastain)

Publicity photo of Samuel Z. Arkoff.

makes it mandatory that the intimate parts of the body – specifically, the breasts of women – be fully covered at all times. Any compromise with this regulation will compel us to withhold approval of your picture.

In accordance with Code requirements, please consult with Dr. Young, of the American Humane Association, as to all scenes in which animals are used.

Page 43: The action at the bottom of this page must not be a kick; if it is just a shove and not excessively brutal, it will be acceptable.

Page 93: Please exercise proper restraint in photographing the fight, to avoid any excessive brutality. Specifically, there must be no kicking, kneeing, gouging, etc.

Page 102: The kick indicated...would not be acceptable.

You understand, of course, that our final judgment will be based upon the finished picture.
The script reproduced herein may have undergone

various revisions for many reasons, but it is evident that Wood made the necessary changes that the PCA required. After all, their endorsement was critical for any film that aspired to mainstream theatrical distribution.

But as much as Wood was pushing *The Phantom Ghoul*, he had not forgotten about the other projects. And he might also have been considering changing *The Phantom Ghoul*'s title to (or even back to) *The Ghoul Goes West*. In a syndicated newspaper column of October 30, 1953, Bob Thomas wrote, "Lugosi said the horror market was on the upbeat. His future films include *The Atomic Monster, The Vampire's Tomb* and *The Ghoul Goes West*." The list was comprised solely of Wood's projects.

And the list of Wood-Lugosi projects was actually longer. In late 1953, Wood snapped still photographs of his actress-girlfriend Dolores Fuller with Lugosi at the Hollywood Historama, a non-profit exhibit on Hollywood Boulevard. Soon thereafter, Wood booked Lugosi into San Bernardino's West Coast Theatre for December 31, 1953, New Year's Eve. Lugosi's personal appearance consisted of little more than delivering a brief speech.

Then, in January 1954, Wood wrote to Samuel French, Inc., a company that had for decades represented and published three-act plays:

Permit me first to introduce myself as Mr. Bela Lugosi's manager. Since Mr. Lugosi has been feeling well for some time and has done two pictures for my company during the past year he wishes again to go into live plays. His first appearance on the stage in some time will be in 2 weeks at St. Louis in the play *Arsenic and Old Lace*.

I am interested in also doing a play to star Mr. Lugosi. The one that made him famous, *Dracula*. I am desirous of any information as to royalties, contracts, etc., which will enable me, if we choose to go ahead, to produce this play for the public with an all-pro cast.

Perhaps Lugosi's brief but successful St. Louis run in *Arsenic and Old Lace* (which had nothing to do with Wood) might have inspired Wood to consider staging his own Lugosi play. At any rate, nothing came of the idea.

Then, Wood returned to the subject of *The Vampire's Tomb* and other unnamed projects for Lugosi. On March

Bela Lugosi and Dolores Fuller at the Hollywood Historama in 1953.

11, 1954, he wrote to Lugosi as part of an effort to keep Lugosi's agent Lou Sherrill out of his negotiations. At that time, Lugosi was in Las Vegas for what became a seven-week run at the Silver Slipper in *The Bela Lugosi Revue*, a show that Wood incorrectly claimed to have developed:

> I haven't mentioned anything to Lou [Sherrill] about anything. I am keeping on the good side of him only about his deals so as we know everything as it happens. As for our deals, that is only yours and my business. I haven't actually mentioned salary to anyone. If the picture goes ten days, you would only work for the six anyway. So we are alright, Bela.
>
> Now Bela, I haven't let you down yet. I'm strictly

on your side, because I know you will do right by me when the time comes, if I need a favor.

> Now Alex [Gordon] is back. He came in Saturday. I asked him why he didn't take the apartment with you, but the question was evaded. However, I suggest we don't get into any arguments about that because the horror picture deal seems to be set and should be ready to shoot about the time you are finished in Las Vegas, of course, giving you plenty of time for a day or two of rest, and several days of study. I'll be able to help you there as I did before. It seems to be *The Vampire's Tomb*, now called by [the title] *The Vampire*, that they are going to do. Ford Beebe is to direct.

Bela Lugosi, Dolores Fuller, and Ed Wood in San Bernardino on New Year's Eve 1953.

...I was contacted by another man I've known for seven years, a man named Frank Winkler, in regards to your doing a picture for him. He was an agent several years back when I went to Seattle to promote fights, wrestling and ice-skating. He is back now and has about decided to do a picture. So I'm looking into this now to see what there it is to offer. Also, you must stay on real friendly terms with Ron Ormond. He has been my very close friend for a long time, many years, and he is putting a few pictures in my hands to do. One   thing – he likes you very much, and I'm almost sure we can swing one of his pictures your way this year.

The content of this letter implies that Gordon's aforementioned discussion of Ford Beebe might really have been a reference to 1954, rather than 1953, with Gordon's on-and-off involvement lasting longer than he recalled.

Then, on March 12, 1954, Wood responded to a Lugosi fan letter on Lugosi's behalf. Along with describing his

work in the *Bela Lugosi Revue* nightclub act in Las Vegas, Wood-posing-as-Lugosi said, "By the way, my next film will be *Bride of the Vampire* to go before the cameras sometime immediately after the completion of my work here at the Silver Slipper." Was *Bride of the Vampire* another possible title for Allied Artists' *The Vampire's Tomb*? Or could this have been a *new* Wood project, one he hoped to develop if he was feeling locked out of the negotiations involving Gordon, Beebe and Allied Artists?

Wood sent yet another letter to Lugosi on March 21, while the actor was still in Las Vegas:

[Alex Gordon] called me again around ten last night and was still in a meeting with Ford Beebe and Harold [Mirisch] at Allied Artists. This is very important to all of us so I didn't press the issue of getting up there [to see you in Las Vegas] – although I will get there before the week is out.

I've been checking all the newspapers and haven't found any of the write-ups yet – buying all these

The building where Wood shot parts of *Glen or Glenda* (1953) and *Plan 9 from Outer Space* (1958). *(Photograph taken by David Wentink)*

newspapers every day gets rather expensive – but we need every bit of publicity on you we can get. I have definitely set a picture for you which will go [into production] within the next sixty days (other than Alex's deal). Now I *haven't* mentioned anything to Lou Sherrill or Alex so I suggest you do not. There is no sense cutting anyone in who has not worked in bringing it about. The money for you is not up to where I want it yet – but you and I will meet with those in charge upon your return next week. They are very impressed with you – your new publicity – and the fact you have remained seven full weeks in Las Vegas – that seems to be some kind of a record for most clubs up there.

Also – a friend of mine – one of the fellows who has put some money into my last picture – and got all his money back from the sale – has given me – or rather okayed to me – $1000.00 to promote the picture, not get started on it. I suggest I take this cash, you and I form sort of an agreement and own the

picture together. Of course, this fellow would have to be cut in too. But the one thing I have always told you – you should own a good piece of one of your pictures since they always make good money. And we can arrange it that way this time along with a sizeable amount of immediate cash.

What was this unnamed project that Wood had ready for Lugosi in sixty days? Perhaps it was *Bride of the Vampire*; perhaps it was another script.

In the meantime, Alex Gordon had his own project underway for Lugosi. He hoped to take some Lugosi footage from the British comedy *Mother Riley Meets the Vampire* (1952) and combine it with new footage, turning the result into a new story, *King Robot*. The project was talked about for several months in 1954, with Lou Rusoff writing a script that was meant to go before cameras in January 1955. By that time, Gordon hoped to include Lon Chaney Jr. and Helen Gilbert in the cast. Here was another project that didn't come to fruition, in this case because Lugosi looked too different from the old footage

Bela Lugosi and "Tommy" Haines in *Glen or Glenda* (1953).

filmed in 1951.

At any rate, Wood seemed to be expanding his efforts to ingratiate himself with Lugosi and to generate revenue for him even outside of film sets. For example, at the end of March 1954, Wood sent the same letter to ten different comic publishers:

Since the advent of TV, the reissues of his old pictures on that medium, two in release, two to be filmed in May, his great horror comedy review recently closing at the Last Frontier Hotel, Las Vegas, Nevada, after a seven week run, and the reissuing of his great *Dracula*, which even now commands greater crowds than ever before, it may be of interest to you that Mr. BELA LUGOSI is interested in talking a deal for a Bela Lugosi comic. If you are interested in further pursuit of a comic of this nature, please contact me.

Given the popularity of horror comic books in the late '40s and early '50s, Wood's idea was a good one. Lugosi's name remained big as a result of theatrical reis-

sues and television broadcasts, and his illustrated presence as either a host of or participant in horror stories would have worked well. But no comic book happened, perhaps because the publishers were already selling huge numbers without paying horror personalities like Lugosi. Moreover, anti-horror sentiment against those same publishers was gaining momentum in 1954. Senator Estes Kefauver's infamous subcommittee hearings on the subject began in April of that year.

Having considered stage, screen, television and comics, Wood next tried to corner the market on horror radio. On April 18, 1954, he wrote to Lugosi:

Here is the first of the *Terror* radio scripts – 15 minutes each. Since … the scripts will be read … you will not have to worry about memorizing them – just be familiar with them. I will get each of the other 12 scripts to you as I write or buy them.

Unfortunately, no copy of the script Wood wrote seems to exist, and certainly no radio show was ever produced.

By the summer of 1954, Wood seems to have returned

his attentions to *The Vampire's Tomb*, presumably because whatever deal Gordon had tried to negotiate with Beebe and Allied Artists fell apart. Once again in charge of the project, Wood began to consider a suitable cast to support Lugosi's character of Dr. Acula.

Gordon had hoped the movie would have starred Lugosi and included Helen Gilbert, Richard Denning, Raymond Hatton, Stuart Holmes, Jack Mulhall and Jack Perrin. But that was not the troupe that Wood chose to form. He wanted such players as Richard Powers (Tom Keene), Bobby Jordan, Lyle Talbot, Frank Yaconelli, Hazel Franklyn and Bud Osborne. He also wanted his girlfriend Dolores Fuller to play the female lead and Vampira (Maila Nurmi) to play a fake vampire.

But Wood changed his mind about the latter two roles, if only due to necessity. Vampira refused to appear, even though Wood sought her as late as August 1954; as a result, Wood considered casting "Devila," a name he concocted for a Vampira knockoff. Devila's real identity is unknown, if she even existed. Perhaps she was nothing more than a name awaiting a suitable actress.

And then there was Wood's own decision to replace Fuller with Loretta King. For years, Dolores Fuller lamented Wood having given the lead role in *Bride of the Monster* to Loretta King, a role that he had in fact written for Fuller. She never felt the same about Wood afterwards, and it was key in her decision to leave him. But the problem Fuller discussed may have had its roots in *The Vampire's Tomb*. On August 2, 1954, the *Los Angeles Times* wrote:

> Dolores Fuller will play a sexy type in *The Vampire's Tomb*, starring Bela Lugosi. She had considered the lead in the picture, but preferred this switch because of its dramatic opportunities. Frank Yaconelli will appear opposite her as a comic killer. ... Loretta King will have the lead opposite Richard Powers [Tom Keene], and Wood is endeavoring to secure Vampira for the picture, which should make it a super event.

Whether or not King's casting had anything to do with it, Wood soon made changes to at least five pages of the script, the copy reproduced herein indicating the revisions with the date August 26, 1954.

Wood's finances for *The Vampire's Tomb* seem to have been largely non-existent. However, the period from July to November 1954 saw more reports on *The Vampire's Tomb* being published than in any other:

> Bela Lugosi, Loretta King, Lyle Talbot, Dolores Fuller and Hazel Franklyn yesterday were signed for roles in *The Vampire's Tomb*, exploitation film to be produced and directed by Edward D. Wood Jr.
> – *Daily Variety*, July 28, 1954

Advertisement published in the *Las Vegas Sun* on February 19, 1954.

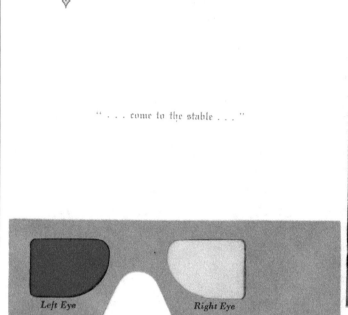

Ed Wood's 3-D Christmas card. *(Courtesy of Roger Hurlburt)*

Bela Lugosi is about to resume his villainy in *The Vampire's Tomb*. And how about Vampira as the female lead?

— *Daily Variety*, July 29, 1954

Loretta King, stage and TV actress, has been cast as the feminine lead with Bela Lugosi in *The Vampire's Tomb*, to be produced by Edward D. Wood Jr., starting early in August.

— *Los Angeles Times*, July 30, 1954

Bela Lugosi, Loretta King, Lyle Talbot, Dolores Fuller and Hazel Franklyn sign for roles in *The Vampire's Tomb*.

— *Variety*, August 4, 1954

Loretta King has been forced to bow out of femme lead stint in Laguna Playhouse's *The Big Knife* due to current thesping in *Vampire's Tomb*, Bela Lugosi starrer, which will conflict with the legit opening next Tuesday.

— *Daily Variety*, August 19, 1954

Vampira is now set in *The Vampire's Tomb*, which will be produced and directed by Edward D. Wood Jr., starting today, with Bela Lugosi, Hazel Franklyn from TV and stage and others in the cast.

— *Los Angeles Times*, August 27, 1954

Producer Edward Wood Jr., who is also directing *The Vampire's Tomb* with Bela Lugosi as the male star and Vampira as one of the principal players, has arranged for Lugosi to do six more features, the second to be filmed at Sedona, Ariz. This will be a spooky western, as yet untitled, which Wood has written.

— *Los Angeles Times*, August 31, 1954

We were trying to determine with Eddie Fox and Bela Lugosi what movie Lugosi had made that had "a lot of coffins" in it. Lugosi (alias Count Dracula) thought a moment, said: "All my pictures had lots of coffins in them." . . .

Published in the *Las Vegas Sun* on February 28, 1954.

THE WAR AGAINST THE IRISH

NEWS WEEKLY • MARCH 15, 1954

TEMPO

Ike's Team
To Keep
Prosperity

RHONDA FLEMING

TEMPO'S
ALL-AMERICAN
BASKETBALL
TEAM

32

Monster movies were coming out of Hollywood in greater numbers than at any time since the days of Dracula, Frankenstein and King Kong. Reason: *King Kong*, re-issued, took in more money in theaters across the country than it had the first time out. Here are Kong's latest rivals.

DRACULA

OGLES ..

...TODAY'S MONSTERS

Bela Lugosi evoked shudders as *Dracula*.

Bulging-eyed monsters from another planet in RKO's *Target Earth*.

Villains of *Black Lagoon* (l.) and *Gorilla At Large* grab girls.

One-eyed monster is Cyclops, in Paramount's production, *Ulysses*.

Bela Lugosi had Ed Wood purchase numerous copies of this issue of *Tempo* magazine published on March 15, 1954.

Not recommended as a bedtime story for kiddies: *The Vampire's Tomb*, co-starring Bela Lugosi and Vampira.
— *Daily Variety*, September 8, 1954

An unknown actress, to be tabbed Devila, will co-star with Bela Lugosi in Edward D. Wood, Jr.'s *The Vampire's Tomb*, slated to roll Oct. 1 at Ted Allan studios. Remainder of cast includes Lyle Talbot, Bobby Jordan, Frank Yaconelli, Dolores Fuller, Loretta King and James Moore. Wood planed to San Francisco yesterday to close financing with Jake Shimano. No release is set.
— *Hollywood Reporter*, September 9, 1954.

The Vampire's Tomb ... to shoot at Ted Allen [*sic*] Studios. (Wide-screen) Starts Oct. 1.
— *Daily Variety*, September 10, 1954

The Vampire's Tomb ... to shoot at Ted Allen [*sic*] Studios. (Wide-screen) Starts Oct. 1.
— *Daily Variety*, September 17, 1954

[This is a reprint of the entry published on September 10, 1954.]

Consolidated Film Lab will process Edward Wood's theatrical film, *The Vampire's Tomb*, toplining Bela Lugosi and Bobby Jordan. *Tomb* rolls Oct. 1.
— *Daily Variety*, September 23, 1954

First to go [into production at the remodeled Ted Allan Studios] will be Edward Wood's *The Vampire's Tomb*, for theatrical release....
— *Daily Variety*, September 24, 1954

Edward D. Wood Jr. will produce *Vampire's Tomb*, starring Bela Lugosi, Devila and Lyle Talbot, for standard and widescreen projection. Two-week shooting sked begins Oct. 4. at the Ted Allan Studios. Deal has been set with Consolidated Film Industries to handle processing on *Tomb* and Wood's next feature, *The Ghoul Goes West*.
— *Daily Variety*, September 24, 1954
[This quotation appears in a separate article than the above quotation from *Daily Variety* on the same date.]

Don Nagel has forsaken acting temporarily to be assistant to E. D. Wood, Jr. on his *The Vampire's Tomb*, due to roll Oct. 18 with Bela Lugosi.
— *Hollywood Reporter*, October 1, 1954

Richard Powers (aka Tom Keene), potential cast member of *The Vampire's Tomb*.

The Vampire's Tomb ... to shoot at Ted Allan Studios. (Wide-screen) Starts Oct. 18.
> – *Daily Variety*, October 1, 1954

Producer-director Ed Wood inked Alexander Laszlo over the weekend to score *The Vampire's Tomb*, starring Bela Lugosi.
> – *Daily Variety*, October 4, 1954

Al Shapiro, Ed Schaft ["planted" in] *The Vampire's Tomb*
> – *Daily Variety*, October 6, 1954

The Vampire's Tomb ... to shoot at Ted Allan Studios. (Wide-screen) Starts Oct. 18.
> – *Daily Variety*, October 8, 1954
> (This is a reprint of the same announcement that appeared in *Daily Variety* on October 1, 1954.]

Conrad Brooks ["planted" in] *Vampire's Tomb*.
> – *Daily Variety*, October 11, 1954

Slated for early production [at Ted Allan Studios] are a theatrical film, Edward Wood's *The Vampire's Tomb*, and the *Hank McCune Show* for television.
> – *Variety*, October 13, 1954

The Vampire's Tomb ... to shoot at Ted Allan Studios. (Wide-screen) Starts Oct. 18.
> – *Daily Variety*, October 15, 1954
> [This is a reprint of the entry published on October 8, 1954.]

Now shooting is: *The Vampire's Tomb* (Bella [*sic*] Lugosi, Devila, Lyle Talbot) - an Edward D. Wood Jr. Production – Wood personally producing and directing.
> – *Film Bulletin*, October 18, 1954

Believing the time is ripe to reintroduce horror on the screen, independent producer Edward D. Wood, Jr., is making *Vampire's Tomb*, with Bela Lugosi, Devila (a girl with a name coined to match her devilish fine appearance) and Lyle Talbot. He will follow it with *The Ghoul Goes West*. Without fee or license, I offer him an idea for a follow-up–*There's No Ghoul Like an Old Ghoul*.

– *Picturegoer*, November 6, 1954

Loretta King ... has signed with Catacomb Pictures to quail before Bela Lugosi's advances in both *Bride of the Atom* and *The Vampire's Tomb*.

– *Los Angeles Times*, November 10, 1954

As you might have expected, *The Vampire's Tomb* will be produced by Catacomb Pictures. How spooky can you get?

– *Daily Variety*, November 11, 1954

Following completion of [*Bride of the Atom*], Edward D. Wood will start immediate production of *The Vampire's Tomb*, also co-starring Lugosi and Miss [Loretta] King.

– *Hollywood Reporter*, November 12, 1954

Despite all of these confident trade reports – which represent something of a testament to Wood's ability to generate publicity – *The Vampire's Tomb* did not go into production in 1954.

Wood did shoot at least two days on *Bride of the Monster* (under its title *Bride of the Atom*) in late October 1954, but then its production screeched to a halt until approximately March 1955, when he finally completed principal photography.

Only a few weeks after the *Bride of the Atom* shoot wrapped, Lugosi made national news due to his drug addiction. On April 22 of that year, he requested that he be committed to a state hospital to be cured. He had already sought help at a private sanatorium, but could not afford to stay there. Commending him for his bravery, Judge Wallace L. Ware ordered Lugosi to the Metropolitan State Hospital in Norwalk, California.

Numerous journalists visited Lugosi during his three months in the hospital, as did at least a few friends, including Ed Wood. Paul Marco once told Jan Alan Hen-

Lyle Talbot, potential cast member of *The Vampire's Tomb*. *(Courtesy of Laura Wagner)*

derson, "Ed and I took the script for *Tomb* to Bela when he was in the county hospital, and we hoped that he would be well enough to finish the picture when he got out, but that never came about." Marco told Tom Weaver, "It was while Bela was in the hospital that we approached him with the script for *The Ghoul Goes West*, a western horror film that Eddie was planning." Here was *The Phantom Ghoul* under the title that more clearly indicated its cross-generic narrative.

Had Wood decided to push *The Ghoul Goes West* instead of *The Vampire's Tomb*? That seems apparent for

Frank Yaconelli, potential cast member of *The Vampire's Tomb*.

three reasons. One is that cowboy film star Gene Autry allegedly expressed interest in co-starring opposite Lugosi. The other – perhaps a direct outcome of the first – is that actor Tony McCoy decided to produce *The Ghoul Goes West* in April 1955, on the heels of completing *Bride of the Atom*. In fact, on April 22, *Daily Variety* announced that McCoy had scheduled the project for "indie production" and had already cast Don Nagel. Thirdly, the combination of press activity and production inactivity on *The Vampire's Tomb* in 1954 may have led Wood to think it was best to shelve it, at least for the time being.

In addition to Marco and Wood's trip to the hospital, Tony McCoy and Loretta King – Lugosi's *Bride of the Atom* co-stars – delivered the *Ghoul Goes West* script to Lugosi. Wood later told Robert Cremer that McCoy arranged the script handover as a publicity stunt to get his own picture in the newspaper. The press quoted Lugosi's response: "To know that people have such faith in me is better than medicine. I will not let them down."

In his book *Lugosi: The Man Behind the Cape* (Henry Regnery, 1976), Cremer wrote: "In the weeks that followed, Bela and the manuscript seldom parted company. He took it with him when he was granted permission

for a stroll around the hospital grounds. Occasionally he would rest on a bench and rehearse his lines." He also spoke about the project in a filmed interview on the day of his release from the hospital.

On August 6, 1955, the *Los Angeles Herald-Examiner* told readers, "In two weeks, Lugosi will start work on a role in the film *The Ghoul Goes West*. He has been studying his part at the hospital." The *Los Angeles Times* reported it would go into production on August 20. "It's very cute," Lugosi told the newspaper. To another journalist, he said, "I get to play an undertaker [in *The Ghoul Goes West*]. That's turning the tables. Three months ago, some of my friends thought I was ready for one."

But once again, a much-talked-about project did not go before the cameras. In her autobiography *A Fuller Life* (BearManor Media, 2009), Dolores Fuller wrote:

> I firmly believe that Eddie's choice of professionals for his movies proves that he would have done very outstanding work if he had been able to attract sufficient financing. He almost did this with his casting of Gene Autry...in what was to be a Republic Pictures production of *The Ghoul Goes West*, but when Autry dropped out, so did Republic.

Fuller added, "I was later told that Alex Gordon, who had introduced Gene to Eddie ... when they were living together, spiked the deal because he became jealous of Eddie's success in making *Glen or Glenda*."

To the press, Lugosi made it seem as if the project might still happen, even if he knew that its chances were bleak. Syndicated columnist Harrison Carroll reported on September 20, 1955, "Bela Lugosi tells me that *The Ghoul*

Barry Fitzgerald will be featured in the Walter Mirisch-Allied Artists production of "The Black Prince," to start at Elstree Studios in England, with Henry Leven directing, Monday.

Loretta King, stage and TV actress, has been cast as the feminine lead with Bela Lugosi in "The Vampire's Tomb," to be produced by Edward D. Wood Jr., starting early in August. She was in "Sabrina Fair" at the Biltmore and has done much TV.

Richard Quine will direct "My Sister Eileen," with Janet Leigh and Jack Lemmon, at Columbia.

Richard Allan, 20th contractee, who was in "Niagara" and

Loretta King

Published in the *Los Angeles Times* on July 30, 1954.

Before Vampira: Maila Nurmi on the cover of a September 1950 magazine. *(Courtesy of George Chastain)*

Ted Allan with Eleanor Powell.

Goes West has been postponed until he can get a look at the script and can be assured of 'enough money to keep me for awhile.'"

The last notable press account of the project came in the *Hollywood Reporter* of October 7, 1955. The trade claimed Wood would produce, but that Harold Daniels would direct. Paul Marco was associate producer, and Lugosi would headline alongside cowboy star Bob Steele. Wood and Daniels would shoot *The Ghoul Goes West* in VistaVision and color later that same month. Allegedly. The project permanently stalled.

And so, after all of his hard work over the course of three years, Wood's only completed Lugosi projects were *Bride of the Atom*, the 1953 appearance in San Bernardino and *Glen or Glenda*. Did Wood have anything to do with Lugosi's only known product endorsement of the era? That is difficult to say, but as of late October 1955, the *Los Angeles Times* announced:

A specialty company is getting up a package they're calling Spooky Foods. Contents: Rattlesnake meat, French fried grasshoppers, snails, alligator soup, Mexican worms and Japanese quail eggs. They're trying to get an endorsement from Bela Lugosi.

Self-portrait of Vampira, painted by Maila Nurmi. *(Courtesy of Dennis Phelps and MonsterMovieMuseum.com)*

A photograph survives of Lugosi with some of the Spooky Foods products, but the extent to which the company used it in advertisements is unknown.

But Wood definitely began speaking about a new Lugosi project in 1955. Entitled *The Final Curtain*, he described it to Robert Cremer as being:

the story of a vaudeville actor who dies on stage but doesn't realize it. He searches through his entire career to find something that his spirit is attracted to. Finally, in the climactic scene, his spirit returns to the live theater where he last performed, and the coffin he used in his act slowly opens and beckons to him. Fade out.

Bela Lugosi at the Los Angeles County General Hospital on April 22, 1955.

Lugosi and the script to *The Ghoul Goes West* at the Metropolitan State Hospital.

Wood's plot was strong. His financing wasn't. And so he returned once again to one of his old projects.

Grave Robbers from Other Scripts

At some point in late 1955, Wood attempted to revive *The Vampire's Tomb*. Paul Marco recalled, "It was for that picture that Ed shot all that miscellaneous footage of Bela, which had no purpose whatsoever outside of maybe *The Vampire's Tomb* would take advantage of *some* of this material."

Alex Gordon wrote much the same in *Fangoria*: "To interest financiers [in *The Vampire's Tomb*, Wood] shot a few scenes of the former Dracula coming and going from his apartment. Eventually this led to *Plan 9 from Outer Space*."

Certainly there can be no doubt that Wood did film footage of Lugosi in a cemetery, as well as at a house that in real life belonged to Tor Johnson's son Carl (as opposed to the apartment that Gordon mentioned).

In fact, it is possible to determine when at least some of the footage was filmed. On November 27, 1955, the *Los Angeles Times* reported, "Patrons at Johnny Davis' Cameo room were, to say the least, startled the other evening when Mr. Bela Lugosi came in for a snack. He'd been on location in a Hollywood cemetery and hadn't bothered to get out of makeup."

Wood later gave a detailed description of the cemetery shoot to Robert Cremer:

The cemetery was very long and narrow, making it difficult to get the right depth of field. There was a road on one side and the housing development on the other, so we finally decided that we would have to 'rearrange' the tombstones to fit our camera angles. We couldn't afford any retakes, so everything had to be perfect the first time. Tor, his son Carl and Bela started dragging the tombstones into position, while [cinematographer William C.

Lugosi with the script to *The Ghoul Goes West*.

Thompson] took the light readings. Bela actually didn't do very much except order Tor and Carl around, telling them where to place the stones. Tor and Carl complained and gave him dirty looks every once in awhile.

As morbid as it all seemed to us carrying tombstones around a cemetery at night, Bela seemed perfectly at home – in a professional sort of way, that is. He walked around apologizing to the resident corpses about the disturbances and promised that we would return their tombstones as soon as we were finished. When Tor and Carl heard *that*, they said, 'You bring them all back on your own time, Bela. We're going to see the osteopath!'

Wood also recalled that a local newspaper later featured a story called something like "Ghouls Invade Cemetery."

But was all of the Lugosi footage *really* intended for *The Vampire's Tomb*? Wood later wrote in his book *Holly-*

wood Rat Race, "Bela died months before I started [*Plan 9 from Outer Space*], but we had made several thousand feet of film in advance. Producers often shoot some footage of the star to help him sell the picture to backers." Gordon and Marco's memories, as well as the content of the cemetery footage, certainly suggest that the images of Lugosi in his cape were meant for *The Vampire's Tomb*.

That said, there are reasons to believe that Wood was already thinking about the project that became *Plan 9 from Outer Space*. One is that the *Vampire's Tomb* script does not include scenes of the type that Wood shot of Lugosi crying at a funeral or coming out of a small home and mournfully picking a flower. This alone is not conclusive evidence, as the *Vampire's Tomb* script reproduced herein might be one of many drafts. Nevertheless, reading *The Vampire's Tomb* makes it difficult to believe such footage would have had anything to do with the Dr. Acula character or the mansion where the script is set.

Perhaps more importantly, there are the memories of

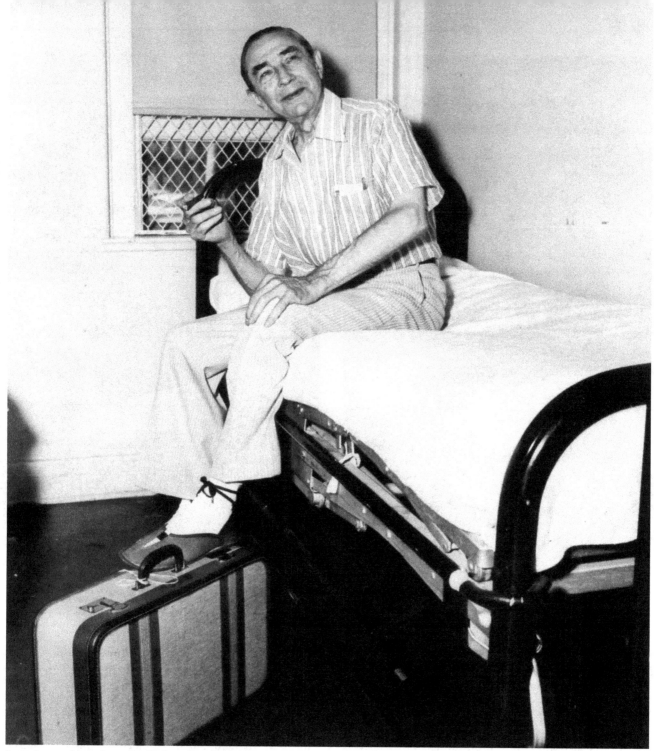

Lugosi preparing to leave the Metropolitan State Hospital on August 5, 1955. *(Courtesy of Dennis Phelps and MonsterMovieMuseum.com)*

Lugosi's friend Richard Sheffield, who was at the cemetery in November 1955 when Wood shot some or all of the footage in question. He recalled the tombstones being moved, admitting, "I purloined some of the grave markers and relocated them in my basement." But he also specifically remembered Wood shooting a few tests of flying saucers that day as well. If correct, Wood may have been thinking less about *The Vampire's Tomb* in November 1955 than about *Grave Robbers from Outer Space*, his title for the film that became *Plan 9*.

Doctors Voodoo and Acula

Unfortunately, scripts do not seem to survive for some of the Wood or Gordon-Wood projects. Indeed, a few of them – like *The Zombie's Curse* – might never have been written. As for *Doctor Voodoo*, Gordon described its plot, which started with the arrival of a mysterious stranger at the once-luxurious mansion of Doctor Markoff (Karloff), a respected physician from London's Harley Street now engaged in research. The stranger is Gerard Lejeune (Bela Lugosi), whose work in distant Hungary once brought him into contact with

Lugosi with Paul Marco, the actor who might have been associate producer on *The Ghoul Goes West*, at a 1954 party.

Lejeune kills Markoff in a last-minute confrontation by shoving him in a pit crawling with Gaboon vipers that the doctor has kept for his secret experiments, and takes the girl away, with the suggestion that she will eventually become a normal person with an appetite for life, love and lust, not necessarily in that order. The last shot shows a Gaboon viper crawling over the nightgown that personified her attachment to Markoff's will.

The story echoes *The Black Cat* (1934), which used the same basic plot, even if in more extreme terms, particularly in that Karloff's character Poelzig was a Satanist who gets skinned alive by Lugosi's Werdegast.

As for *Dr. Acula*, Gordon does not seem to have ever spoken about the announced television series in any detail, but he did recall the feature-length script:

The Vampire's Tomb was to star Lugosi as a famous actor who invites a group of friends to his house in the country for a weekend. Mysterious murders, apparently caused by a vampire, begin to occur, and there are visions of a beau-

Markoff years ago. Markoff had fallen in love with Lejeune's young wife and the duo had fled to London. World War I had intervened and it made it impossible for Lejeune to seek out his wife and persuade her to return to him, but some years later, he received a deathbed letter from the young woman in which she begged his forgiveness and told him of the existence of a daughter.

It is this child that Lejeune has come to trace, but Markoff tells him regretfully that she died in the great flu epidemic of the immediate postwar years. That night, alone in his eerie room, Lejeune sees a vision of a beautiful teenage girl wearing an angora nightgown, but before he can fully come to his senses and turn on a light, the vision has disappeared. Eventually, Lejeune discoverers traces of the girl's existence, and, in a final showdown, he finds her confined to her quarters in a trance. Markoff has kept her under his hypnotic spell to prevent her from leaving him and to retain her will under his complete control.

Lugosi advertising "Spooky Foods."

'FLY' ALSO SHOWING

'Plan 9' Special Effects Excellent

By JAMES MEADE
The San Diego Union's Theater Writer

"Plan 9 From Outer Space," now at the Tower Theater, is another one of those deals in which superior intelligences from other planets are determined to straighten out the earth's numbskulls on a few matters.

It seems scientists of the earth have been messing around with atom and hydrogen explosions long enough to make their planetary neighbors fear they may set off the big chain reaction. the one that will explode the sun and destroy the universe.

To offset this, Eros (Dudley Manlove) and Tanna (Joanna Lee), are sent in a flying saucer to institute Plan 9. Apparently the other eight plans misfired so maybe these spacemen are not so smart, after all.

Plan 9 calls for raising all the dead on earth to destroy other earthlings. A start is made in a San Fernando Valley cemetery and the spacemen never get to Forest Lawn. a ressurection that would cause more trouble in Hollywood than this film will.

Vampira

This fiendish idea is fatal to passersby and the spacemen apparently had not considered at all the dismay it would cause in probate courts and insurance companies.

The film features three good ghouls. Vampira. the best-looking spook around. and the late Bela Lugosi. a veteran chiller, cast a great many effective leers. Tor Johnson apparently deserted wrestling to play the heavy.

Whoever devised the technical effects for the film can take a bow for the flying saucers look believable. The interiors and costumes are less effective.

John Brockinbridge as the Ruler apparently is an old-fashioned spaceman for he sports a halberd on his tunic. The halberd is a medieval weapon now used only for display by the Vatican's Swiss guards. Manlove and Miss Lee have the usual bolt-of-lightning symbol.

It seems difficult to devise a scientific-looking interior without giving the impression of a storeroom for juke boxes and pin ball machines.

* * *

"That was my first American picture and it has outgrossed anything I've done since." Canadian-born Patricia Owens said of "The Fly," which is the second feature at the Tower. Miss Owens was in town last week on behalf of the Tri-Hospital building fund.

A re-issue, "The Fly" tells the story of man who invents a machine that can break up matter and reassemble it elsewhere. The result is a fly with a man's head.

Vincent Price, Herbert Marshall and Al Hedison co-star in the film.

* * *

James Garner, the star of television's "Maverick," is pleased with his assignment

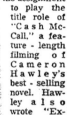

Garner

to play the title role of "Cash Mc-Call," a feature - length filming of Cameron Hawley's best - selling novel. Hawley also wrote "Executive Suite" which starred James Stewart and June Allyson.

"We're hoping it will be another 'Executive Suite,'" Garner said on the Warner Bros. Studio set recently. "McCall is a high-financier who buys and sells corporations at the drop of a hat."

The story tells what happens when McCall falls in love with Natalie Wood, who plays the daughter of a rival industrialist.

Garner was just recovering from the fact that he had not won the Emmy for best actor in a leading role a continuing series. Those on the set could not console him with the thought that "Maverick" had won an Emmy as the best western series.

"Let's face it," he said. "I lost and I'm a poor loser." (Raymond Burr as "Perry Mason" was awarded the Emmy for best series actor).

---

tiful girl, clad in an angora nightgown (Wood's trademark), wandering through the gardens of the estate. Eventually, it is revealed that the killings are not due to the activities of the undead but [to] the daughter of a famous actress ruined by the actor. She pretends to be a vampire in order to lay the blame for the evil deeds on the party's host.

Gordon also remembered, "Eddie decided to rework the *Vampire's Tomb* script," a fact that seems evident by comparing the script reproduced herein with the above description.

Wood apparently had an attachment to the title *The Vampire's Tomb*, as variations like *Tomb of the Vampire* and *Bride of the Vampire* appear only briefly in primary sources. More interesting, perhaps, is that its narrative roots go much deeper than 1951. Consider the tale's setting, as noted in the surviving script:

A once proud mansion, now old and gloomy, near ruin. The grass surrounding the semi-circle driveway is high and burned brown by the long hours of the sun's scorching heat without proper care. The drive is directly in front of the large wooden front door of the two-story mansion. A private cemetery can be seen off to the far left and a long winding lake beyond that. There are trees, vines, and brush intermingled among the grave stones of the cemetery. The night is very dark with heavy rain clouds in the sky. However the mansion is streaked in light as lightning suddenly flashes across the sky followed by deep, rolling thunder claps. It is at this time, during one of the lightning flashes, that a giant bat flies into view – hovers in the sky a moment – then heads in a streak towards the old house.

A number of heirs convene on the night before the reading of Aunt Lucille's will—all but Lucille's long-lost sister Helen. The one road to the mansion is washed out, and there is no telephone.

A male and female vampire appear near the home. The female vampire, hovering over Barbara in her bedroom, clearly resembles Aunt Lucille. Then a scream rings out from the cemetery. Near a cliff, a hat belonging to an heir named Flinch is discovered, but his body is nowhere to be found. Fear grips the family, some of whom bear an awful secret. All of the heirs save Barbara murdered Lucille for her money. The plot thickens.

The Vampire's Tomb features decent dialogue and a fairly strong understanding of Hollywood story structure. It might have made an interesting film, if only because it had been

Article published in the *San Diego Union* on May 18, 1959.

Lugosi, Dolores Fuller, and Ed Wood composing unfinished cinematic symphonies.

made twice before: first as director Tod Browning's silent film *London After Midnight* (1927) with Lon Chaney, in which a detective poses as a vampire to solve a murder case. Then Browning split the detective and fake vampire into two separate roles for the remake *Mark of the Vampire* (1935), with Lionel Barrymore as the former character and Lugosi as the latter.

In creating the role of Dr. Acula, Wood seems to have drawn upon the earlier films. The detective and fake vampire would be the same character, with Dr. Acula relying on the fake Lucille vampire not unlike *London After Midnight* relying on the equally fake Bat Girl (Edna Tichenor). To add a new dimension to the story, Wood co-opted the basic "old dark house" formula that pervaded the U.S. stage and screen in the 1920s and '30s. And instead of an individual murderer like Browning used, Wood had several operating in collusion, all gathered for the reading of a will, trapped in an old mansion with a terrible storm raging outside.

Professor Smoke

Recalling *The Ghoul Goes West*, Alex Gordon wrote: "In this – a horror-western – mysterious vampire-like killings occur on a ranch, and there are several suspects. It turns out that a vampire, buried in an old mine, returns to life when the mine is exploded for its vein of gold." Here was a fascinating plot, something of a Western riff on the wartime bombing events in *The Return of the Vampire* (1943).

But as with *The Vampire's Tomb*, it is apparent from two surviving Wood scripts – one titled *The Ghoul Goes West*, reproduced in this volume, and another titled *The Phantom Ghoul* – that the story changed dramatically. It features no vampire, but instead two ghouls: Tanz and Karl make their first appearance on page one, robbing a grave in a small cemetery. They are not unlike Lobo (Tor Johnson) in *Bride of the Monster*.

Of the two scripts, *The Phantom Ghoul* was perhaps written first. In it, the female lead is Sally; in *The Ghoul Goes West*, she is Nancy. But in Scenes 12 and 14 of the script reproduced in this volume, the name Sally accidentally reappears, only to be crossed out by hand and replaced with Nancy. (All that said, the fact this version of *The Ghoul Goes West* was apparently typed and revised after *The Phantom Ghoul* says nothing about various other drafts that Wood might have written between 1951 and 1955.)

Doctor Voodoo's plot echoed aspects of *The Black Cat* (1934), which starred Boris Karloff.

Double S Ranch. A reference to New York in *The Phantom Ghoul* is "back East" in *The Ghoul Goes West*. Both are Westerns, but *The Ghoul Goes West* is more firmly rooted in the nineteenth century.

The Final Curtain

Unfinished symphonies are sometimes more famous than those which were completed, as in the case of Schubert's *No. 8 in B Minor*, which is famously heard in the Lugosi *Dracula* (1931). While we can ruminate on how its unwritten movements might have sounded, it nevertheless remains one of the great "What If"s of the musical world.

Perhaps Wood's final project to star Lugosi during the actor's own lifetime was one that he didn't even write. In 1956, Lugosi's teenage friend Michael Spencer typed a paragraph-long treatment for a horror movie called *Repeat Performance* on his old Underwood typewriter. On a visit to Lugosi's apartment, Spencer found the actor with Ed Wood:

> They had been reading a one-paragraph idea I had written for a film for Bela, and Wood wanted it. I said, 'Sure, it's yours.' Still apprehensive, Wood asked if I would take payment of the symbolic one dollar to make it legal. I accepted, hoping this was going to help Bela's near-terminal career.

Other differences between the two scripts are also worth noting. The saloon bartender has a very prominent speaking role in *The Phantom Ghoul*, but not in *The Ghoul Goes West*. In the latter, most of his dialogue goes to a character named Melody, the female saloon owner, who was presumably written to create another much-needed female role. And while a castle features in both, *The Ghoul Goes West* usually refers instead to a haunted mine.

Otherwise, the key variances involve the story's vague time setting. Both are clearly situated in the rural west, but *The Phantom Ghoul* includes cars, a truck and even an oxygen mask designed for use by high-altitude pilots; in *The Ghoul Goes West*, these are horses and a wagon (as well as mention of a stagecoach). There is a dude ranch in *The Phantom Ghoul*; in *The Ghoul Goes West*, it is the

Forrest J Ackerman, Hope Lininger Lugosi, and Richard Sheffield, pictured here years after Lugosi's death.

Maila Nurmi's final resting place. *(Photograph taken by David Wentink)*

Wood never made the film, but – even if it was merely a coincidence – *How to Make a Monster* (1958) used the same basic storyline.

Lugosi died on August 16, 1956. In a 1959 magazine, Wood's friend Conrad Brooks wrote, "By his side was a half read script for a film called the *Final Curtain*." Wood told Robert Cremer that Lugosi was clutching the script pages when his widow found him. In his book *Hollywood Rat Race*, Wood gave a somewhat different account, claiming it was found beside Lugosi's bed, opened to page six. (By contrast, Lugosi's last wife Hope insisted on numerous occasions that there was no script nearby when she found her husband dead.)

Surprisingly or not, *Final Curtain* became a film after Lugosi's death, a 1957 short intended as a pilot for a television program called *Portraits in Terror*, which was to feature "original stories and screenplays written, produced, and directed by Edward D. Wood Jr." Duke Moore stars, with the voice of Dudley Manlove providing the character's interior thoughts. A new world appears inside a theater once everyone has gone home for the night, "that of the spirit and the unseen."

Final Curtain opens with a text crawl that speaks to many things, ranging from vampires of the type Lugosi played to dialogue similar to that which Criswell speaks in *Night of the Ghouls* (1958).

But it also seems uniquely suited to provide an Ed

Woodian description, epitaph even, of the status of *The Vampire's Tomb* and *The Ghoul Goes West* and of all film scripts that never quite make it to the screen, of all the unfinished cinematic symphonies that one has to strain so hard to hear:

Even the devil rejects them. Doomed to haunt the earth throughout the endless reaches of time.

The creatures in this story of terror were --

Once human ----

Now --- monsters ----

In a void between the living and the dead.

Creatures to be pitied.

Creatures to be despised.....

CRYPTS NOTES on

WOOD'S **THE GHOUL GOES WEST**
and
THE VAMPIRE'S TOMB

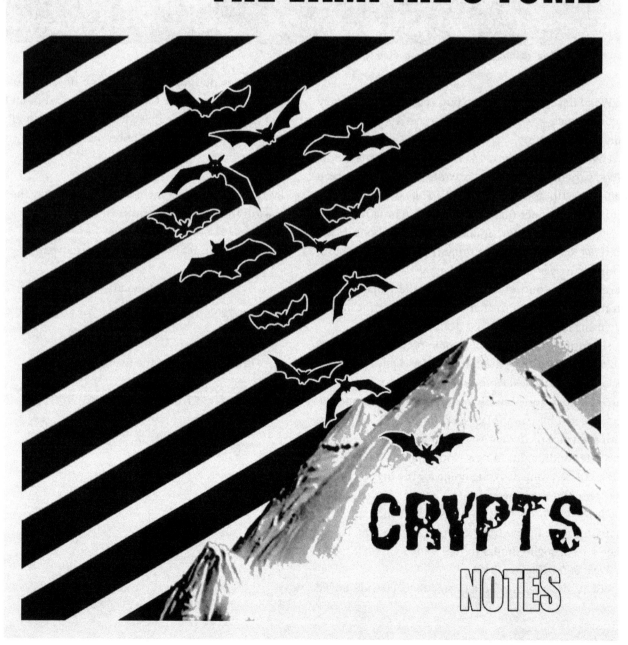

CRYPTS
NOTES

Annotated Synopses

The Ghoul Goes West and The Vampire's Tomb

By Tom Weaver

The words **REGISTERED 1951** on the title pages of the two Ed Wood scripts reproduced in this book constitute a puzzler. If we could be sure that these scripts were indeed written in 1951, a *lot* of Ed Wood-Bela Lugosi-Alex Gordon history might need to be re-written, because an examination of these scripts upsets the "conventional wisdom" apple cart. Not just "upsets" it, but pours gasoline on it, lights it and rolls it off the edge of a cliff!

The problem, in a nutshell, is this: All "The Books" say that Wood and Alex Gordon met in connection with the making of the Western *The Lawless Rider* in 1952, and that Gordon subsequently introduced Wood to Lugosi. But how can that be correct when *The Ghoul Goes West*, supposedly written in 1951, features a character who talks and acts like a stereotypical Bela baddie and is packed with moments lifted from past Lugosi movies? The first paragraph of the *Vampire's Tomb* script calls for the words "BELA LUGOSI in" to fill the screen before the title appears. Why would Ed Wood, in 1951, write Bela Lugosi vehicles, if Lugosi was someone Wood had never met and was making no effort to meet? Could he have been associated with Lugosi even before Alex Gordon was?

I find it hard to believe they were written in 1951, but don't ask me why Wood would put "1951" on the

covers of scripts written after that year. Perhaps in 1951 he wrote scripts with these titles and, after he entered the Belasphere, he rewrote and "Lugosified" them? The task of trying to connect the dots in the weird world of Edward D. Wood Jr. rivals the lunacy of Calvin and Hobbes' Calvinball.

The Ghoul Goes West

The title suggests a takeoff on the English ghost comedy *The Ghost Goes West* (1936) but *The Ghoul Goes West* is actually *Bride of the Monster* (1956) in cowboy hat and Western chaps. In *Bride of the Monster*, Lugosi is a foreigner-scientist, banished from his homeland, who has set up shop in a desolate American locale and has henchman Tor Johnson kidnapping locals for his experimental use (he intends to create a race of supermen). In *The Ghoul Goes West*, the Lugosi-like main character is a foreigner-scientist, banished from his homeland, who has set up shop in a desolate American locale and has his *two* Tor Johnson-like henchmen stealing corpses for his experimental use (he intends to create a race of supermen). In both movies, the scientist holds a woman captive throughout, her lawman boyfriend at last arriving to rescue her and battling the henchman/henchmen. As mentioned above, *Ghoul*'s script is also filled with short scenes, bits of "business" and dialogue that will have you flashing back to past Lugosi flicks, from *White Zombie* and *Murders in the Rue Morgue* (both 1932) to *Voodoo Man* (1944) and *Abbott and Costello Meet*

Bela in approximately 1955 or '56, after Hollywood put him out to polka-dotted pasture. There'd be no more starring roles in new movies, not even in Ed Wood movies, in his limited future.

Wood's colleague and crony Alex Gordon (left) with his friend and longtime boss Gene Autry. Rumor has it that Autry was interested in the hero spot in *Ghoul Goes West*.

Frankenstein (1948), and even to a couple of his serials.

Below are synopses of *The Ghoul Goes West* and *The Vampire's Tomb*. They've been written (1) so that future researchers will find in this book short, user-friendly recaps of the plots of these two scripts, and (2) so that I could insert a number of observations and do some peanut-gallery kibitzing of my own. My comments are in **bold**.

The Ghoul Goes West Synopsis

The story begins at night in a small cemetery where a giant of a man ("well over six foot tall and weighing perhaps three hundred pounds") with a lantern stands over a grave in which a second person, unseen, is digging. When the giant's accomplice climbs out of the

grave, we see that he "is as tall as perhaps a bit taller than the other." **The script later describes the second giant as an eight-footer, which certainly *is* "a bit taller," no "perhaps" about it. An opening scene of grave robbers in a lonely cemetery calls to mind the 1931 *Frankenstein*.** They carry the unearthed coffin on their shoulders to their horse-drawn wagon and ride away. Nearby is the small shack of cemetery caretaker Ezra, who lies collapsed in the doorway battered and bloody.

Ezra revives and staggers on foot to the small mining community nearby. Finally he reaches Sheriff Chance Hilton's office and collapses in the doorway. **This guy must just *like* to lie in doorways.** Deputy Tom helps Ezra to his feet and seats him in a chair. Fortified by a

Picture Tor Johnson-like heads on *Frankenstein*'s Henry and Fritz and you may have some idea how *The Ghoul Goes West*'s opening scene, with grave robbers Karl and Tanz, might have looked.

Years before Wood conceived of his roadside kidnappers Karl and Tanz, John Carradine and Pat McKee played identical characters in Lugosi's *Voodoo Man*.

slug from a pint bottle of whiskey, Ezra tells Deputy Tom that the grave robbers have struck again (the third time in two weeks), bashing him in the head on this go-round. Deputy Tom knows that Chance is at Lover's Leap with his girl, so he unlocks a cell door and tells prisoner Skimpy to fetch him. Skimpy, serving ten days for some drunken misdemeanor, is bewhiskered and nervous "but a nice little guy." **Whenever he's part of a scene, I picture "Gabby" Hayes.**

At Lover's Leap, a cliff-top spot, Chance and his girl Nancy Corbet **(or Corbett—they alternate)** snuggle at the base of a tree. Nancy, wearing a blouse topped with a fuzzy pink *angora* **(what else?)** cardigan, just inherited the Double S Ranch from her deceased Uncle Pat. Chance mentions a "haunted" mine up in the buttes, abandoned when strange noises frightened away the workers. Skimpy arrives and fills Chance in about the grave robbers. Nancy tells Chance she'll find her way home alone, and he advises her to hurry: "Make like the Lone Ranger." **The Lone Ranger, the fictional character created for radio in 1933? I guess *The Ghoul Goes West* would have been one of those "shared universe" movies.**

Nancy heads home on horseback through the woods on a narrow road. Her horse "bolts" slightly when, on the road ahead, they see the giants and their wagon. One giant has the horses pull the wagon off the road as much as possible, as though they're making room for Nancy to pass, which the frightened girl tries to do—but once she's within the taller giant's reach, "reach" he does, pulling

her from her horse. **A pair of dumb galoots, waiting at night on a lonely road to seize a passing girl for their mad doctor master, recalls Toby and Grego (John Carradine and Pat McKee) snatching girl motorists in Lugosi's *Voodoo Man* (1944).**

Chance arrives at his office where Doc Simpson is patching up Ezra. Ezra rants that he's quitting his caretaker job ("As of when I got hit my resignation became final...") and claims that the grave robbers "was as dead as the ones they was diggin' up and stealin'." Chance, Ezra, Doc Simpson and Deputy Tom head for the cemetery.

Drawn by coal-black horses, the giants' wagon (with the coffin and Nancy under a tarpaulin in the back) heads up a mountainous road with a dangerous cliff on one side. At the top is a mine shaft, "a foreboding sight of disaster and horror"(!). A struggling Nancy is dragged down a mine corridor to a cobwebby chamber where a man is loudly and wildly playing a pipe organ, his head swaying to the weird music. **Monster Kids may think of Lugosi's Dr. Vollin, pumping away at the organ as Jean (Irene Ware) looks on in awe in *The Raven* (1935).** The organ player, in striped trousers and lounging jacket, is Professor Smoke, the local undertaker. His two giants are named Karl and Tanz; Tanz is "the shorter of the two giants" and Karl is "the tallest [sic] of the two giants." **I'm wondering if Wood would have had Tor Johnson play Karl or Tanz.**

Wood calls for an extreme closeup of Professor Smoke's eyes in a shot where he fixes Karl with a hypnotic stare and gives him an order. **Movies in which Lugosi has**

After Dr. Vollin (Lugosi) tickles the ivories in *The Raven* (1935), Jean (Irene Ware) says he's almost a god. Lugosi as Prof. Smoke would have again played the organ–and been god-like (raising the dead)–in *The Ghoul Goes West*.

a big brutish henchman or henchmen, and movies in which he has hypnotic powers, are too numerous to list. **The way Wood indicates an extreme closeup of** *only Professor Smoke's eyes* **calls to mind** *White Zombie*, **perhaps the only movie where Lugosi the Hypnotist is seen in** *that* **tight a closeup...until Wood and Lugosi did it in** *Bride of the Monster*. Professor Smoke is polite enough with Nancy, but she senses that she's the prisoner of this weirdo, and she *is*. **When Professor Smoke is done talking with Nancy, he orders Tanz, "Take her to my quarters!" In** *Bride of the Monster*, **when Vornoff is done with Janet, he orders, "Lobo! Take the girl to my quarters!"**

Next we see Professor Smoke hovering over an operating table in a small laboratory, working on someone (presumably the body exhumed by Karl and Tanz). We can tell by the way he closes his eyes and sighs, and later looks at the floor with "saddened eyes," that whatever he was trying to do, he failed. **This evokes a memory of** *Murders in the Rue Morgue*: **Dr. Mirakle's failed experiment with the blood of the Woman of the Streets (Arlene Francis), and the way he becomes emotional when he realizes she has died.** Professor Smoke tells the giants, "Get rid of it" (the body), and they

drop it through an opening in the floor into a "bottomless pit." **In** *Rue Morgue*, **Mirakle tells his henchman Janos (Noble Johnson), "Get rid of it" (the body of the Woman of the Streets), and Janos drops it through a trap door into the river. Regardless of whether** *Ghoul Goes West* **was written in 1951 or later, either way it was pre-***Shock Theater***. Wood's ability to remember so many individual Lugosi movie scenes, and in this case even a short line of dialogue, is impressive.** The Professor enters the room where Nancy is imprisoned and sadly makes a speech **reminiscent of Dr. Vornoff's "I** *have* **no home" speech in** *Bride of the Monster* **(see page 24 of the script)**, complete with references to his experiments prompting his exile from his home country. He also mentions his inability to control the brains of his creations, **this dialogue reminiscent of** *Abbott and Costello Meet Frankenstein's* **Count Dracula (Lugosi), fixated on finding a new, simple, compliant brain for the Monster.** The Professor cannot control the giants without the use of drugs, regularly administered; **we get the feeling that if they regained their souls, they would tear the Professor to pieces—shades of Lugosi's**

Wood describes Professor Smoke's eyebrows as black and bushy; perhaps Wood was recalling Bela's caterpillar eyebrows in *Murders in the Rue Morgue*.

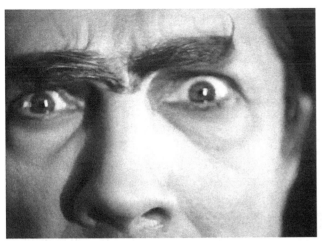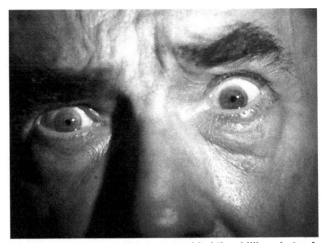

The eyes have it: The *Ghoul Goes West* script calls for closeups of Lugosi's eyes that would have resembled the chilling shots of Murder's (Lugosi) eyes in *White Zombie* (left), an effect Wood also used in *Bride of the Monster* (right).

Murder in *White Zombie*. We also flash back to the serial *SOS Coast Guard* (1937) and Lugosi's human slave Thorg (Richard Alexander), his scarred head a visual reminder of Lugosi's mutilation of his mind. **Throughout the 12 chapters of *SOS Coast Guard*, Thorg gives Lugosi nothing but "If looks could kill" looks while at the same time obeying him like a dog**.

As Chance, Doc, Ezra and Deputies Tom and Steve search the graveyard for clues, Professor Smoke makes an unexpected appearance; he wears a long black cloak and a friendly smile. **A cloaked, smiling Professor Smoke in a shabby little cemetery of wooden crosses... how can we *not* recall *Plan 9 from Outer Space's* (1958) cemetery footage with Lugosi enthusiastically swanning around as the cloaked, back-from-the-dead Old Man?** Professor Smoke plays dumb so Chance fills him in on what happened. Ezra mentions having seen the giants, and the Professor now regards him as though he poses some kind of threat.

It's morning before Chance arrives back at his office. Doc Simpson arrives with the bad news that Nancy never arrived back at her Double S Ranch. Her foreman Marty Bullock tells Chance that he has some of his men searching the hills for her already. At the spot where Nancy was abducted, Chance later finds the tracks of wagon wheels.

Back in town, Ezra the caretaker is dressed up and carrying a suitcase, preparing to leave town. On his shoulder perches his small pet bird, **a quirky touch reminiscent of the aptly named Police Capt. Robbins (Harvey B. Dunn) having a pet bird in his office in *Bride of the Monster*. Ezra calls his bird Fooey;** according to the American Film Institute, the bird in *Bride of the Monster* was named Fooey in real life. Perhaps a pet bird named Fooey was part of Ed Wood's past or present life. Chance wants Ezra to stick around a bit longer so, because Ezra is toting an unloaded gun, Chance threatens to jail him for carrying a concealed weapon if he won't stay willingly. Chance tells the distraught Ezra to go to his cemetery shack and fetch him the last couple months of burial records. Later that day, Ezra is walking back to town with Fooey on his shoulder and the records under his arm when Professor Smoke rides up behind him on his hearse wagon and offers him a ride. Ezra reluctantly climbs aboard.

Chance cooks up a plan to catch the grave robbers, sharing it with his deputies and Doc Simpson. That night at the saloon, Nancy's foreman Marty, very drunk, grabs one of the chorus girls, fighting off the bartender and other men. Even saloon owner Melody can't calm him down. Chance arrives, and Marty says some things that make it clear that he resents that Nancy is Chance's girl. The two men fight, with Chance prevailing. Marty is about to hand Chance his gun butt-end first, when he suddenly spins it around and fires four times at the lawman. Doc Simpson pronounces Chance dead as Deputies Tom and Steve haul Marty to jail. Melody, who loved Chance, is especially upset. Doc Simpson says that Chance's wish, should he be killed, was to be buried immediately, so a sunset funeral is announced.

At Professor Smoke's undertaking parlor, with just Simpson and the Professor in the room, Chance sits up smiling. The Professor is nonplussed. Chance and Simp-

Surely *Bride of the Monster*'s Harvey B. Dunn and Fooey (the bird) would have played cemetery caretaker Ezra and *his* bird Fooey.

son explain that they've devised a plan to catch the grave robbers: Marty pretended to shoot and kill Chance so that Chance could be buried alive with an oxygen mask and an air bottle and await the grave robbers, who (he hopes) will take him to Nancy. **In the 1800s or when-ever *Ghoul Goes West* is set, were there really oxygen tanks and masks with capacities of "several hours"? I'd bet there weren't. The eight-foot, scientifically created giant Karl doesn't faze me, but the oxygen tank does!** Meanwhile, back at the jail, Marty is worried by an unexpected development: Angry townsfolk are starting to act like they might throw him a party. A necktie party.

Professor Smoke drops in on his prisoner Nancy to sadistically tell her that Chance has been murdered by her foreman Marty, adding, "But do not fear—you will see him again—when I have his coffin brought here tonight—" When the Professor notices that Karl is being disobedient, there's a scene where we get to see every step of the process as the undertaker fetches a hypodermic needle, selects a bottle from a shelf, pierces the cork with the needle, carefully fills the barrel and gives Karl an injection. **If Wood wrote this borderline "How To" scene after the world knew of Lugosi's addiction and how drug-fuddled he'd become, it's in pretty poor taste.**

The Professor goes back to his undertaking parlor and, when Chance isn't looking, takes the bullets out of his gun and damages the oxygen apparatus. He then seals Chance in his coffin. Karl and Tanz enter the room and carry Chance's coffin away. Later, at Chance's funeral, a different coffin is buried. Melody whips the mourners into a frenzy with talk of stringing up Marty, and they rush back into town to do so. The men use a pole as a battering ram on the sheriff's office door; Doc and the deputies decide to reveal that Chance is still alive, a good plan except they all get knocked out by the rioters. Marty screams that Chance isn't dead, that it's all a plan to catch the ghouls, but he's dragged outside. With Melody in charge, the mob is about to stretch Marty's neck when Doc and the deputies reappear and insist that Chance is alive in his grave, awaiting the ghouls. (Marty to Melody: "When this is all over I'm goin'a paddle you good.") Melody agrees that they'll all go to the cemetery to see if the story can be verified; if it can't, Marty will swing from a cemetery tree. **Melody is eager to hang Marty, perhaps partly just for the fun of it, and she even threatens to have Deputy Tom killed. In a movie about a corpse-robbing murderer-mad scientist, *she's* the most detestable character!**

Imagine everyone's surprise when the coffin is opened—and it contains the body of the shot-in-the-back Ezra and his still-living bird Fooey. Taking advantage of the confusion, Marty makes a break, jumps on a horse and gallops off, members of the mob in pursuit. Meanwhile, Chance—still in his coffin—is on an operating table in the mine while Professor Smoke again pounds away at the organ. Nancy, escaping from the Professor's quarters, realizes that someone is in the coffin and unlocks it. Chance, gasping for air, lifts the lid and sits up.

Back at the sheriff's office, Skimpy shows up and claims that he heard screams and organ music emanating from the haunted mine; Doc realizes at once that it must be the grave robbers' hideout. Meantime, at the mine, Tanz walks in on Chance and Nancy and goes on the attack. Chance mostly dodges to stay out of the way of Tanz, who moves like a wrestler. **Okay, there's my answer; Wood would have had Tor Johnson play Tanz.** Tanz falls through the floor into the bottomless pit. **The script description of Chance, bleeding, his clothes torn, makes me think of Dick Craig**

(Tony McCoy) at the end of his lab fight with Lobo (Tor Johnson) in *Bride of the Monster*.

Chance and Nancy sneak up on the organ-playing Professor Smoke, but he's cool as a cucumber because he knows Karl is still around to protect him. Karl makes an appearance and begins stalking the sheriff as Smoke explains that he transplants glands into his subjects, making them two, three, four times as big and strong as a normal person, and immune from illness. Nancy says, "He's mad," **even though...ummmm...Nancy? He's not *talking* about doing it, he's *done* it! Professor Smoke's speech about glands calls to mind the gland-happy scientist (John Carradine) in *The Unearthly* (1957), a movie that already reeks of Ed Wood influence even though there doesn't seem to be any proof that Wood had anything to do with it.** Just as Karl gets his big hands on Chance, Marty rides up to the mine, the posse right behind him. Marty runs into the mine, closing and locking the double doors, and now joins with Chance in fighting Karl. Melody dynamites the door, and Karl is destroyed by the blast. As Professor Smoke drags Nancy out of the organ room through a secret door, Melody and the angry townsmen surge in; when they get a gander at Chance, they realize their lynch mob fun is over. Nancy gets away from the Professor, who climbs up onto his hearse wagon and hightails it down the winding mountain road. Chance pursues him on horseback. When Smoke sees the deputies and Doc riding up the incline toward him, he loses control. The hearse crashes end over end down the cliffside. **It's very much like a serial villain demise, and reminiscent of Bela's death by airplane crash in *The Phantom Creeps* (1939)—a favorite of Ed Wood's.**

In the happy ending, Marty comically chases after Melody, apparently intent on paddling her the way he threatened, Skimpy says and does silly "Gabby" Hayes-type stuff, and Chance and Nancy snuggle.

Professor Smoke's gland-transplanting surgeries seem identical to those of *The Unearthly*'s Charles Conway (John Carradine).

A thought that occurred to me while reading *The Ghoul Goes West*: At about the midpoint, I realized that I wasn't finding as much Ed Wood clunker dialogue as I'd expected. In fact, none of the dialogue was jumping out at me as outstandingly awful. Where was the wealth of "Wood-sian" gobbledygook? It had become conspicuous by its *absence*. How was this possible?

One likely explanation: *Ghoul Goes West* has a Western setting, most of the characters are simple, plain-spoken folks, and apparently Wood could write that kind of Z-movie dialogue just fine. The only character who speaks awkwardly is Professor Smoke, and since I hear Lugosi in my mind's ear as I read the Professor's lines, even *this* dialogue sounds okay because I'm used to it from Lugosi; throughout his career, he was frequently stuck with awkward dialogue. (And even when the dialogue *was* okay, Lugosi had the ability to make it *sound* awkward!) It was when Wood wrote dialogue for modern-day policemen and psychiatrists and other professionals that he over-thought and tried to impress and ended up with a hot mess.

Take the Ed Wood Dialogue Challenge: Re-watch one of the worst-of-the-worst Woods and, every time a line

"THE PHANTOM GHOUL"

FADE IN:

1. EXT. SMALL CEMETERY - MEDIUM CLOSE - PANNING - NIGHT

As the camera pans a small western style cemetery to show rough crosses, wooden head boards, a scattered granite head stone here and there and one or two big marble monuments. The cemetery holds the stillness of the dead except for the soft scraping of a spade as it digs into the earth. As the camera comes to rest on the action the scraping changes to the sound of a spade hitting then scraping on wood. The camera moves in until, clearly, we see a giant of a man well over six foot tall and weighing perhaps three hundred pounds. He is holding a lantern over an open grave. He sits the lantern down and tosses a rope into the grave. For another long moment he looks deep into the grave where his accomplice works. The man who at this point comes out of the grave is a giant some eight feet tall. He tosses the spade to the ground and dusts his hands together. Both men move one on each end of the grave and lift up the ropes readied there for them......

DISSOLVE TO:

2. EXT. SAME - MEDIUM LONG SHOT

As we see the two men, a coffin securely on their shoulders, as they walk through the cemetery.....

DISSOLVE TO:

3. EXT. CARETAKER'S SHACK - CEMETERY - MEDIUM CLOSE - DOLLY TO CLOSE

On a team of horses and a wagon as the two giants carrying their ghoulish burden move into the scene at the rear of the wagon. Quickly they deposit the casket into the wagon then get onto the wagon seat. They drive off. As the wagon is driven off scene we can see that hidden behind it was a small cemetery

CONTINUED

---

14. MEDIUM WIDE ANGLE

The deputy selects a key from his ring. He inserts it into the lock and twists it. The cell door comes open. The little man grabs his hat and jams it down over his ears. The deputy puts a small ignition key into his hand....

DEPUTY
Take the Sheriff's car - an make it fast ------

SKIMPY
Sure...

TOM
An on the way stop an tell Doc. Simpson to hightail it over here pronto....

SKIMPY
Sure.....

The little man moves off fast as Tom, the deputy, walks back to Ezra.....

EZRA
Think he can find Chance alright?

TOM
Like he said - If he can't - nobody can......

DISSOLVE TO:

15. EXT. LOVER'S LEAP - MEDIUM CLOSE - NIGHT

A spot high on a lone cliff which looks out over a vast stretch of land far below. A lone tree stands a few feet back from the cliff's edge. Beyond the tree a pair of saddled horses can be seen quietly grazing. Beneath the tree, seated on the ground, their backs against the tree trunk is a young man and a young girl. The girl, Sally, wears riding trousers, boots, and an angora vee-necked sleeveless sweater over a long sleeved rayon blouse. The young

CONTINUED

---

18. CONTINUED

CHANCE
Guess that's because it has so much more freedom out here. It can just saddle up and roam all over the place and not be cluttered up with streets and houses....All but for that old castle up in the buttes....Guess that one dark spot don't matter much --- The old moon just rides off around it.....

SALLY
Tell me about the castle....

19. CLOSE SHOT - CHANCE

CHANCE
Not much to tell - nobody's used it for years. An old Scotsman came to this country years ago and brought his castle - stone by stone - with him. He had it rebuilt up in the buttes just like it had been in Scotland. The old boy died twenty years ago. Nobody ever claimed it - so there it sits - kind of spooky like - getting old and musty year after year......

20. CLOSE TWO

SALLY
Sounds romantic.....

CHANCE
I don't think you'd find it very romantic......

SALLY
Let's ride up there one day soon.

CONTINUED

Three pages from Wood's *Phantom Ghoul* script: the mood-setting opening page; page 6 where Skimpy is given the keys to the sheriff's car (rather than a horse) to go fetch him; and page 8 where the sheriff describes the Scottish castle brought to America stone by stone and reconstructed here (Wood probably stole this idea from the 1936 ghost comedy *The Ghost Goes West*).

delivered by a Timothy Farrell or a Lyle Talbot or a Kenne Duncan sounds ungrammatical or hilariously bizarre or even completely senseless, now replay it in your mind's ear *in the voice of Bela Lugosi*. If you're like me, each line instantly becomes completely okay, even natural when coming from Bela!

Before we move on to the synopsis of *The Vampire's Tomb*...

The Phantom Ghoul

Also still extant, and in the collection of Gary Rhodes, is a different draft of the above-described *Ghoul Goes West* script, this one titled *The Phantom Ghoul*. It's 90-something percent the same as *The Ghoul Goes West* but the differences are worth mentioning, which is what I'll do below. The "big news" in this draft is that we learn that Ed Wood intended for Lon Chaney Jr. to play the role of foreman Marty.

"The storrry must be *told*"—again: What follows is

a slightly abridged duplication of the *Ghoul Goes West* synopsis above *except*—things that are in the *Ghoul Goes West* draft but not in *Phantom Ghoul* are ~~crossed out~~, things that are in *Phantom Ghoul* but weren't in *Ghoul Goes West* are **bold**.

The Phantom Ghoul Synopsis

The story begins at night in a small cemetery where a giant of a man ("well over six foot tall and weighing perhaps three hundred pounds") with a lantern stands over a grave in which a second person, unseen, is digging. When the giant's accomplice climbs out of the grave, we see that he "~~is as tall as perhaps a bit taller than the other.~~" **is a giant some eight feet tall**. They carry the unearthed coffin on their shoulders to their horse-drawn wagon and ride away. Nearby is the small shack of cemetery caretaker Ezra, who lies in the doorway battered and bloody.

Ezra revives and staggers on foot to the small mining community nearby. **Along with a few horses, there are a couple of automobiles and a pick-up truck parked on the street and a sheriff's car in an alleyway. One of the reasons I think this *Phantom Ghoul* draft may have preceded the *Ghoul Goes West* draft is that, in *Ghoul Goes West*, Wood writes about trails and vehicles as though it's the automobile age: a "one-lane" road, vehicles that "screech" when they're at top speed and "screech" to a stop, etc. Reading *Ghoul Goes West*, I get the impression that it's a rewrite of an earlier script that featured cars.** Finally he reaches Sheriff Chance Hilton's office and collapses in the doorway. Deputy Tom helps Ezra to his feet and seats him in a chair. Ezra tells Deputy Tom that the grave robbers have struck again, bashing him in the head on this go-round. Deputy Tom knows that Chance is at Lover's Leap with his girl, so he unlocks a cell door and tells prisoner Skimpy to fetch him. Skimpy, serving ten days for some drunken misdemeanor, is bewhiskered and nervous "but a nice little guy." **Deputy Tom gives Skimpy the key to the sheriff's car.**

At Lover's Leap, a cliff-top spot, Chance and his girl ~~Nancy Corbett~~ **Sally Corbett** snuggle at the base of a tree. ~~Nancy~~, **Sally**, ~~wearing a blouse topped with a fuzzy pink *angora* cardigan~~, just inherited ~~the Double S Ranch~~ **a dude ranch** from her deceased Uncle Pat. Chance men-

tions an old castle up in the buttes, MacGregor Castle, brought to America stone by stone by an old Scotsman who died 20 years ago. Skimpy arrives and fills Chance in about the grave robbers. ~~Nancy~~ **Sally** tells Chance she'll find her way home alone.

~~Nancy~~ **Sally** heads home on horseback through the woods on a narrow road. ~~Her horse "bolts" slightly~~ **She pulls up** when, on the road ahead, ~~they see~~ **she sees** the giants and their wagon. One giant has the horses pull the wagon off the road as much as possible, as though they're making room for ~~Nancy~~ **Sally** to pass, which the frightened girl tries to do—but once she's within the taller giant's reach, "reach" he does, pulling her from her horse.

Chance arrives at his office where Doc Simpson is patching up Ezra. Ezra rants that he's quitting his caretaker job and claims that the grave robbers "was as dead as the ones they was diggin' up and stealin'." Chance, Ezra, Doc Simpson and Deputy Tom head for the cemetery.

Drawn by coal-black horses, the giants' wagon (with the coffin and ~~Nancy~~ **Sally** under a tarpaulin in the back) heads up a mountainous road with a dangerous cliff on one side. At the top is MacGregor Castle. A struggling ~~Nancy~~ **Sally** is dragged ~~down a mine corridor~~ **into the castle and then** to a cobwebby chamber where a man is loudly ~~and wildly~~ playing a pipe organ, ~~his head swaying to the weird music~~. The organ player is Professor Smoke, the local undertaker. His two giants are named Karl and Tanz.

Wood calls for an extreme closeup of Professor Smoke's eyes in a shot where he fixes Karl with a hypnotic stare and gives him an order. Professor Smoke is polite enough with ~~Nancy~~ **Sally**, but she senses that she's the prisoner of this weirdo, and she *is*.

Next we see Professor Smoke hovering over an operating table in a small laboratory, working on someone (presumably the body exhumed by Karl and Tanz). We can tell by the way he closes his eyes and sighs, and later looks at the floor with "~~saddened eyes~~," **"a saddened face,"** that whatever he was trying to do, he failed. Professor Smoke tells the giants, "Get rid of it" (the body) ~~and they drop it through an opening in the floor into a "bottomless pit". The Professor enters the room where Nancy is imprisoned and sadly makes a speech, complete with references to his experiments prompting his exile from his home country. He also mentions his inability to control the brains of his creations. The Professor can-~~

~~not control the giants without the use of drugs, regularly administered~~. The Professor enters the room where ~~Nancy~~ **Sally** is imprisoned and talks with frustration (but no clarity!) about his continued failures.

As Chance, Doc, Ezra and Deputies Tom and Steve search the graveyard for clues, Professor Smoke makes an unexpected appearance. The Professor plays dumb so Chance fills him in on what happened. ~~Ezra mentions having seen the giants, and the Professor now regards him as though he poses some kind of threat.~~ **The Professor leaves in his small black coupe.**

It's morning before Chance arrives back at his office. Doc Simpson arrives with the bad news that ~~Nancy~~ **Sally** never arrived back at her ~~Double S Ranch~~ **dude ranch**. Her foreman Marty Bullock **(Lon Chaney Jr.)** tells Chance that he has some of his men searching the hills for her already. At the spot where ~~Nancy~~ **Sally** was abducted, Chance later finds the tracks of wagon wheels.

Back in town, Ezra the caretaker is dressed up and carrying a suitcase, preparing to leave town. ~~On his shoulder perches his small pet bird.~~ Chance wants Ezra to stick around a bit longer so, because Ezra is toting an unloaded gun, Chance threatens to jail him for carrying a concealed weapon if he won't stay willingly. Chance tells the distraught Ezra to go to his cemetery shack and fetch him the last couple months of burial records. Later that day, Ezra is walking back to town with ~~Fooey on his shoulder and~~ the records under his arm when Professor ~~Smoke rides up behind him on his hearse wagon and offers him a ride. Professor~~ Smoke's coupe comes along and the Professor offers him a ride. ~~Ezra reluctantly climbs aboard.~~ **A grateful Ezra climbs in.**

Chance cooks up a plan to catch the grave robbers, sharing it with his deputies and Doc Simpson. That ~~night~~ **afternoon** at the saloon, ~~Marty, very drunk, grabs one of the chorus girls, fighting off the bartender and other men. Even saloon owner Melody can't calm him down. Chance arrives, and Marty says some things that make it clear that he resents that Nancy is Chance's girl.~~ **Chance confronts a very drunk Marty about carrying a gun in a public place.** The two men fight, with Chance prevailing. Marty is about to hand Chance his gun butt-end first, when he suddenly spins it around and fires four times at the lawman. Doc Simpson pronounces Chance dead as Deputies Tom and Steve haul Marty to jail. ~~Melody, who loved Chance, is especially upset.~~ Doc Simpson

says that Chance's wish, should he be killed, was to be buried immediately, so a sunset funeral is announced.

At Professor Smoke's undertaking parlor, with just Simpson and the Professor in the room, Chance sits up smiling. ~~The Professor is nonplussed. Chance and Simpson explain that they've devised a~~ **The Professor has also been made aware of Chance's** plan to catch the grave robbers: Marty pretended to shoot and kill Chance so that Chance could be buried alive with an oxygen mask and an air bottle and await the grave robbers, who (he hopes) will take him to ~~Nancy~~ **Sally**. Meanwhile, back at the jail, Marty is worried by an unexpected development: Angry townsfolk are starting to act like they might throw him a party. A necktie party.

Professor Smoke drops in on his prisoner ~~Nancy~~ **Sally** to sadistically tell her that Chance has been murdered by her foreman Marty, adding, "But do not fear—you will see him again—when I have his ~~coffin~~ **body** brought here tonight—**later**...." When the Professor notices that Karl ~~is being disobedient~~, **has disobediently picked up a bottle on nitroglycerine,** there's a scene where we get to see every step of the process as the undertaker fetches a hypodermic needle, selects a bottle from a shelf, pierces the cork with the needle, carefully fills the barrel and gives Karl an injection. **Professor Smoke is angry that he needs "such things as this" (the drug injections) to control his giants.**

The Professor goes back to his undertaking parlor and, when Chance isn't looking, takes the bullets out of his gun and damages the oxygen apparatus. He then seals Chance in his coffin. Karl and Tanz enter the room and carry Chance's coffin away. Later, at Chance's funeral, a different coffin is buried. ~~Melody~~ **Skagley the bartender** whips the mourners into a frenzy with talk of stringing up Marty, and they rush back into town to do so. The men use a pole as a battering ram on the sheriff's office door; Doc and the deputies decide to reveal that Chance is still alive, a good plan except they all get knocked out by the rioters. ~~Marty screams that Chance isn't dead, that it's all a plan to catch the ghouls,~~ **Marty insists that Chance isn't dead, only faking,** but he's dragged outside. With ~~Melody~~ **Skagley** in charge, the mob is about to stretch Marty's neck when Doc and the deputies reappear and insist that Chance is alive in his grave, awaiting the ghouls. (~~Marty to Melody: "When this is all over I'm goin'a paddle you good."~~) **Marty to**

96. CONTINUED

speed and cuts out behind the corral heading out across the open country.

DISSOLVE TO:

97. EXT. PASTURE LAND - MEDIUM WIDE

As Chance plows across the picturesque countryside. He makes a sudden swerve and hits a dirt road....

98. CLOSE RUNNING SHOT

With Chance spurring the horse on to great speed along the road for a ways then he again cuts the horse off the road to head out again across country. The CAMERA CAR stops and the CAMERA holds on the East end of the horse going West until he is nearly out of sight....

DISSOLVE TO:

99. EXT. RANCH HOUSE SPREAD - MEDIUM WIDE

Of a low, nice looking ranch house. Four or five dude cowboys and girls are seated about at the corral and the guest house itself. A couple of nice looking automobiles are parked in various spots. Chance can be seen in the distance as he cuts across the open land behind the ranch house. He speeds in and pulls up in front of the ranch house.....

100. MEDIUM CLOSE

As Chance gets quickly out of the saddle. The door of the Ranch house opens. Marty Bullock (LON CHANEY) the foreman, comes out to meet Chance...Marty is a big, rough looking man, but a well meaning man that gets things done - quick - and efficiently....

CONTINUED

308. CONTINUED

holds his punch - realizing he is beaten before he starts in this case. Sally stifles a slight scream as her hand goes to her mouth...The monster, Karl, towers over both of them...The Professor moves into the shot...Chance turns on him.

CHANCE
Guess you know best - What trial....

PROFESSOR
But I don't mind you knowing my reasons for what I have done. That is - since you won't be telling anyone....

309. CLOSE SHOT - PROFESSOR

PROFESSOR
You will remember that the bodies taken from the grave were - a horse riding victim - an automobile accident victim and a fight victim - all accidental deaths - good sound bodies except for that which was destroyed and the cause of death. All the other organs were in perfect shape. Those who died of disease or old age would be useless to me....

310. CLOSE TWO SHOT - CHANCE & SALLY

PROFESSOR (o.s.)
Some time ago I perfected the use of organs and glands from the bodies of the accidental deaths to use in another body, making that body two - three - even four times as great as a normal - healthy body....

311. CLOSE SHOT - PROFESSOR.

PROFESSOR
I perfected the way to make a giant of a man - a man any

311. CONTINUED

PROFESSOR (cont'd)
country would give a fortune in money and glory to possess. With such a giant man which ever country gave enough, could rule the world.....

312. CLOSE SHOT - SALLY

SALLY
He is mad...

313. CLOSE SHOT - PROFESSOR

PROFESSOR
Mad - my experiments have been a success twice - Tanz, whom you subdued - and Karl who now gazes upon you. Is that the work of a mad man? I am sorry that I've had to do things the way I did - but radical science frowns upon such as my work. But then this past work was so much easier..I had to kill the victims myself in the early days in order to produce Tanz and Karl - but one little thing stands in my way of complete success - and that is the reason for the bodies of late - Even with all my projection I have no control over my two subjects without the use of hypnotic drugs that I slip into their arms once every forty-eight hours...Strange isn't it - To perfect one such as he and still not be his complete master without the use of drugs.. But such are the rewards of a scientist......

314. CLOSE GROUP SHOT.

CHANCE
How long do you think you can get away with this....?

CONTINUED

Three more *Phantom Ghoul* pages: page 31 where Wood indicates that he intends to cast Lon Chaney as Marty Bullock, and pages 96 and 97 where Professor Smoke talks about his grisly life-restoring procedure and his motives.

Skagley: "When this is all over and you're alone—I'm gonna' tear the hide from you in strips." ~~Melody~~ **Skagley** agrees that they'll all go to the cemetery to see if the story can be verified; if it can't, Marty will swing from a cemetery tree.

Imagine everyone's surprise when the coffin is opened—and it contains the body of the shot-in-the-back Ezra[1] ~~and his still-living bird Fooey~~. Taking advantage of the confusion, Marty makes a break, jumps on a horse and gallops off, members of the mob in pursuit **in their cars**. Meanwhile, Chance—still in his coffin—is on an operating table in the ~~mine~~ **castle** while Professor Smoke again pounds away at the organ. ~~Nancy~~, **Sally**, escaping from the Professor's quarters, realizes that someone is in the coffin and unlocks it. Chance, gasping for air, lifts the lid and sits up.

Back at the sheriff's office, Skimpy shows up and claims that he heard ~~screams and organ music~~ **"a hootin' and**

1 In the *Phantom Ghoul* script, Doc Simpson says of Ezra, "He's been shot between the eyes." Someone, presumably Wood, changed it by hand to "He's been shot in the back."

Chance has as much chance in a fight against Tanz as Dick did in his *Bride of the Monster* battle with Lobo.

a hollerin'" emanating from the ~~haunted mine~~ **castle**; Doc realizes at once that it must be the grave robbers' hideout. Meantime, at the ~~mine~~ **castle**, Tanz walks in on Chance and ~~Nancy~~ **Sally** and goes on the attack. Chance mostly dodges to stay out of the way of Tanz, who moves like a wrestler. ~~Tanz falls through the floor into the bottomless pit.~~ **After a long fight, Chance lands a knockout punch and Tanz topples to the floor. Chance and Sally wrap chains around him.**

Chance and ~~Nancy~~ **Sally** sneak up on the organ-playing Professor Smoke, but he's cool as a cucumber because he knows Karl is still around to protect him. Karl makes an appearance and begins stalking the sheriff as Smoke explains that he transplants glands **and organs** into his subjects, making them two, three, four times as ~~big and strong as a normal person, and immune from illness; "Think of how this would benefit all of humanity."~~ **great as a normal, healthy body; "I perfected the way to make a giant of a man—a man any country would give a fortune in money and glory to possess. With such a giant man, whichever country gave enough could rule the world..."** ~~Nancy~~ **Sally** says, "~~He's mad.~~" **"He is mad..."** ~~Just as Karl gets his big hands on Chance, Marty rides up to the mine, the posse right behind him. Marty runs into the mine, closing and lock-~~

~~ing the double doors, and now joins with Chance in fighting Karl. Melody dynamites the door, and Karl is destroyed by the blast. As Professor Smoke drags Nancy out of the organ room through a secret door, Melody and the angry townsmen surge in; when they get a gander at Chance, they realize their lynch mob fun is over. Nancy gets away from the Professor, who climbs up onto his hearse wagon and hightails it down the winding mountain road. Chance pursues him on horseback. When Smoke sees the deputies and Doc riding up the incline toward him, he loses control. The hearse crashes end over end down the cliffside.~~ **Doc, the deputies and Skimpy appear, their guns drawn. Karl moves toward them, unfazed by one of Tom's bullets, but Doc puts a bullet in his forehead that drops him. Meanwhile, Professor Smoke has dragged Sally outside. He casts her to the ground and drives off in his coupe. Chance jumps in his car and pursues him down the mountain road. By taking a short cut, Chance gets ahead of the Professor's car and then speeds toward him in reverse. Smoke gets rattled, tries to turn around but instead goes backwards off the edge of the cliff. The car is smashed to bits in the fall.**

As dawn breaks, Our Heroes head back toward town to see what's happened to Marty. The sound of a gunfight draws them to Sally's ranch where Marty is in the ranch house, holding off his would-be lynchers. Skagley and the others are shocked by Chance's reappearance, which ends the gun battle. Marty comes out of the house babbling Lennie-like: "Chance—Chance—Tell 'em you ain't dead—" Skagley is placed under arrest and the others shooed away.

In the happy ending, ~~Marty comically chases after Melody, apparently intent on paddling her the way he promised,~~ Skimpy says and does silly "Gabby" Hayes-type stuff, and Chance and ~~Nancy~~ **Sally** snuggle.

The Vampire's Tomb

When reading *The Ghoul Goes West–The Phantom Ghoul*, it's fun to I.D. the past horror movies from which Wood apparently scavenged all the bits and pieces of his plot. *The Vampire's Tomb* offers no such challenge because here Wood did some one-stop shop(lift)ing: It's a disguised remake of Lugosi's *Mark of the Vampire* (1935). Yes I know *Mark of the Vampire* was a remake of Lon Chaney's

Grrrrrrl on girl: *Mark of the Vampire*'s sometimes feral-looking vampiress (Carroll Borland) seemed to have fangs only for the hapless heroine (Elizabeth Allan). This is echoed by the vampiress' fixation on Barbara in Wood's *The Vampire's Tomb*.

812-118

London After Midnight (1927) so perhaps I should say that *Vampire's Tomb* is a disguised remake of *that* movie. But I have no idea whether Wood ever saw *London After Midnight*; he was a toddler when it was new, and where would he have seen it afterwards? To me, it seems infinitely more likely that he saw, and did his borrowing, from Bela's *Mark of the Vampire*. So I'm proceeding under that *assumption*.

How much is *The Vampire's Tomb* like *Mark of the Vampire*? *The Vampire's Tomb* includes a Girl Vampire with long black hair and grave clothes who throughout the movie creeps around a cemetery and in and out of the mansion where it's set (and twice appears to try to bite the heroine). This matches everything that Luna the vampire girl does in *Mark*. On top of this, *Vampire's Tomb* features Lugosi as a caped, vampiric-looking character doing some of the same things the actor did as the vampire Count Mora in *Mark*. If Wood *had* produced *The Vampire's Tomb* and a print turned up in 2016, a Monster Kid could watch it *without sound* and peg it as a *Mark of the Vampire* ripoff! And Wood's Mora and Luna counterparts are just the start of the *deja view* experience. (However, as Gary Rhodes points out, one actor playing vampire and vampire-hunter is *London After Midnight*, not *Mark of the Vampire*.)

The Vampire's Tomb does feature tried-and-true horror flick elements *not* found in *Mark of the Vampire*: The reading-of-a-will and greedy heirs in a creepy mansion reeks of *The Cat and the Canary*, innocents trapped by a wild storm in a house inhabited by a strange homicidal family is *The Old Dark House*, etc. But mainly it's *Mark of the Vampire*, enough so that if you don't know by the bottom of page 20 exactly how it'll end, you should be required to surrender your Monster Kid I.D. badge, decoder ring and beanie.

The script makes the reader wonder if Dr. Acula is a vampire or a vampire-hunter. It might have been fun, had the movie been made, to see Lugosi as a Van Helsing type. The actor would even have spewed Van Helsing-like dialogue, like "The strength of the vampire comes from the fact no one will believe in him" (page 37), a close copy of Van Helsing's *Dracula* line "The strength of the vampire is that people will *not* believe in him." On page 38 Dr. Acula says the alternative to staking a vampire is to remove the head from the body, a comment perhaps inspired by a *Mark of the Vampire* line: Prof. Zelen, who is Van Helsing in everything but name, says that the vampires' "heads must be severed with one clean stroke."

Wood dips into "werewolfology" for his page 36 line "Who-so-ever is bitten by the vampire, himself becomes a vampire…"; that's a takeoff on Maleva's "Whoever is bitten by a werewolf and lives, becomes a werewolf himself" in *The Wolf Man* (1941)—yet *another* movie with Lugosi. Wood avoids an obvious temptation in a scene (page 61) where Dr. Acula is offered a drink: He declines with the line "Never touch it, thank you," instead of the expected comeback… Well, *you* know.

Wood had actors in mind for all the characters in *The Vampire's Tomb* so, even though the movie was never made, I've included the actors' names in this synopsis so that, in your mind's eye, you can put faces on most of the characters—the same faces Wood put on them. (The fact that Loretta King is on Wood's front-of-the-script castlist means that the handwriting on that particular page *can't* be from 1951: Wood and King met in 1954.)

Not surprisingly for Wood, the door of the mansion's liquor cabinet gets a much more frequent work-out than the door of the mansion, the door of the tomb and every other door in the story. Don't play a drinking game where you take a drink as often as the characters do, because you'll soon be seeing pink Lugosis. But this *is* surprising: The word angora can be found nowhere in this script. Heroine Barbara *does*, however, rock "a fluffy marabou bed jacket" and, in a later scene, fur mules.

The Vampire's Tomb Synopsis

Wood calls for the *Vampire's Tomb* credits to be superimposed over a shot of Dr. Acula (Lugosi) in a windy cemetery at night. Following his gaze, the camera pans to the right and fixes on a tomb as a Girl Vampire (Devila) "in the long flowing roles of the dead" exits the structure and begins prowling in the cemetery. **When I picture in my mind's eye this action playing behind superimposed credits, I feel like I'm watching the opening of a TV horror anthology series.**

Lightning flashes and thunder rumbles outside an old two-storey mansion. A giant hovering bat checks out the house **in the same way that the Dracula bat "cases" the Edlemann house in *House of Dracula* (1945) and the Dracula bat spies on Prof. Stevens in *Abbott and Costello Meet Frankenstein*.** The Girl Vampire peers through French windows at two men and a younger woman in the library. **A vampire spying through a window at the inhabitants of a man-**

In the days before drones, Dracula himself was a spy in the sky, checking out his *Abbott and Costello Meet Frankenstein* lab through its skylight.

sion is from *Mark of the Vampire.*

The owner of this estate, Lucille, died two months ago, and tomorrow is the reading of her will. The trio in the library are her husband Dr. Judson Ruppert (former East Side Kid Bobby Jordan), his brother Flinch (Duke Moore) and their sister Diana Cordoni (Dolores Fuller), a hard-drinking Hollywood actress. They, and others, are responsible for Lucille being fatally poisoned; they also made sure her cause of death was listed as a heart attack so that they could get her money. Flinch alludes to the danger of one of the heirs bumping off other heirs in order to increase his or her slice of the pie.

Also there for the will-reading are Lucille's niece Barbara (Loretta King), her handsome young boyfriend Lake Lyon (Richard Powers) and Barbara's uniformed maid Paula (Mona McKinnon), none of whom know that Lucille was murdered. **Mona McKinnon later played a Paula for Wood in *Plan 9 from Outer Space.*** Barbara is asleep in her room when the Girl Vampire enters and glides toward the bed. Barbara's about to get it in the neck when she awakens, screams and faints. **The girl-on-girl vampire action is reminiscent of Luna's two attacks on Irena in *Mark.*** Lake pounds on the door, scaring off the Vampire. The room becomes crowded as elderly housekeeper Emma (Hazel Franklyn),

Judson, Flinch and Diana arrive. The frightened Barbara insists that the ghostly-looking intruder was her Aunt Lucille. **In *Mark,* Irena's father Sir Karell dies under similarly mysterious circumstances, then returns to haunt his own house.** The sound of a man's scream comes from outside, and Lake and Judson rush to investigate. Judson sees the Girl Vampire in the cemetery but doesn't tell Lake. On the edge of a cliff they find the hat of Flinch, who must have taken a fatal plunge. **"The *hat* of Flinch"—remember that.**

Rain is falling when two more guests arrive: another Ruppert brother, attorney Boris (Lyle Talbot), and Diana's husband, undertaker Frank (Frank Yaconelli). Standing unseen in the shadows of the garage is Dr. Acula, who holds his cape up over the lower part of his face (***Abbott and Costello Meet Frankenstein,* anyone?**) as he spies on Boris "with hatred." Boris and Frank were also "in on" Lucille's murder, as was Emma, now in Barbara's bedroom sitting watch over the endangered girl *a la* **Mina's nurse in *Dracula* and Irena's maid Maria in *Mark of the Vampire*.**

The fiendish family decides to cover up the inexplicable demise of Flinch the way they did their murder of Lucille: Boris will handle the legal details, Judson will make out

By covering most of his face, Lugosi drew all audience attention to his eyes in *Abbott and Costello Meet Frankenstein.*

a death certificate and Frank will take care of the body, once they find the body. They now talk about getting rid of Lake, Barbara and Paula. Lucille's will left pretty much everything to her sister Helen ("Who hasn't been seen or heard of in years…") and Barbara—but Boris has changed it so that Lucille's killers are her beneficiaries.

Standing outside in the storm, under a tree in the cemetery, is Dr. Acula. The script calls for a shot of his hypnotic eyes to carry over into the next shot, which shows Barbara in her bed. **That would have been reminiscent of a shot of Murder's (Lugosi) eyes superimposed over action in *White Zombie*.** Like a sleepwalker, Barbara wanders away from the house until Lake and Judson catch up with her. Barbara: "It was as though [Lucille] was calling to me from the very tomb itself…" **Did you just flash-back to Mina sleepwalking out onto the lawn, toward Dracula (Lugosi), in *Dracula*, or Irena sleepwalking out onto her terrace, toward Luna, in *Mark*? Incidentally, now that we know that the Girl Vampire is Lucille, I wonder if Wood took the name from *Dracula*'s Lucy (but didn't want to "go" with Lucy in that era when *I Love Lucy* ruled TV).**

Judson, Boris and Frank slog through the rain to Lucille's vault to make sure she's in her coffin, **reminding readers of the *Mark of the Vampire* scene of Prof. Zelen and Baron Otto on a similar mission to Sir Karell's tomb**. And, yes, there she is, in tattered black shrouds, her hair disheveled and lips bright red. Everyone is startled when Dr. Acula appears in the tomb doorway, "his long black cape hanging loosely down his back (*a la* Dracula)." After some introductions, Dr. Acula examines Lucille and declares that she is a vampire—pointing to the wet hem of her dress as proof that she has been out tonight. At Dr. Acula's request, Frank fetches a stake and a rock; they're presented to Judson, but he can't do it and hands off the grisly chore to Dr. Acula. While Judson, Boris and Frank wait outside, Dr. Acula gets into position to stake Lucille, and then tosses the stake and rock aside. Lucille slowly sits up in the coffin. Outside, the Rupperts are already discussing the liquidation of Dr. Acula.

After Dr. Acula emerges from the tomb, the men head back toward the house, "the wind pushing Dr. Acula's cape up behind him, giving him the appearance of a giant bat." In the brush, *some*thing is following them. Dr. Acula sees that it is the Girl Vampire; he "smiles, calmly—knowingly" and says nothing to the others. The four reach the house as the Girl Vampire "moves dream-like among the headstones"—**like Luna again. Well, everything the Girl Vampire *does* is like Luna**.

At this point, the number of characters begins dropping…quickly:

 Emma mounts a staircase and, near the top, sees some off-screen figure who fills her with horror. "You're…You're dead…" she whispers, just before a thrown knife pierces her heart. Paula sees the Girl Vampire and screams, **reminiscent of the *Mark of the Vampire* scene where servants Jan and Maria spot Lugosi's Count Mora in the house**.

 Even though the storm has probably made the roads impassable, a fed-up Boris decides to leave. He goes out to the garage and is about to drive away when he sees someone off-camera and becomes extremely nervous. A shot rings out, Boris slumps onto the wheel and the car crashes through the back wall of the garage and falls down the cliffside to the lake.

 When Diana opens a closet, the camera becomes the eyes of someone *in* the closet. Diana, horrified, faints. **This made me think of the "Murderous Cameraman in My Bedroom" scenes in 1944's *The Lodger*, the camera stalking the street singer (Doris Lloyd), and 1946's *The Spiral Staircase*, the camera spying on the lame girl (Myrna Dell).**

With dawn approaching, Dr. Acula tells Frank that he's hatched a new plan to dispatch Lucille and enlists his help. The two hike back to her tomb to await her return. When Dr. Acula opens her coffin, Frank is shocked to see Lucille inside. Then Dr. Acula hits him with, "It was arsenic poisoning, wasn't it?" Frank folds under pressure—but then pulls a gun. As Frank backs toward the opened doorway, preparing to shoot Dr. Acula, a shot from outside, coming in through the door, spins Frank around. Then the shooter—the supposedly dead Flinch Ruppert—enters and puts a second bullet into Frank as he dawdles toward death.

Holding Dr. Acula at gunpoint, Flinch cops to killing

his fellow "share holders" Emma, Boris and Diana, whose body is in a drawer in that very tomb. **Oh, what a "surprise": The guy we thought was the first victim is actually the killer, right out of Agatha Christie's *And Then There Were None*.** When Judson unexpectedly appears, he and Flinch level their guns at each other. Judson says he realized that Flinch wasn't dead when he found in the house a shoe matching Flinch's shoe found at the edge of the cliff**...writer Wood forgetting that at the edge of the cliff, Flinch's hat, not a shoe, was found.** From outside, Lake shouts, "Who's out here!!! Speak up!!!" which gives Flinch his chance to shoot the distracted Judson.

Now it's Flinch's turn to be distracted: Lucille opens the coffin and sits up, glaring at him. Flinch screams, drops the gun and bolts from the tomb, tangling with Lake outside as Barbara watches. Flinch runs, Lake chases him and the men again go fist to fist outside the garage. **Wood doesn't fully describe their battle, instead indicating in all-caps "FIGHT SEQUENCE TO BE DIRECTED TO THE DISCRESTION [sic] OF THE DIRECTOR."** The fight takes them into the garage. One of Lake's punches knocks Flinch into a pile of old tires and out the Boris'-car-sized opening at the back of the structure. Down the cliff he goes.

By daylight, deputy sheriffs are removing Diana's body from the tomb; Judson, still alive, will be patched up at the hospital in preparation for his future appointment with the hangman. Barbara and Lake are on hand when the sheriff (Bud Osborne) chides Dr. Acula, "Can't you private detectives ever find a case that ain't all cluttered up with murdered bodies...?" A deputy is frightened by the approach of the Girl Vampire, but she's actually Dr. Acula's client, Lucille's lookalike twin sister Helen in a black wig. Helen suspected that Lucille was murdered and hired Dr. Acula, who came up with the idea of Helen playing the resurrected Vampire Lucille, in order to put Lucille's killers on edge. "Clever—am I not...?" Dr. Acula smiles. **The Vampire's Tomb has the same two climactic surprises as *Mark of the Vampire*: The Van Helsing character is actually an investigator cracking a murder case, and the back-from-the-dead murder victim-turned-vampire is actually someone who's the murder victim's spitting image. Give Ed Wood his due: His variation on *Mark*'s surprise ending is an improvement. In** *The Vampire's Tomb*, **the lookalike is Lucille's twin sister, whereas in *Mark of the Vampire* the murdered Sir Karell's exact lookalike (and exact sound-alike) is just some cop named Franz!**

That **said, however, at least in *Mark of the Vampire*, Irena was "in on" the deception, which retroactively explains why she seemed to be in the power of the vampires, her sleepwalking excursion, etc. In *The Vampire's Tomb*, Barbara's "slave of the vampire" interludes are inexplicable.**

Wood did eventually ~~pay tribute to~~ **rip off** *Mark of the Vampire*: He followed *Bride of the Monster* and *Plan 9* with 1958's *Night of the Ghouls*, a semi-sequel to *Bride* that has a few similarities to *Mark*...if you look for them. In *Night of the Ghouls*, the old Willows Place, Dr. Vornoff's *Bride of the Monster* hideout, is shunned and feared by locals the way the vampire-haunted mansion was in *Mark*. Ghostly figures drift in and out of shadows and fog in shots too much like those in *Mark* to chalk up to coincidence. And the whole spook business is really just an elaborate scam.

Only two 35mm prints of *Night of the Ghouls* were ever made, and who knows if Wood ever saw it: It went unreleased for over a quarter-century. By the time it emerged from *its* crypt, Ed Wood was in his.

Ed Wood promised Lugosi the moon but couldn't deliver. Except for *Bride of the Monster*, all that their four-year association yielded for Bela was a strange supporting role in *Glen or Glenda* and a few scraps of footage used in *Plan 9*. Like unfinished symphonies, the rest...was silence.

Bela Lugosi, would-be star of *Final Curtain*, pictured here with Dolores Fuller at the Hollywood Historama in late 1953.

The Almost, Penultimate Final curtain

By Lee R. Harris

At the end of 1956, the greatest days of Ed Wood's creativity were ending. *Plan 9 from Outer Space,* shot in the third week of November, was being edited with an eye toward a March or April 1957 premiere.

To consider *Plan 9* Ed's creative peak, you'd have to see his anti-achievements as amounting to a "peak," and reveal some decline in the quality of his movies following the alleged Worst Film of All Time. In 1957 the skid amounted to the production of a Wood-scripted film (*The Bride and the Beast*) about a gorilla's obsession with a woman's angora sweater, and in 1958 making *Night of the Ghouls* with his usual stock company and crew. *The Sinister Urge* (1960) was one of the last old-fashioned exploitation films, and Wood's last legitimate directing credit. All that came after, until his 1978 death, were scripts for other producers, fast-buck pornographic fiction for magazines and novels, and softcore and hardcore loops and features.

Occasionally there were sad references to the headier days of the '50s, as in 1971's *Necromania*: Apprehensively entering a satanic bordello-sex clinic, actor Ric Lutze says, "At any moment, I expect to see Bela Lugosi as Dracula."

Neatly cleaving the era of Good Ed and Bad Ed is the 1957 television pilot *Final Curtain.* Lugosi is said to have been reading the script at the moment of his August 16,

Opening title to the film, a pilot for Wood's television series *Portraits in Terror*.

1956, demise, and while this is still debated, there's no doubt that Wood wrote it with Lugosi in mind.

For over 20 years, *Final Curtain* was as impossible to see as *Night of the Ghouls,* which incorporates some of its footage. Wood told actress Valda Hansen that he was withholding *Ghouls* from release "because of the way they want to deride me," but the truth is that he couldn't afford the lab fees. *Ghouls* was rescued from limbo for home video release in the 1980s, but the two known prints of *Final Curtain* remained in the hands of private collectors.

After the May 2006 death of veteran Wood actor Paul (Kelton the Cop) Marco, his great-nephew Jason Insalaco cleaned out Marco's West L.A. apartment and made a unique discovery. In the drawer of a bedside stand was a letter from Wood, detailing his plans for selling *Final Curtain* to television. This set Insalaco on a dogged mission to locate the 22-minute, nearly 50-year-old film.

His search eventually led him to one of the aforementioned private collectors and a pile of deteriorating 35mm reels smelling of vinegar. A couple of the cans were tantalizingly marked **WOOD – Final Curtain**. Insalaco purchased the footage and contacted friend Jonathan Harris to set about restoring this obscurity.

Somewhere en route to *Final Curtain*'s December 2011 premiere at the Slamdance Film Festival, it underwent a trick as old as the movie biz itself. In a digital-age equivalent of the nickelodeon era problem of prints

James "Duke" Moore, the intrepid lieutenant from *Plan 9 from Outer Space* (1958), roams the deserted theater in *Final Curtain*.

being swiped for a few hours and duped at a lab, someone absconded with *Final Curtain* and put it on YouTube. Insalaco and Harris, interviewed for the book *The Cinematic Misadventures of Ed Wood* (BearManor Media, 2015), have no idea when or how this happened.

The technological advancements since Ed Wood's death have brought his films to his true audience. In his time, watching a movie in his home meant 16mm projected through a haze of cigarette smoke. Immediately following his December 10, 1978, passing came the VCR (called "VTR" at the time). Just as the video revolution brought us Wood's then-mythically rare *Glen or Glenda* (1953), the Internet now enables us to see *Final Curtain*. The print, save for intermittent scratches on the right side, is exceptionally clear and bright. (Insalaco and Harris claim their version is even better.)

Viewing *Final Curtain*, one is struck by the familiar stamps of Ed's auteurist personality. There's stock footage of lightning flashes, reliance on narration, a child's sense of spookiness, and terribly overwrought writing. A tuxedoed actor, Duke Moore, roams an otherwise deserted theater where his play has just closed. Every menacing sight and sound compels him further toward some unseen supernatural goal, unknown to him until he finds a casket in a prop room and climbs in. Forever! (*Night of the Ghouls* ends with phony spiritualist Kenne Duncan being shut in a casket, only against his will.)

Setting the mood before we first see Duke Moore three minutes into the film, and intercut with him throughout, are innumerable shots of inanimate objects. Just as Milton's *Paradise Lost* sets itself in "caves, dens, ferns, bogs, and shades of death," *Final Curtain* establishes its mood with water pipes, paint-chipped windows, weighted sandbags, ropes, pulleys, lighting panels, ripped-up theater seats, chandeliers, the backs of scenery and water coolers. Shot in one day at Santa Monica's long-gone Dome Theater (3014 Ocean Front Promenade), there is but one moment of sync dialogue, when Moore lets loose an unearthly scream at 5:15 into the proceedings.

While several of Wood's older male actors were veterans of the B Westerns he loved as a kid (Bud Osborne, Tom Keene, Kenne Duncan), all of Duke Moore's acting jobs were in Eddie projects. He is especially beloved for his line in *Plan 9*, "One thing's sure. Inspector Clay's dead – murdered – and *somebody's responsible!*" The *Final Curtain* narration refers to his "starring role [in the play] as the vampire," but Moore looks about as suave and vampiric as Don Knotts.

Narrating is Dudley Manlove, Eros from *Plan 9*. ("Your stupid minds!") A voiceover artist heard on TV commercials for Dove for Dishes and Ivory Soap, Manlove dabbled in on-camera acting in films as big as *Ten North Frederick* (1958) and TV shows like *Dragnet*. (His last screen appearance was in Andy Warhol's favorite film, 1962's *The Creation of the Humanoids*.) He announces his role in *Plan 9*, standing up straight and enunciating his lines. For *Final Curtain* he shows more dramatic range, but in getting Wood's words up off the page, it becomes comical. (See the manuscript's paragraph which begins with "What is this blackness?")

When Ed Wood set his mind to it, he could produce frightening, unnerving images. Sixteen minutes into *Final Curtain*, Moore opens a door "easily, without a sound" (although its hinges groan as loudly as Castle Dracula's). Inside he finds the pale, long-haired mannequin of a female vampire, used in the play. He examines and caresses the figure, and when he turns to leave, she smiles at him and beckons with "come hither" hand gestures. In *Final Curtain*, the actress is billed as Jenny Stevens. This scene was included in *Night of the Ghouls*, in which she also plays "The Black Ghost"; there she is billed as Jeannie Stevens. (No connection is made between the two characters.)

Since this was intended as a TV pilot, it begs a few logical questions. Although television was much different in the '50s, *Final Curtain* – intended to sell networks or syndicators on a series called *Portraits in Terror* – seems weak as a pilot. Twenty-two minutes of a single character's thoughts, and no dialogue, seems unlikely to attract sponsors. It's a long haul before we get to the arresting weird-out of Jenny/Jeannie Stevens coming to life.

You also have to wonder about this as an intended

Scaffolding looms over Santa Monica's Dome Theater in 1957 as Ocean Park Pier is transformed into Pacific Ocean Park. The theater was closed during construction, which is when Ed Wood shot *Final Curtain* there.

vehicle for Bela Lugosi. The John Barrymore of Hungary dwarfs Dudley Manlove as an actor, but bringing *Final Curtain's* turgid monology to life is still a monumental task. Visually it would have been interesting to see Lugosi's broad theatrical gestures in reaction to the unseen midnight threats.

Final Curtain's longtime repository, *Night of the Ghouls*,

The Dome Theater, adjacent to Pacific Ocean Park, looks forlorn and abandoned in *Final Curtain*.

Jenny Stevens doesn't do a very good job of holding still as the vampire mannequin.

Billed as Jeannie Stevens in *Night of the Ghouls* (1958), Jenny also appears as the Black Ghost.

is dull. It not only lacks *Plan 9's* fever-pitch histrionics but plays as if Wood had been saddled with an unwanted homework assignment. Duke Moore plays Police Lt. Daniel Bradford, dressed in a tux (to match the *Final Curtain* footage) as he prepares to go to an opera opening, but is assigned to investigate the haunted Willow Lake house instead. The theater's upstairs rooms become the sinister house by the lake, the con artist clairvoyants' hideaway. As he explores, Moore's narration supplants that of Dudley Manlove.

The *New York Times'* story on the *Final Curtain* restoration (January 31, 2012) calls the Slamdance screening its first public showing. In this instance the towering oracle of journalism was in error. The film had "escaped" at least once, showing at UCLA's Ed Wood Film Festival in 1981. Los Angeles artist and author Tony Mostrom attended the fest, his only knowledge of Ed Wood coming from the Medved brothers' *The Golden Turkey Awards* the year before.

"It was more incredibly, satisfyingly seedy than I expected," Mostrom says of *Final Curtain*. "That sensa-

> After Bela's remarkable recovery he began a new picture, PLAN 9 FROM OUTER SPACE, the first film to combine horror and science fiction. I also appeared in this picture, and it was my fifth with "the grand old man of horror". Between takes Bela, with a tired look on his face, expressed the fondness which he had for his work. He seemed to realize that the end was near, and his 73 years showed on his face. During the location shooting in the cemetery Bela became ill, and never recovered. He passed away peacefully, in his bed, to the great grief of all who knew him. By his side was a half read script for a film called the FINAL CURTAIN.

From Conrad Brooks' article in *World Famous Creatures* #3 (1959).

tion of 'Ed Wood's badness is even better than I expected it to be.' Having only seen *Plan 9* on television, it just gives off this '50s, black and white, late night film quality. Which I later thought came to greater fruition in [Wood's] *Jail Bait* [1954]. *Final Curtain* had a lot of that *Jail Bait* atmosphere. Bad writing, just the stillness of the shots – it was more intensely Ed Wood than *Plan 9*."

To horror movie fans, Lugosi's death has been mythologized to the extent of Rudolph Valentino's in 1926. The claim persists that Lugosi died clutching the script of *Final Curtain*. It first appeared in *World Famous Creatures* #3 in 1959, with actor Conrad Brooks saying, "He passed away peacefully, in his bed, to the great grief of all who knew him. By his side was a half read script for a film called *The Final Curtain*."

Brooks fits the description of a "fringe" Hollywood character and has expended great energy cementing his Ed Wood legacy, but I have never known him to fabricate any stories. That the above quotation came just three years after Lugosi's passing lends the anecdote some credence. It was vigorously denied by Lugosi's widow Hope, but she was a cantankerous contrarian who would dispute anything from those closest to the actor.

The flowery, Victorian mental picture of Count Dracula dying while reading something titled *Final Curtain* does seem poetic, with black and white Tim Burton art direction and sad music. The info since 1956 suggests that it could be true, although with Lugosi in boxer shorts and liquor bottles hidden near the bed.

What is beyond dispute is that the following is a manuscript from Ed Wood's own typewriter. The last page looks somewhat faded because it is a carbon copy, probably due to a revision. Since Hope rid herself of most of Lugosi's belongings to start anew after his death, it

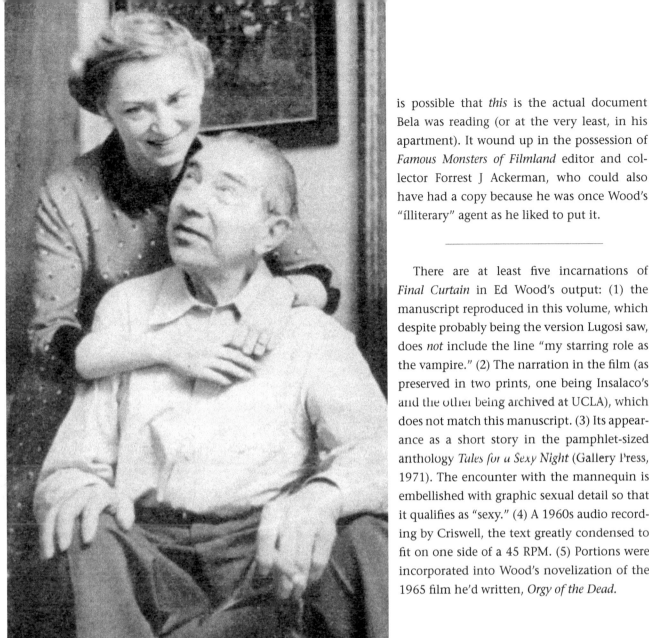

Lugosi and his final wife, Hope Lininger.

is possible that *this* is the actual document Bela was reading (or at the very least, in his apartment). It wound up in the possession of *Famous Monsters of Filmland* editor and collector Forrest J Ackerman, who could also have had a copy because he was once Wood's "illiterary" agent as he liked to put it.

There are at least five incarnations of *Final Curtain* in Ed Wood's output: (1) the manuscript reproduced in this volume, which despite probably being the version Lugosi saw, does *not* include the line "my starring role as the vampire." (2) The narration in the film (as preserved in two prints, one being Insalaco's and the other being archived at UCLA), which does not match this manuscript. (3) Its appearance as a short story in the pamphlet-sized anthology *Tales for a Sexy Night* (Gallery Press, 1971). The encounter with the mannequin is embellished with graphic sexual detail so that it qualifies as "sexy." (4) A 1960s audio recording by Criswell, the text greatly condensed to fit on one side of a 45 RPM. (5) Portions were incorporated into Wood's novelization of the 1965 film he'd written, *Orgy of the Dead*.

From the anthology
Tales for a Sexy Night
(Gallery Press, 1971).

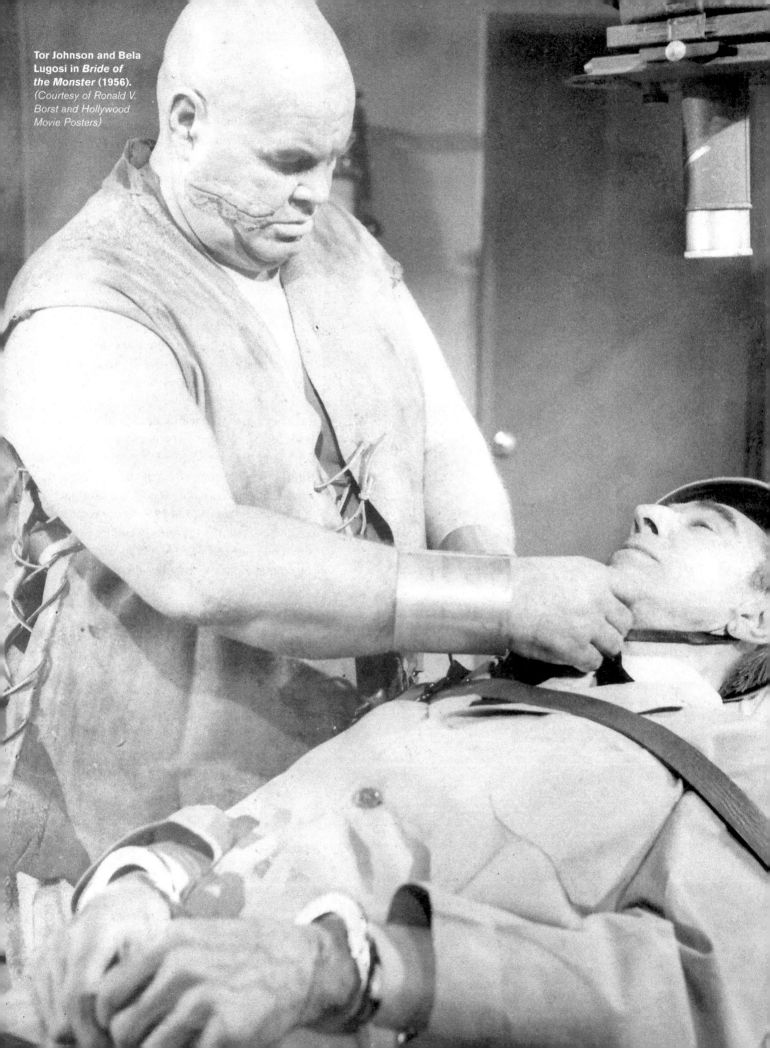

A Tale o' the Cock: My Weekend with ED WOOD

By Robert Cremer

In the course of my research on a family-authorized biography of Bela Lugosi in the early 1970s, it became immediately apparent to me that an enigmatic director by the name of Ed Wood Jr. was inextricably linked with the actor. Through the recollections of Bela's fourth wife Lillian, it was clear that the relationship between Wood and Lugosi was not just professional in nature, but also very personal. Until her divorce from Bela in 1953, Lillian was party to many evening get-togethers where Bela and Ed discussed film projects over bowls of one of Bela's favorite dishes, fish-head stew.

An interview with Ed Wood was, therefore, absolutely essential to illuminate so much of Bela's professional and – from the main focus of my biography – his personal life.

The decided lack of concrete information about Ed Wood left me with rumors and hearsay that had coursed through Tinseltown for years. Had he really convinced Bela to paint his Christmas tree black as a publicity stunt for Wood's next film project? Had the chiropractor of Wood's wife Kathy really supplied Lugosi with his habit-forming pain medication Demerol? And perhaps the most important question: Was Wood Bela's professional savior in his later years or his downfall? I had to meet the man to answer these questions – a man who, rumor had it, had even set his apartment on fire to collect insurance for financing his next film.

The 36 hours of interviews I conducted with Ed Wood Jr. in the summer of 1974 at his apartment in the San Fernando Valley, just outside Los Angeles, were not focused primarily on stories from the rumor mill, but rather on the critical – even pivotal – role Wood played in Lugosi's later years after a decade-long battle with the narcotic Demerol that Lugosi used as a pain medication. Lugosi's son Bela Jr., who arranged the interviews with Ed Wood for our collaborative book, was convinced of Wood's importance in his father's life. He also maintained that Wood exacerbated his father's dependency on habit-forming pain medications through his personal contact with a supplier. Nevertheless, Bela Jr. wanted all aspects of his father's life illuminated, not with supposition or hearsay, but with facts.

The tale of this very long and strenuous weekend of interviews began on a Friday at Ed Wood's watering hole, the Tail o' the Cock, a popular eatery in the 1970s on Ventura Blvd. in the Valley. Jim Beam was Wood's liquid refreshment of choice and he left no doubt as the first interview continued that it was his only liquid of choice. A glass of water was brought with every one of his drinks, and every time he pushed it to the far side of the table. Small talk broke the ice when Wood began describing his fascination with film legend Orson Welles. "Now there was someone who did it all," he said. "He wrote, directed, produced and starred in his films," Wood added – as if Welles were a well-kept secret. "You know, he's always been my idol and, when I look at my own career," he philosophized, "we have a lot in common. Yeah, really!"

Ed Wood and Bela Lugosi at Paul Marco's Christmas party in 1954. *(Courtesy of Paul Marco)*

Paul Marco, Hope Lugosi, Jerry Cooper, and Bela G. Lugosi. *(Courtesy of Dr. Robert J. Kiss)*

He was probably reacting to my expression of surprise which I couldn't camouflage well enough. "I have also produced, directed, written the screenplays and acted in my films," he noted with such self-assurance, I quickly got the impression that Wood actually saw himself as an unofficial protégé of Welles.

Having made the connection with his own career in his opening gambit, Wood continued to talk about his films. "Now *Bride of the Monster* was, you know, a humdinger at the box office, but *Plan 9* was the most challenging," he noted. "When Bela passed away, I had to use the footage we shot with a double to get it in the can. Not easy, I tell you, but we did it!" he declared triumphantly with a fist held above his head. When Wood asked me if I had seen the films, I said I had and added that Lugosi's monologue in *Bride of the Monster* was particularly trenchant, given his own persecution in Hungary after World War I and the necessity to flee to the United States.

With this remark, Wood's mood changed – suddenly and drastically. "Yeah," he mumbled, "you're writing the book about him with the family. You know all that stuff. You know what bothers me about that?" he asked after a long pause. "What bothers me about that is that *you* are writing the book and *not me!*" I was surprised at his aggressive tone, but didn't interrupt him.

"Who, *who* was really there for him when he needed work? You wanna know who? *Me*. That's who!" he said with a decided emphasis on "me." "He did two pictures with other studios in 1952," he elaborated, "with Fernwood and Realart Pictures. *Old Mother Riley Meets the Vampire*," he continued, "and *Bela Lugosi Meets a Brooklyn Gorilla* were an insult for an actor of his caliber. And he knew it. The way he was treated during the filming of *Glen or Glenda* with me was a different ball game from those two cheap films he made. I wanted to produce films with him that would pull him out of his slide. Nothing more, nothing less. I just didn't want to see him taken advantage of any more."

Bela Lugosi and Ed Wood with William C. Thompson and George Weiss on the set of *Glen or Glenda* (1953).

Paul Marco and Bela Lugosi attend Ed Wood's marriage to Norma McCarty in 1956.

His statement was very convincing, although I found it difficult to determine whether he was speaking of Lugosi or of himself. Who was pulling whom out of his slide? Of course, Ed Wood would also profit from his association with an actor like Lugosi who possessed such name recognition in Hollywood and might open doors and jump-start Wood's financially strapped film projects.

It is true that Wood wooed Lugosi in a way that other producers and studios did not. Wood explained: "They didn't have to deal with Lugosi as a major actor, because he needed work. They had him by the balls. Humphrey Bogart often said that his 'F*** you' fund always made it possible for him to say no to film roles he felt would damage his career. Bela had to say yes." That was Ed Wood's forte with Lugosi. He frequently invited Bela and his wife Lillian to dinner to discuss film projects. He insured that Bela regularly received his pain medication for sciatica which had plagued him since the 1940s. In short, he made Lugosi feel as if he were the actor he used to be, in his heyday as Dracula. While Lugosi's son saw the relationship in an overwhelmingly negative light, Ed believed wholeheartedly that he had made a Herculean effort to rebuild the self-esteem of a broken actor and had offered Lugosi hope for a dignified Hollywood comeback. Wood emphasized that this was *not* on the agenda of the B-movie studios that used Lugosi on occasion.

"Hell, I even arranged a benefit viewing of the film *Bride of the Monster* in LA for Bela that was sold out two hours in advance and netted Bela money he desperately needed," he added as proof of his commitment. "Did any of the other studios do that for him? Did they? No!" he exclaimed, slamming his hand down on the table, nearly spilling his drink. Nevertheless, it is also conceivable that Lugosi's last speaking role in Wood's *Bride of the Monster* was probably instrumental in the film being regarded as the only Wood film that was halfway successful at the box office. One fact was undeniable: Ed Wood's relationship to Bela was definitely not that of a savior or guardian angel, but rather one of a symbiotic nature; simply put, one of mutual survival.

"We got together quite often and bounced film ideas off each other," Wood reminisced. "Boy, those were unforgettable times. When we got to talking, you could see the gleam in Bela's eyes as if he was a million miles away. You wanna know why? Because we weren't talking about minor roles for him – the kind that the studios were offering him where he sometimes didn't even have a speaking role, like in *The Black Sleep* – but starring roles where Bela would get the top billing he deserved," Wood noted. It became immediately apparent as Wood said this that his eyes also began to gleam – just like Lugosi's in days of yore.

DRIVE-IN
AUSTIN
THEATRE
1 MILE WEST ON CACHE RD

OPENS 7:00 P.M.
STARTS AT DARK
ENDS TONIGHT

HENRY FONDA — ANTHONY PERKINS
—in—
"TIN STAR"
—plus—
CORNEL WILDE IN
"OMAR KHAYAM"
FOR FRIDAY NITE ONLY

SPOOKARAMA!
Ghost Convention!

REST
IN
PEACE

4 THRILLING HORROR SHOWS
"Blood of Dracula"
"I Was A Teenage Frankenstein"
"Creature From The Black Lagoon"
"Bride of The Monster"

WE
GUARANTEE FOR
ALL YOU..
"BOIS & GOILS"
A MOST
EXCITING TIME

At
Dark
Chilling
Admission
Only
50c

I asked Wood about the state of Bela's health during his association with Wood as his medical addiction to Demerol had visibly taken its toll on the actor. Wood responded, "Oh, I can't say that his health was a big deal. It was never a regular topic with us, except in discussions about a film project where Bela was concerned about his stamina. You know, with specific scenes where he wanted to be sure that he could deliver the goods and meet his own very high standards. For example, he was very concerned about his long monologue in *Bride of the Monster*, because he noticed that his memory wasn't what it used to be, but in that case his health was no problem at all. He delivered the entire monologue in one take – letter perfect!

"On the other hand," Wood added, "there was little doubt that Bela had major health problems related to his sciatica and dependence on pain medication. I helped Bela to get the medications he needed when necessary, for example, when he was literally crippled with pain during the night filming in Griffith Park for *Bride of the Monster*. Otherwise," Ed explained, "he would not have been able to shoot his scenes. Sometimes he was doubled over with pain and simply couldn't walk, let alone concentrate on his role. As I said, this was not a chronic problem, but there were times when he was paralyzed with pain."

After staring into his bourbon glass for inspiration, Wood continued to describe his success formula with Lugosi. "You know," he reflected, "creative people like Bela and me [*sic*] are very vulnerable. We all share high professional hopes and when others – critics, for example – don't see it that way, it can really get to ya. I knew Bela well and saw how painful it was for him to remember his salad days as a major actor and then have to face the humiliation of critics in his later years. That's why I always went out of my way to

**Published in the *Lawton Constitution*
(Lawton, OK) on August 28, 1958.**

treat him like the star he really was." Lillian Lugosi verified this in her recollections. "Oh, yes, when we went to Ed's for dinner, Bela was treated like a VIP. Ed went out of his way to show Bela the respect that he had missed for quite a long time. Whatever Ed Wood's motivations were, he always treated Bela with respect and, you could even say, reverence." From this one might even get the impression that Wood was on a mission: to resurrect the film career of Bela Lugosi singlehandedly.

After I got five hours of sleep, our interview continued on Saturday at Wood's San Fernando Valley apartment. His abode was modest and Spartan in furnishings: a lonely couch in the living room, a table and four chairs in the adjacent dining area, a bedroom with bed and commode and a naked kitchen, full of empty cabinets. My impression was that Wood spent little, if any, time in the apartment. He introduced me to his wife Kathy who lay on the bed smoking cigarettes and watching TV. Then he showed me a bookshelf filled with his pornographic novels, of which he was extremely proud. When he excused himself for a moment, I asked if I could get myself a glass of water. "Sure," he said with another sweeping gesture of his arm, "help yourself!" I finally found glasses in a cabinet – but nothing else. When I turned on the water faucet and nothing came out, I looked in the refrigerator for bottled water. The refrigerator was, alas, as empty as the cabinets. Rumors to the effect that Wood was plagued by financial problems would explain both the lack of food and running water in the kitchen.

The first item on our agenda was the payment for Wood's interviews. He had requested that he be paid in cash. As he looked at the money in his hand, his eyes began to gleam once again and he got that "Lugosi faraway look" he described so vividly the day before. Before we could begin the day's interviewing, he rushed to the phone in the kitchen. He was clearly just as "wired" as the telephone as he ordered not one but two cases of Jim Beam and, of course, he wanted it delivered. In an instant, Wood also became a different person – a producer of status in his own mind. With money in his hand, Wood seemed at peace. The deep furrows on his forehead disappeared and the ensuing interview proceeded quite differently from the night before. The bitterness of the previous evening had disappeared and was replaced by his regaling me with his minor coups in film production.

A number of stories followed about how he was always able to keep his production budgets low by outfoxing the city, the police department and his paltry entourage of investors. For example, Wood beamed as he related the details of how he shot scenes for *Bride of the Monster* in Griffith Park at night without purchasing a shooting permit from the City of Los Angeles. He let out a massive belly laugh when he recounted the flooding he caused by damming up the creek running through the park for the film's octopus scenes. His story about the police car used in *Plan 9 from Outer Space* was again punctuated by laughter. "Actor Tor Johnson's son Carl worked for the police department in the Valley," Wood whispered as he leaned closer to me. "He got us the car without the police department ever finding out about it. Then I told our cinematographer Bill Thompson that he should be sure to keep the insignia on the side of the car illegible in all shots. He did." Laughter. "Maybe it was because the shots were out of focus. You know, his eyesight wasn't what it used to be. He even had to read his light meter with a candle sometimes." Again, laughter.

Then he leaned even farther over the table and said, "Speaking of *Plan 9*, I have a copy of the film, you know. Yep. I borrowed it from the Oklahoma State University Library…and never returned it!" After the two cases of bourbon were delivered – and paid for – Wood excused himself again and went back to the telephone. A few calls later he returned and said, "I just talked with a few of the cast members from *Plan 9* to see if they would be interested in coming over to see the film again. They're coming this evening – Lyle Talbot [who played General Roberts], Maila Nurmi [Vampire Woman], Jeron Criswell [who played himself] and Paul Marco [Kelton the Cop]."

In anticipation of the evening to come, Wood broke out the bourbon for the continuation of the interview. Wood spoke quite freely about the problems he encountered financing his films. "You know," he began, "being an artist isn't all it's cracked up to be when your need for money to finance your projects makes you kind of a whore." His laughter was suddenly absent and his expression had changed to one of irritation. "I have sacrificed a helluva lot in my life for my work. Why, I had to agree to give relatives of backers major parts in movies, although they couldn't act worth a s***. I had to cut corners constantly. When the Cadillac hubcaps we used for flying saucers in *Plan 9* were damaged beyond re-use in a major scene, we had to steal some quickly for a retake, because

Robert Cremer and Bela G. Lugosi

studio time was so expensive that the time needed to buy new ones would have practically bankrupted us. We had to improvise constantly, because we couldn't afford the equipment we needed. That hurts, man. I tell ya. You have a vision of your product and how it should look and then … bang! It's something completely different. Your artistic vision becomes a nightmare. And it's out of your control."

What visions Wood had for *Bride of the Monster* or *Plan 9 from Outer Space* are anybody's guess, but one cannot say that quality was irrelevant to him. Whatever visions he might have had were clearly compromised by his financial limitations. There was no doubt in my mind that Wood truly saw himself as the protégé of Orson Welles, but without the means to realize his mission in life. Wood spoke of his films as parents speak about their children, almost lovingly. They *were* his children, each with unique characteristics that made every one of them memorable, at least in his own mind. Similarly he exuded optimism about his planned productions as if his severe financial problems were indeed a thing of the past now that he had been paid for the interviews. Little did anyone know that he would die of a heart attack in just four years at the age of 54. One such project, a screenplay entitled *I Woke Up Early the Day I Died*, could be viewed as an apocalyptic script for Wood.

Wood had arranged for a projector to be delivered for the evening viewing of *Plan 9* with cast members. I asked him if we shouldn't get something to eat for the evening as we had not eaten a thing all day. He made another grandiose gesture with his arm and said, "Let 'em eat bourbon," his laugh once again returning. The cast members arrived promptly for the screening of what some critics have rated as one of the worst movies of all time, but that criticism played no role here. As Wood greeted each of them warmly, it was apparent that he and his actor-entourage were in a universe all their own – totally protected from such criticism. In his role, Wood was not just a one-man show as writer, producer and director, but also king of his realm – replete with subjects like Talbot, Marco, Nurmi (aka Vampira) and Criswell.

Talbot was reserved but good-natured and loved to joke with the other cast members. Marco was short and made up for this by talking constantly and mostly about himself. He was extremely fidgety and had trouble sitting quietly through the film. Nurmi was very dignified and turned heads just as she probably did many times at Hollywood cocktail parties. She was soft-spoken, but had a deadly sense of humor. She rarely commented during the viewing of the film, but was quite vocal otherwise. Criswell conducted himself like an ambassador – always in control, always gracious and always with a strategically correct comment about the film and the actors.

Marco immediately began reminiscing about the film

and quickly triggered a mutual backslapping orgy, the likes of which I had never experienced. However, this was only a pale prelude to the running commentary that unfolded with the opening credits projected on a decidedly soiled movie screen. During an early scene where a pilot first sights a UFO, for example, Marco trumpeted his praise of director Wood with the words, "Ed, you've really got the touch. It's so realistic – the cockpit, the UFO, everything." Murmurs of agreement rumbled through the living room. Wood himself was mesmerized by his own consummate artistry in using such a convincing double for Lugosi, who had died before production began. Exterior scenes filmed with Lugosi with narration by Criswell were intercut with those of the double used during production. A superficial comparison of the two would lead one to exactly the opposite conclusion of that of Paul Marco, but we were, after all, in a different world that evening – Wood's world.

Asides were made, naturally, regarding the police car and also the cemetery set. Wood joked about how the tombstones needed for the narrow lot that doubled as the cemetery had to be "borrowed" from a real cemetery – much to the consternation of families who visited deceased family members only to find a number of the tombstones were in different locations and some missing altogether. Lyle Talbot quipped, "Ed, you know it was a real shame that you made headlines, but couldn't take credit for them!" Wood's hoax caused an uproar in the local press, which was consolation enough for him. "The main thing," Wood retorted, "was that we did it and they never knew who was responsible!" Talbot was deeply moved by the Criswell monologue which introduced the film:

> Greetings, my friend. We are all interested in the future, for that is where you and I are going to spend the rest of our lives. And remember, my friend, future events such as these will affect you in the future. You are interested in the unknown, the mysterious, the unexplainable. That is why you are here.

Personally, I was speechless that this monologue evoked such an emotional reaction from Talbot, but it was a good reminder about how I had to phrase my questions to the cast. Diplomacy, as embodied by Criswell, was the order of the day. When the accolades subsided, I ventured my first question concerning the rapid changes in the scenes between night and day where it appeared that the scenes were contiguous and there was no major passage of time. Murmur filled the room immediately as if the cast had never noticed this. One could possibly argue convincingly that they, in fact, hadn't. Wood, however, took immediate charge of the situation, quieted the cast down and announced, "That was Bill [Thompson]. Poor guy had bad eyesight – I mentioned that to you, didn't I? – and he sometimes read the exposure on the light meter with a candle and sometimes not. Just depended on the ambient light available. Still he was a great cinematographer, really one of the best." Others quickly chimed in, voicing their agreement. So, there you have it. Wood proved conclusively that he could cut corners anywhere and in any way he had to.

What became unavoidably clear on that evening after my further questions about technical aspects of the film was that neither director nor cast actually saw what unfolded on the screen at 24 fps. No one was bothered by the fact that the house where the pilot, who sighted the UFO, lived with his wife was directly adjacent to the cemetery, but later Kelton the Cop (Paul Marco) found it necessary to drive the pilot's wife from their house to the cemetery in his police car. Police chief Tor Johnson's emergence from an open grave, which was unmistakably far too small for the massive frame of a professional wrestler, was similarly heralded as a major highlight of the film. Perhaps there is no better example of the corners Wood had to cut and the compromises he had to make with his artistic vision in order to get *Plan 9 from Outer Space* in the can.

As the bourbon flowed, the tongues wagged. Each of the cast members discussed future film projects with Wood that made their mouths water. Marco, for one, saw an endless string of roles for his character Kelton the Cop. Criswell was enthused about Ed's ideas for more films dealing with the occult, and he spoke with enthusiasm about his prologue to Wood's 1958 entry *Night of the Ghouls*. He also mentioned Wood's plans for two films – *The Vampire's Tomb* and *The Ghoul Goes West* – which might involve Criswell's rhetorical talents.

The final round of interviews began on Sunday morning at his apartment. Wood had a glass of bourbon on the table when I arrived and looked as if he had not slept. He was visibly agitated again. When I mentioned the film

LUGOSI
The Man Behind the Cape

The authorized, intimate, shocking story
of the man who was Dracula

Robert Cremer
Introduction by Bela Lugosi, Jr.

Robert Cremer's groundbreaking book, published by Henry Regnery in 1976.

ideas Criswell had mentioned the night before, *The Vampire's Tomb* and *The Ghoul Goes West*, every trace of the optimism and exuberance he had exhibited the evening before was gone. "Production was hampered by the lack of necessary funding," Wood began. "I had no idea when or how we could get the cash together to begin filming, but my headliners, Loretta King and Tony McCoy, visited Bela at Norwalk State Hospital [where he was undergoing treatment for medically incurred drug addiction] and told him that we were holding production up on *Ghoul* until he was released and could join the cast. Okay, it was a little white lie they used for their own publicity purposes, but I let it go, because I knew that Bela needed news like that to give him the hope and courage to beat his addiction."

When I asked him what had become of *The Vampire's Tomb* and *The Ghoul Goes West*, he just shrugged his shoulders and said, "I've got the scripts, cast and production personnel ready to go. I just don't have the bucks from the backers. I'm sure they'll be great films if I can finally get them in the can." A trace of optimism returned to his face, seemingly undaunted by his constant nemesis, money, but nothing could conceal the fact that Wood looked much older than his 50 years. Of course alcohol played a role, but the feeling he conveyed was that of frustration over his financial limitations. He ruminated on still other ideas and film projects waiting in the wings, waiting for backers. It was clear that Ed Wood felt misunderstood by the Hollywood mainstream, which he firmly believed never understood his artistic talent. It is ironic in hindsight that he didn't live to see the film biography of his life, 1994's *Ed Wood*, earn two Academy Awards.

At the end of our last interview, Wood became emotionally overwrought at the thought of one of his most personal unfinished projects: his own biography of Bela Lugosi. "I don't know why I agreed to these interviews, you know, because I'm giving away unique information for a very personal project of mine. No one should write a book about Bela but me, because I was there for him when all the chips were down and no one cared about him," he noted bitterly. "What I know about Bela no one else knows and now it will appear in a book, but not mine!"

If there were one overriding reason for him granting these interviews, disclosing his personal information and giving up the dream of writing his own book about Lugosi, it was this: his pressing need for money.

Coming back one last time to Bela Lugosi's memorable monologue in *Bride of the Monster*, "One is always considered mad, when one discovers something which others cannot grasp," I asked myself, while walking back to the car after our last interview, if that line wasn't more a personal statement of Wood's regarding his feeling of being misunderstood and unappreciated in Hollywood than just a line in a script. The line was, after all, penned by Ed Wood himself.

An imagined movie poster for the unproduced Lugosi film *The Ghoul Goes West*, as created for this book by George Chastain in 2016.

"THE

GHOUL

GOES

WEST "

By
EDWARD D. WOOD, JR.

REGISTERED, 1951

"THE GHOUL GOES WEST"

CAST LIST

PROFESSOR SMOKE	(The Undertaker)
MARTY	(The Foreman)
CHANCE HILTON	(The Sheriff)
MELODY	(The Saloon Owner)
NANCY CORBETT	(The Girl)
DOCTOR SIMPSON	(The Doctor)
EZRA	(The Cemetery Caretaker)
SKIMPY	(A comic drunk)
TOM	(A Deputy Sheriff of Experience)
STEVE	(A Young Deputy)
HOPE	(A Dance Hall Girl)
KARL	(A Giant)
TANZ	(A Giant)

"THE GHOUL GOES WEST"

FADE IN:

1.   EXT. SMALL CEMETERY MEDIUM CLOSE PANNING NIGHT   1.

The camera pans a small western style cemetery to
show rough crosses, wooden head boards, a
scattered granite head stone here and there and
one or two big marble monuments. The cemetery
holds the stillness of the dead except for the
soft scraping of a spade as it digs into the
earth. As the camera comes to rest on the
action the scraping changes to the sound of
a spade hitting then scraping on wood. The
camera moves in until, clearly, we see a giant
of a man well over six foot tall and weighing
perhaps three hundred pounds. He is holding a
lantern over an open grave. He sits the lantern
down and tosses a rope into the grave. For another
long moment he looks deep into grave where his
accomplice works. The man who at this point
comes out of the grave is as tall as perhaps a bit
taller than the other. He tosses the spade to the
ground and dusts his hands together. Both men
move one on each end of the grave and lift up
the ropes readied there for them....

                              DISSOLVE TO:

2.   EXT. SAME MEDIUM LONG SHOT   2.

We see the two men, a coffin securely on their
shoulders as they walk through the cemetery...

                              DISSOLVE TO:

3.   EXT. CARETAKER   SHACK CEMETERY MEDIUM CLOSE   3.
DOLLY TO CLOSE

On a team of horses and a wagon as the two giants
carrying their ghoulish burden move into the scene

                              (CONTINUED)

Gary D. Rhodes   85

3.   CONTINUED: 3.

at the rear of the wagon. Quickly they deposit the
casket into the wagon then get onto the wagon seat.
They drive off. As the wagon is driven off scene
we can see that hidden behind it was a small cemetery
caretaker's shack. It is a one room affair with the
yellowed lights of an oil lamp coming through the
battered window which is framed by a dirty piece of
cloth one might refer to as a curtain... Half in
and half out of the doorway, battered, bloody and
bruised lies the caretaker. He is a man in his late
sixties wearing a faded work shirt and overalls.

He stirs and rolls over on his back then with much
effort he moves to a sitting position. His hands
go to his injured head. Slowly he rises to his feet.
Every movement, no matter how slight, seems to be
great pain to him. Once on his feet he staggers
towards the CAMERA.

                                        DISSOLVE TO:

4.   EXT. SMALL WESTERN TOWN MEDIUM WIDE NIGHT   4.

The town is a small western mining community.
Its false front buildings and hitching rails
are quite reminiscent of the early period it
represents. The street is completely void of
pedestrians, although there are several horses
in front of the gaily decorated noisy saloon.
Gas lights burn brightly through the saloon
windows, and drifting out into the night air
we hear a bawdy piano and the loud voices of the
clientel. Other horses are hitched in various
places on the street. " A wagon, half loaded
with bales of hay is parked at the hay and grain
company ramp, waiting for morning and completion
of the loading process. A saddled horse can be
seen tied to the hitching rail in front of the
jail, sheriff's office combination. A small
yellowed light burns inside showing through the
barred window of the jail. On the far edge of
town suddenly appears the staggering figure of
the cemetery caretaker. He makes his way
laboriously, stumbling along the straight center
of the street...

                                        (CONTINUED)

4.   CONTINUED:

Melody, the lusciously, beautiful girl saloon owner
steps out onto the boardwalk. (This is in close
to the camera). She does not see Ezra's tortured
movement far down along the street. She lights
the two gas lanterns hanging suspended from the
roof, then turns and enters back into the noisey
saloon. Ezra again stumbles and falls....

5.   MEDIUM CLOSE DOLLY   5.

Ezra is sprawled in the dirt. He gets heavily to
his feet and continues on. As he turns to his
right, towards the lighted sheriff's office and
jail, he pauses to catch his breath then continues
on towards the door.

6.   INT. SHERIFF'S OFFICE ESTABLISHING NIGHT   6.

A deputy sheriff, a man in his middle forties is
leaning back in a swivel chair, his feet up on the
roll top desk before him. His hat is pulled down
over his face and his hands are folded over his
middle. Over the desk can be seen pasted to
the wall both old and new wanted posters.

To the left of the deputy is the one cell jail.
A man lies on the bunk already asleep with a thick
army blanket over him. One small heavily shaded
oil lamp is suspended down from the ceiling - the
only light in the poorly lighted room. A long,
wooded table, litered with books, papers, wanted
posters, etc., is jammed up against the wall between
the desk and the cell. The door opens with the
quick violence of being shoved heavily. The slamming
of the door against the wall is enough to shake the
wood and glass cabinet which holds several pistols
and rifles. The old caretaker sprawls across the
threshold. The deputy comes back to the world
quickly... He pulls back his hat....

7.   CLOSE SHOT TOM   7.

Tom looks to Ezra, the old caretaker.

8.   MEDIUM CLOSE EZRA   8.

Laying prone across the threshold.....

9.   MEDIUM WIDE ANGLE   9.

The deputy moves quickly from his chair to the
fallen caretaker. He helps him to his feet and
escorts him to a chair where he seats him. When
he is safely in the chair the deputy moves to the
desk and throws open a drawer. He pulls out a
pint of whiskey and uncorking it he moves back
to the caretaker.

10. CLOSE TWO SHOT   10,

Extremely weak the old man is aided in holding
the bottle to his lips as he swallows a long slug.
He sighs as the bottle is removed from his lips.
His voice is weak and strained as he tries to talk.

                    EZRA
          Them grave robbers again!

                    TOM
          Take it easy, old timer.

                    EZRA
          Got me this time.. Banged
          on the door and bashed me in
          the head. Jist like that -
          banged on the door and when
          I went for a look see - BANG -
          my lamps went out - Where's
          the sheriff?

                    TOM
          He took a night off for a
          change.

                    EZRA
          Iff'n you know where he is -
          You'd best get hold of him,
          Tom.

                    TOM
          You're right - but I just
          can't go off and leave the
          office..

Studying, he turns to look towards the cell which
houses the off scene prisoner.

11.   CLOSE SHOT SKIMPY   11.

Now we can really see the old coot. Be-Whiskered-
nervous - but a nice little guy. He is fully
clothed in rugged Western attire and a leather
vest. An empty old holster and belt are strapped
around his middle with the holster being
tied down tightly to his leg. He sits on
the edge of the bunk, wide-eyed at the dialogue
he is hearing...

12.   MEDIUM CLOSE   12.

Tom moves across the room to the cell.

                      TOM
             You sober, Skimpy?

The wheezened little man jumps to his feet and
moves up close to Tom. His ever moving hands grip
the bars. He speaks, seriously.

                    SKIMPY
             After four days in this corn-
             traption, deputy Tom, how else
             could I be.. Ttweren't like
             this in the old days when Chance's
             Pa was sheriff...

                    TOM
             Chance's Pa's been dead a long
             time and Chance is Sheriff
             now... Besides, if you'd keep
             out of that saloon everytime
             you come to town, you wouldn't
             get in jail....Know where
             Lovers' Leap is....?

A glimmer of almost embarrassment comes into the
old man's weather beaten eyes.

                    SKIMPY
             Oughtta' - spent 'nuff time
             out there when I was younger...
             Out on the Double S spread,
             south of town a spell.

                    TOM
             Sheriff's out there with Miss NANcy
             ~~Sally~~ watchin' the moon come
             up - Think you can find him?

                             (CONTINUED)

12.   CONTINUED:

                         SKIMPY
              Think I can ? - - Deputy Tom--
              Iff'n I can't - nobody can...

13.   MEDIUM WIDE ANGLE

       The deputy selects a key from his ring. He inserts
       it into the lock and twists it. The cell door
       comes open. The little man grabs his hat and
       jams it down over his ears...

                         TOM
              Take my horse - an make it
              fast.

                         SKIMPY
         Sure....

                         TOM
              On the way outta' town stop
              and tell Doc Simpson to
              hightail it over here,
              pronto...

                         SKIMPY
         Sure..

       The little man moves off fast as Tom walks back
       to Ezra.

                         EZRA
              Think that old galoot can
              find Chance?

                         TOM
              Like he said - if he can't -
              nobody can...

                                        DISSOLVE TO:

14.   EXT. LOVER'S LEAP MEDIUM CLOSE NIGHT

       A spot high on a lonely cliff which looks out
       over a vast stretch of land far below. A lone tree
       stands a few feet back from the cliff's edge. Beyond

                                        (CONTINUED)

14.   CONTINUED: 14.

       the tree a pair of saddled horses can be seen quietly
       grazing. Beneath the tree, seated on the ground,
       their backs against the tree trunk is a young man
       and a lovely young girl. The girl, Nancy Corbet,
       wears riding trousers, boots and a blouse topped with
       a fuzzy pink angora cardigan. The young man is wearing
       a neat western outfit. His western style hat lays
       on the ground near his hand. ~~Sally~~'s hair is long
       and lays in folds over her shoulders. Her hair
       snuggles in close on Chance's shoulder and his
       arm is around her.

                              NANCY
                              ~~SALLY~~
                    The big city called me --
                    so I went -- bag and baggage...

                              CHANCE
                    Then what happened?

                              NANCY
                    The usual thing -- The rent
                    was due -- I was nearly broke --
                    so when I was notified of
                    Uncle Pat's death and that
                    he had left me his Double S
                    Ranch, I decided on the wide
                    open spaces...

15.   CLOSE SHOT CHANCE   15.

                              CHANCE
                    Lucky for me you did,....

16.   CLOSE SHOT NANCY   16.

       She smiles, snuggling deeper in his shoulder. Her
       eyes leave his face and look to the full moon in the
       sky above them...

                              NANCY
                    It's beautiful - Isn't it..!

                              CHANCE
                    It's the same moon you saw
                    back East...

                                        (CONTINUED)

16.   CONTINUED: 16.

                              NANCY
                    It looks so much bigger -
                    brighter - more friendly.....

                              CHANCE
                    Guess that's because it has
                    more freedom out here. It
                    can roam all over the place
                    and not be cluttered up with
                    streets and houses..Nothin'
                    to stop it 'ceptin maybe
                    the old haunted mine up in
                    the buttes - Guess that one
                    dark spot don't matter much -
                    The old moon just saddles
                    up and rides off around it.

                              NANCY
                    Tell me about your haunted
                    mine.

17.   CLOSE SHOT CHANCE   17.

                              CHANCE
                    Not much to tell - - Once
                    it was a big producer like
                    the other mines in this
                    section - - Then the miners
                    began hearing strange noises -
                    Just the wind in the caverns
                    of course, but they got
                    frightened and nobody would
                    work it anymore - - so there
                    it sits - getting old and musty
                    year after year - - Kind of
                    spooky like --

18.   CLOSE TWO   18.

                              NANCY
                    Sounds romantic...

                              CHANCE
                    I don't think you'd find it
                    very romantic.

                                        (CONTINUED)

18.   CONTINUED: 18.

                         NANCY
              Let's ride up there some
              afternoon...

                         CHANCE
              Allright...

       The sound of horses hooves, traveling fast, is
       heard.

19.   LONG SHOT   19.

       Skimpy, riding fast, as he comes up the steep
       grade to Lover's Leap.

20.   MEDIUM WIDE   20.

       Chance and Nancy get to their feet. Chance moves
       towards the approaching horse. The horse and rider
       move into the scene.

21.   MEDIUM CLOSE   21.

       Skimpy pulls up. With Nancy close behind, Chance
       moves up to the rider.

                         CHANCE
              Breaking jail and horse
              stealing is a bad offense,
              Skimpy...

                         SKIMPY
              Ahhhh - Sheriff - I ain't
              done none of them things...
              Deputy Tom sent me up to
              find ya...

                         CHANCE
              What's up?

                         SKIMPY
              Them spook varmits done
              lifted another of Ezra's
              graves. Old Ezra - he looked
              in a right bad way. Tom told
              me to say you should beat
              it back to town, pronto...

22. CLOSE GROUP 22.

> CHANCE
> Get our horses, will you,
> Skimpy?

> SKIMPY
> Sure...

Skimpy moves out of the scene towards the off
scene horses. Chance smiles after the little man
then turns to take Nancy's shoulders in his hands.

> CHANCE
> I'm sorry, Nancy.

> NANCY
> You go ahead - I'll get to
> the ranch alright.

> CHANCE
> I hate to leave you alone - -
> With these ghouls on the loose.

> NANCY
> Don't worry about me, Chance,
> I'll be at the ranch and
> safely tucked in bed within
> twenty minutes.

> CHANCE
> Make like the Lone Ranger.

> NANCY
> As fast as my horse will
> run.

She moves her lips upwards as he brings his down
to meet hers. The kiss is interrupted by Skimpy
returning with the horses.

23. WIDER ANGLE 23.

> Chance gets quickly into the saddle. He looks
> to Skimpy.

> CHANCE
> Be sure you come back --You
> still have six days to do...

> (CONTINUED)

23. CONTINUED: 23.

                              SKIMPY
                            (dejectedly)
            Yeah....

Chance turns his mount into the direction, then
takes off. Nancy watches him for a long moment.
Both have turned to watch Chance ride off, then
Skimpy turns seriously to Nancy.

                              SKIMPY
            Miss Nancy - I don't want to
            go again' your way of thinkin' -
            but maybe I should ride to
            your outfit with you.

                              NANCY
                            (cute-tongue
                            in cheek)
            It's not quite in your direction,
            Skimpy.

                              SKIMPY
            I ain't in no hurry to get
            back to jail --- 'sides I
            ain't got nothin' but time -
            for the next six days
            anyhow...

                              NANCY
                            (cute -tongue
                            in cheek)
            You'd better ride a straight
            line back to town - We wouldn't
            want Chance mad at us -- Don't
            worry, Skimpy ---I'll be
            alright....

                              SKIMPY
                            (sadly)
            Just as you say, Miss Nancy...

24. MEDIUM WIDE ANGIE   24.

Skimpy helps Nancy into her saddle then he gets
into his own. He salutes her quickly then they ride
off in different directions.

                                        DISSOLVE TO:

25. EXT. WOODED ROAD MEDIUM CLOSE MOVING NIGHT   25.

THE CAMERA is set up on the front of Nancy as
she rides at a trot over the narrow one lane
road. The trees and brush of a thick forest
are on both sides of her. Suddenly after riding
for several long, silent, except for the
hoof beats, minutes, she pulls up sharply and
looks with growing fear to the road ahead. Her
horse has bolted slightly.

26. MEDIUM SHOT   26.

Stopped in the middle of the road is the wagon
and giants we have seen before at the cemetery.
Their eyes are straight at the off scene girl.

27. CLOSE SHOT NANCY   27.

Looking towards the men and wagon off scene.
Her face has become a mask of fear.

28. MEDIUM SHOT   28.

A moment longer the two giants sit motionless,
then the man holding the reins snaps the horses
into motion and pulls the wagon as far off the
road as he can. The room on the road is opened
just enough for the girl and horse to pass -but
pass so that the horse will be but scarce inches
away from the wagon.

29. MEDIUM CLOSE DOLLY   29.

Summing up as much courage as she can muster,
Nancy prods her horse forward at a slow pace.
She tries to keep from looking at the two men,
but try as she may her eyes continually dart
to their direction.

30. CLOSE SHOT   30.

On the passive faces of the two giants as they
silently watch the girl's approach.

31.   MEDIUM CLOSE DOLLY   31.

Nancy moves her horse cautiously forward. She
reaches the horses of the wagon. She moves on -
slowly - cautiously - then she is abreast of the
driver. Now her eyes are straight ahead on the road.
She suddenly rises in the saddle to kick the horse
forward but the taller of the two men in that same
instant stands up, reaches over and drags the girl
from her horse. Her hat falls almost unnoticed
into the brush beside the road. Nancy's horse
takes off at top speed up the road. Wrestling in
the giant's arms, Nancy screams as we ....

                                        FADE TO:

32.   EXT. SHERIFF'S OFFICE MEDIUM WIDE NIGHT   32.

Chance races his horse into town. He dismounts
on the run, ties up, then heads for the door to
the Sheriff's office.

33.   INT. SHERIFF'S OFFICE MEDIUM WIDE NIGHT   33.

Chance throws open the door letting it slam shut
behind him. He moves directly to Tom who stands
near a middle aged doctor that is working on the
bandages at Ezra's injured head. The old
caretaker is much better now, having had
treatment and time to rest.

                    CHANCE
            How is he, Tom?

34.   CLOSE GROUP   34.

                    TOM
            Better ask the Doc.

                    DOCTOR
            He'll be ready for work again
            by tomorrow night.

                            (CONTINUED)

34.   CONTINUED: 34.

                              EZRA
                            (quickly)
                    No sir-eee...Three times in
                    the last two weeks them
                    graves out there in the
                    cemetery has been robbed...
                    but...I quit.. As of when I
                    got hit.. my resignation became
                    final...

                              CHANCE
                    Did you see who hit you, old
                    timer?

                              EZRA
                    You bet yer life I did - and
                    it was a fearful sight I
                    ain't gonna' forget 'till
                    the day I become jist like
                    'em..

                              CHANCE
                    I don't get you?

                              EZRA
                    They was as dead as the
                    one's they was diggin' up
                    and stealin'...

                              CHANCE
                    How bad did that hit on the
                    head affect him, Doc?

                              EZRA
                    It ain't no hit on the
                    head makes me think I see'd
                    things.. two of them they was.
                    Both as big as a house - One
                    even bigger than the other.
                    Must a been fifteen feet tall....

35.   CLOSE TWO   CHANCE & TOM   35.

        Chance looks to Tom, questioningly. Tom shrugs
        his shoulders hopelessly. Then both look back to
        Ezra.

36.   CLOSE SHOT EZRA

                         EZRA
               Think what ya like - but
               I'm tellin' ya he was - and
               the other must a been ten
               foot up - both with faces
               as white as snow and eyes a
               lookin' out like the black
               holes in a skull - no siree-
               I ain't goin' back to that
               grave yard for nuttin' or
               nobody.....

37.   MEDIUM GROUP

                         CHANCE
               You'll have to go back
               once more, Ezra - with us -
               to show us where it happened.

                         EZRA
               That much I'll do - but I'm
               leavin again when you do...

Chance turns towards the doctor.

                         CHANCE
               Is it alright if he goes...?

                         DOCTOR
               I guess so - long as he
               doesn't bump his head again
               for a few days..

Ezra hops down out of the chair and moves with
Tom towards the door. The doctor takes Chance
lightly by the arm.

                         DOCTOR
               Mind If I trail along,
               Chance - - This talk of
               fifteen foot men interests
               me...
                         CHANCE
               Me too...
                         (laughs)
               Come on, Doc.

They move towards the door.

38. EXT. SHERIFF'S OFFICE MEDIUM WIDE   38.

     Skimpy rides into the scene as the four men come
     out of the sheriff's office. He gets off the horse
     and walks towards Chance after he has tied the reins
     to the hitching rail. Doc,Ezra, and Tom get into
     the saddles of their horses.

39. CLOSE TWO CHANCE & SKIMPY   39.

                         CHANCE
                Miss Nancy get home alright?

                         SKIMPY
                She rode off alone - Didn't
                want me to go with her...

                         CHANCE
                You'd have made a good Army
                runner.

                         SKIMPY
                Shucks, the army ain't no
                place for me.

                         CHANCE
                Anyway - you can forget
                the other six days -- but stay
                out of Melody's saloon...

                         SKIMPY
                Gosh, thanks, Sheriff -- and
                I sure will stay outta the
                saloon -- first thing it
                gets daylight I'm packin'
                my mule and headin' for the
                buttes to do some prospectin' --
                Say -- Chance -- Mind if I
                sleep in the jail tonight --
                ain't got no hotel money...

                         CHANCE
                      (with a soft smile)
                Okay - but round up Steve
                first and tell him to meet
                us out at the cemetery...

                         SKIMPY
                Sure thing...

                         CHANCE
                Your gun is in my desk...

                              (CONTINUED)

39.   CONTINUED: 39.

                              SKIMPY
                I know...

        Skimpy moves off scene quickly. Chance smiles broadly,
        then walks off scene towards his horse...

40.   MEDIUM WIDE ANGLE   40.

        Chance gets into the saddle and rides off quickly
        in the direction of the cemetery with the others
        following....

                                              FADE TO:

41.   EXT. OPEN ROAD MEDIUM LONG NIGHT   41.

        The wagon drawn by the team of coal black horses
        makes its way carefully over a long stretch of open
        road. On both sides of the road, stretched far
        into the night are the long rolling plains of the
        vastness of the west.

        The giants are on the drivers seat of the horse,
        drawn vehicle, but Nancy is not where she can be
        seen. Presumably she is tied up in the rear of
        the wagon under the tarpaulin which hides the
        coffin.

                                              DISSOLVE TO:

42.   EXT. SIDE ROAD MEDIUM CLOSE NIGHT   42.

        The wagon is pulled into the scene and turns to the
        side, dirt road. As it enters the road it comes
        to a full stop....

43.   CLOSE TWO   THE GIANTS   43.

        They look up towards the crevices... in the
        distance.

44.   EXT. MINE   44.

        LONG SHOT   NIGHT

        Of a dreary looking mine shaft, steeped in shadows,
        a foreboding sight of disaster and horror.

45.   CLOSE TWO   GIANTS   45.

        The giants look again to the road and the horses
        are whipped up to start the wagon moving again
        along this branch road.

46.   MEDIUM CLOSE   46.

        The wagon starts its ascent up the little
        mountainous road. We will notice here the
        dangerous cliffs on the side of the road -
        (to be used as the spot for crash sequence
        in the tag.)

                                        DISSOLVE TO:

47.   EXT. MINE SHAFT   MEDIUM CLOSE   NIGHT   47.

        The wagon is pulled into the scene and is brought
        to a halt. From within the cavern we hear
        the weird strains of organ music. The giants
        get out of the drivers seat and move to the rear
        of the wagon. The tarpaulin is thrown back and
        Nancy is dragged to the ground by the larger of
        the two giants. She wrestles and fights against
        the giant, but her fighting is as much use in
        the battle as a butterfly's wings are against the
        tough hide of an elephant. She is half carried, half
        dragged towards the mine shaft opening.

48.   INT. MINE ORGAN ROOM LONG SHOT   48.

Nancy never ceases in her struggle to free
herself from her captors. They drag her through
the mine corridor into a big cavern - at the end
of which can be seen the figure of man playing at
a big pipe organ. The weird organ music is
tremendous within this echo chamber. Nancy slowly
looks up. Her struggles slowly cease. The giants
have come to a full stop. Nancy's questioning eyes
focus straight ahead into the CAMERA.

49.   MEDIUM CLOSE   49.

On the back of Professor Smoke who is wildly
playing the pipe organ. His head sways to the
weird music as if in some kind of trance. His
nimble fingers race across the keyboard. He hits
the deep notes with much vigor and zest.

50.   WIDER ANGLE DOLLY TO MEDIUM SHOT   50.

The CAMERA follows behind the giants and Nancy
as they move again into the big empty stone
room. Empty except for Professor Smoke at the Pipe
Organ. The pipes are hidden in the wall. The man
does not turn around as they approach. The music
becomes low and weird. Nancy frightened, but amazed
now at this atmosphere of the cave stone and cob webs
of the room and the strange man playing the organ.
She suddenly becomes quiet, ceases her struggles
and becomes wide-eyed. They stop close behind the
man. The man still does not turn towards the CAMERA,
nor does he stop playing the organ as he speaks...

                    PROFESSOR
          I trust your journey
          was successful.

                    TANZ
                    (the shorter
                    of the two giants)
          In - Wagon - outside..

                    PROFESSOR
          Good...

                    KARL
          Girl - saw - us -- Bring - Her
          - Here...

51.   MEDIUM CLOSE PROFESSOR SMOKE   51.

He stops playing suddenly.

                    PROFESSOR
            Girl... What Girl...?

Slowly he turns around to face them (CAMERA). (It
will be noted wherewith that Professor Smoke wears
the striped trousers he will use later as the
undertaker.) Over his white shirt and string tie
he wears a velvet lounging jacket. His coal black
hair is combed smoothly back over his head. His
eyebrows are black and bushy. For the first moment,
as he turns and faces the off scene girl, his
features are steeped with anger, slowly, then his
features relax, soften -- he smiles...

                    PROFESSOR
            Good evening, Miss Corbet....

52.   CLOSE THREE SHOT GIANTS & NANCY   52.

Nancy is puzzled at the recognition from this
stranger. She takes a step forward. Tanz steps
forward as if to block her forward movement...

                    NANCY
            How do you know me...?

53.   CLOSE SHOT PROFESSOR   53.

He puts his hand up to stop Tanz.

54.   CLOSE THREE GIANTS & NANCY   54.

Tanz catches the Professor's signal and moves
back. The girl walks on.

55.   CLOSE TWO PROFESSOR AND NANCY   55.

She stops, in close to the Professor. The
Professor is smiling - his eyes gleaming at
the lovely girl.

                    PROFESSOR
            It is my business to know
            most everyone in our small
            community. Even a new arrival...
            like yourself.

                              (CONTINUED)

55. CONTINUED: 55.

He turns on Karl, the tallest of the two giants.
His eyes narrow....

56. EXTREME EYE CLOSE   PROFESSOR   56.

Showing only the Professor's hypnotic stare as he
speaks to Karl...

                         PROFESSOR
             Karl - Tend to that little
             matter now....

57. MEDIUM CLOSE   57.

The giant, his face hard with almost a determined
look of defiance on it.

58. EXTREME EYES CLOSE   PROFESSOR   58.

His eyes become even more narrow.

                         PROFESSOR
             I tell you to go - - Do as
             I say...

59. MEDIUM WIDE ANGLE   59.

The giant holds his look of defiance a moment
longer, then seems to weaken under the Professor's
hypnotice stare, then abruptly he turns and leaves
the room. The Professor gets off the organ bench
and moves to stand with the girl.

60. CLOSE TWO PROFESSOR & NANCY   60.

His eyes gleaming in an almost wicked smile.

                         PROFESSOR
             It seems to be time for Karl to
             have his -- treatment -- In the
             short time of our acquaintance I
             grew to know your Uncle very well --
             When he died it was I who buried him -
             Permit me to introduce myself. I am
             Professor Smoke -- Undertaker...

                                           (CONTINUED)

60.   CONTINUED: 60.

                          NANCY
               You mean to keep me here?

                          PROFESSOR
               I'm sorry it has become
               necessary-- but it has become
               necessary...You have seen my
               men at work - and more so --
               now that you have seen me
               here..
                      (shrugs)

61.   CLOSE SHOT   NANCY   61.

                          NANCY
               By daylight, Chance will have
               a posse out covering this whole
               territory....

62.   CLOSE SHOT   PROFESSOR   62.

                          PROFESSOR
               Be that as it may -- in the
               meantime you will remain here-
               as my guest.... Tanz....

63.   MEDIUM CLOSE   GROUP   63.

       The giant moves up to take the girls arm. She begins
       her futile struggle again...

                          PROFESSOR
               Take her to my quarters -
               Make yourself as comfortable
               as possible, Miss Corbett. I
               have other work to do now...

       The giant takes the sturggling girl out of the scene.
       The Professor watches for a long moment, then starting
       to take off his jacket, he moves towards a door on the
       far right side of the room....

                                        DISSOLVE TO:

64.   INT. SMALL LABORATORY EXTREME CLOSE   64.
       PROFESSOR

       The Professor wears the smock of a laboratory
       technician now - although only his face can be
       seen in this shot. He is bending over the
       operating table. His face is tense, his eyes
       mere slits in his head, as he works. Then it
       would appear that he has failed in what he does.
       He closes his eyes and sighs deeply.

65.   MEDIUM WIDE ANGLE   65.

       To take in the laboratory. The two giants
       stand, one on each end of the operating table,
       while the Professor stands mid-way along it. He
       pulls back the sheet to cover the body. He walks
       to a desk and sits down. He makes some notes in a
       big ledger then turns back to the giants...

                    PROFESSOR
             Get rid of it....

       The two giants move toward the operating table as
       the Professor gets up and walks towards a bolted
       door on the right side of the room. He turns back
       to face the giants who now hold the covered body.

                    PROFESSOR
             Put it with the rest - in the
             bottomless pit...

       The giants move with their covered burden to a large
       stone slate. They lay the body down. Tqnz moves to a
       wall and pulls a lever. The floor stone raises up...
       They lift the body and let it slide from under the
       covering into the pit... The Professor turns again
       to the door.

66.   INT. PROFESSOR'S ROOM   MEDIUM WIDE   66.

       Nancy is asleep on the cot. The bolt is heard to
       be thrown out of place. Nancy wakes up with a
       start. The Professor enters the room and closes
       the door behind him. Nancy sits on the edge of the
       bed. The Professor pulls a chair from under the
       desk and pushes it up beside the bed. He sits in it
       and after a moment of looking to the terrified girl
       he lets his eyes look silently to the floor.

67.   CLOSE SHOT   PROFESSOR   67.

His saddened eyes look to the floor.

                        PROFESSOR
                        (slowly)
        Once more it seems I have failed.

He looks to the girl. He smiles wearily...

                A long time ago, in my home
                country, far across the ocean, I
                discovered the secrets of making
                man's body strong - almost
                impregnable. I was exiled for
                my imagination. I came to this
                country then - to this little
                community, where I could con-
                tinue my experiments in relative
                safety and secrecy - but still
                one little factor remains to be
                found before I attain complete
                success. --- The brain of my
                subject. I cannot control
                their brain without the use of
                drugs.....
                        (suddenly becomes
                        strong)
                ....But it will not always be
                so...One day I will succeed...
                Until then - I must continue
                my work... I am not a cruel man,
                Miss Corbet -- I have a great
                love for my fellow man and his
                well being....In the long run
                humanity will benefit from my
                work --- The end will justify
                my means....

68.   MEDIUM WIDE ANGLE   68.

The Professor stands up and violently tosses the
wooden chair away from him. He turns to walk
towards the door.

69.   CLOSE SHOT   NANCY   69.

Her eyes wide in amazement - wonderment, at the
actions of the man.

70.   CLOSE SHOT   PROFESSOR   70.

At the door, he turns to look back to the girl.

                    PROFESSOR
          Upon my return, we will talk
          again.

He goes out of the door and closes it quickly.
The bolt is heard to slide into place.

71.   CLOSE SHOT   NANCY   71.

She gets up from the bed - her eyes looking towards
the closed door. She turns to look around the room.

72.   PANNING SHOT   72.

From Nancy's viewpoint of the room the walls are
the walls of the mine. An impossible place to
escape from.....

73.   MEDIUM WIDE ANGLE   73.

Hopelessly, Nancy sits back on the bed, her
hands go restlessly to her lap.

                                        FADE TO:

74.   EXT. CEMETERY   MEDIUM CLOSE   NIGHT

The cemetery is now flooded with the light of
many torches and oil lamps. Chance, Doc and
Ezra stand in a small group while the two
deputies, Tom and Steve are looking over the
soft ground at the foot prints imbedded there
 near the opened grave. Doc stays more or less
to the background out of the way but ready to
answer any questions should one be put to him.
Ezra sticks close to Chance's elbow... Tom gets
up from a squatting position and walks back to
where Chance stands....

                    TOM
          They're mighty big footprints...

                    EZRA
I told ya' they would be....

                              (CONTINUED)

74.   CONTINUED: 74.

Chance turns full on Ezra....

                    DOC
          Whose grave was this?

                    CHANCE
          You'd better get your record
          book from the shack, Ezra....

                    EZRA
          Don't need no book to tell who
          was buried here. It was Jim
          Thomas - got killed in that
          stampede day or two ago. Buried
          him just 'afore sunset tonight.

Tom turns and moves back to where the other deputy
is standing.

                    PROFESSOR (o.s.)
          Perhaps I can be of assistance..?

Chance and Ezra turn to face the off scene voice...

75.   FIGURE CLOSE SHOT   SMOKE   75.

The Professor now wears the dark, neatly pressed
suit if an undertaker. His smooth black hair is
covered with a dark Homburg. He carries a can
over his arm. A long black cloak is fastened
about his neck and hangs loosely and long over
his shoulders and down his back. He is smiling -
a short of weird - friendly smile - As he stands,
just inside the light of the torches, the fog of
the night and the cemetery behind him, it gives
a completely weird feeling - an eerie sight to
behold.

                    PROFESSOR
          In passing I saw your apparent
          activity....

76.   MEDIUM CLOSE   76.

Chance walks into the scene. Ezra follows
 closely behind him. Chance moves in close to
the Professor.

                              (CONTINUED)

76.   CONTINUED: 76.

                              CHANCE
                        (indicating grave)
                We've had another visit from the
                grave robbers.

                              PROFESSOR
                Why--this is the grave of Jim
                Thomas.--His family will be
                quite disturbed -- It was only
                earlier this evening we put him
                to rest.

77.   MEDIUM CLOSE   EZRA   77.

                               EZRA
                They weren't just grave robbers,
                Professor Smoke!!! Them ghouls
                was giants. Big as any three
                men I ever see'd.

78.   CLOSE SHOT   PROFESSOR   78.

                             PROFESSOR
                You saw them?

                The Professor is noticeably concerned....

79.   CLOSE SHOT   EZRA   79.

                               EZRA
                Sure I see'd 'em - and if me an
                them never meets again - that's
                too soon for me.

80.   CLOSE SHOT   CHANCE   80.

                              CHANCE
                Ezra took quite a beating. I
                guess they figured him for dead.

81.   CLOSE SHOT   EZRA   81.

                He re-acts to this thought as if it was the
                first time he has realized his previous danger.

                                                   (CONTINUED)

81.   CONTINUED: 81.

                              EZRA
                    Never did think of it like
                    that.

82.   CLOSE SHOT   PROFESSOR   82.

                            PROFESSOR
                    You are indeed a lucky man.

83.   CLOSE GROUP   83.

                              EZRA
                    An I'm gonna' stay that way -
                    Professor - you can get
                    yourself another caretaker -
                    I ain't puttin' in another
                    night around this bone yard...

                            PROFESSOR
                    Oh, come now, Ezra...

                              EZRA
                    I mean it...

                            PROFESSOR
                         (turning to Chance)
                    What could anyone possibly
                    want with dead bodies...?

                            CHANCE
                    I guess that's my job to find
                    out.

                            PROFESSOR
                    Yes -- Yes -- Indeed it is...
                    If I can be of no assistance
                    then I will be on my way...

                            CHANCE
                    Isn't much anyone can do to
                    help right now, Professor --
                    Just routine.

                            PROFESSOR
                    Goodnight...

                                        (CONTINUED)

83. CONTINUED: 83.

The Professor turns and leaves the scene. Ezra
and Chance turn to watch him go. After a moment,
Ezra speaks.

                         EZRA
               He's as spooky as them he
               buries.

                        CHANCE
               Maybe you're looking more
               to the work the man does than
               to the man himself...

                         EZRA
               Say it anyway you like -it
               still comes out the same -
               He's jist one spooky cuss...

Chance smiles at the old caretaker's distress....

84. EXT. CARETAKER'S SHACK MEDIUM CLOSE NIGHT   84.

Professor Smoke comes out of the cemetery, stops,
looks back towards the cemetery proper. He smiles,
then moves towards his hearse wagon.....

85. MEDIUM WIDE ANGLE   85.

The Professor gets on the wagon and takes off...

86. EXT. CEMETERY MEDIUM GROUP CHANCE EZRA   STEVE TOM 86.

Chance is looking to the open grave. He turns to
Steve...

                        CHANCE
               Looks like a long night --
               Steve - you ride on back to
               the Office...
                            STEVE
               Right...

Steve walks off scene...

                                    DISSOLVE TO:

87.   EXT. SHERIFF'S OFFICE MEDIUM CLOSE DAY   87.

        Chance and Tom ride in and pull up at the
        hitching rail. They tie up then move to enter
        the Sheriff's office.

88.   INT. SHERIFF'S OFFICE MEDIUM CLOSE   88.

        Chance and Tom come into the room. Steve, the
        deputy, sits at the desk. He gets up as they
        enter. Chance goes to his desk, pushes his hat
        to the back of his head then looks to the deputy,
        Steve....

                        CHANCE
                Anything new from this end?

                        STEVE
                Quiet all night, except for
                Skimpy's snoring -- He sure
                can snore up a storm...

        Chance turns to look towards the empty cell with the
        messed up jail cot.

                        CHANCE
                Where is he now...?

                        STEVE
                Gone back up in the buttes
                huntin' gold -- Same as
                he does everytime we let him
                out of jail...

                        CHANCE
                        (to Tom)
                You'd better go on home and
                get some sleep. Steve can
                take over now...

                        TOM
                I'm not tired. Kinda' like
                to stick it out if you don't
                mind.

                        CHANCE
                Have it your way.

                                (CONTINUED)

88.   CONTINUED: 88.

A horse is heard to race in and pull up. Steve is
now at the curtain. He pulls back to look out.

                    STEVE
          Doc Simpson.. he's sure in a
          hurry.

The men turn towards the door as the footsteps are
heard on the board walk outside. The door opens and
the doctor enters. He goes directly to Chance. His
face holds a serious look.

                    DOC
          Brace yourself, Chance.

                    CHANCE
          What is it....?

                    DOC
          Nancy never got home last
          night.

89.   CLOSE SHOT   CHANCE   89.

Chance gets to his feet immediately. He faces the
Doctor.

90.   MEDIUM CLOSE   90.

                    DOCTOR
          Her horse came in sometime
          during the night - - nobody
          saw it until this morning.
          Still had the saddle on.

                    CHANCE
          How'd you find out?

                    DOCTOR
          Lem's been down with the flu --
          I went out to check on him
          around daylight - Just after
          I left you at the cemetery...

                              (CONTINUED)

90.   CONTINUED: 90.

Chance turns quickly to Steve, then to Tom.

                         CHANCE
                Steve -- You stay here. Tom.
                Round up some men and meet me
                at her ranch.

Chance turns and runs quickly from the room; Tom
following immediately after....

91.   EXT. SHERIFF'S OFFICE MEDIUM WIDE DAY   91.

Chance comes out, Tom directly behind him. Both
men swing quickly into the saddle. Tom gets out in
one direction and Chance heads in the other. The
CAMERA stays with Chance.

                                        DISSOLVE TO:

92.   EXT. PASTURE LAND MEDIUM WIDE   92.

Chance plows across the picturesque countryside.
He makes a   sudden swerve and hits a dirt road.

93.   CLOSE RUNNING SHOT   93.

With Chance spurring the horse on to greater speed
along the road for a short distance, then he again
cuts the horse off the road to head out again across
country. The CAMERA CAR stops and THE CAMERA holds on
THE EAST END OF THE HORSE GOING West, until he is
nearly out of sight.

                                        DISSOLVE TO:

94.   EXT. RANCH HOUSE SPREAD MEDIUM WIDE DAY   94.

Of a low, nice looking ranch house. Four or five
cowboys can be seen in the background at various
jobs. Chance heads in towards the front hitching
rail.

95.   MEDIUM CLOSE   95.

Chance pulls in and quickly gets out of the saddle.

                                        (CONTINUED)

95.   CONTINUED: 95.

The door of the ranch house opens. Marty Bullock,
the foreman, comes out to meet Chance.. Marty is a
big, rough looking man, but a well meaning man that
gets the job done, quickly and efficiently...

                        MARTY
             My boys are combing the hills
             for her now. They'll find her
             if she's to be found.

                        CHANCE
             When Tom and the possee get
             here send them out to the
             South Wagon road...

                        MARTY
             Okay, Chance.

Chance swings around from the man and gets back in the
saddle. He swings his mount around and heads out in
the opposite direction from which he has come.
Marty moves off as if towards the corral...

                                        DISSOLVE TO:

96.   EXT. ROAD RUNNING SHOT MEDIUM CLOSE DAY   96.

With Chance prodding his horse along a dirt road.
There is open country on both sides of him.

                                        DISSOLVE TO:

97.   EXT. WOODED ROAD MEDIUM CLOSE RUNNING DAY   97.

This is the same spot as used in scene 25,
with the exception it is daylight and Chance
is coming from the opposite direction from that
which Nancy had been riding. He is moving in the
direction the horse and wagon of the giants had
been driving. His horse is now moving at a slow
gallop. He is watching the woods on both sides of
him - carefully - watchfully. Then his eyes lower
to the road before him. Suddenly he pulls up. The
CAMERA CAR stops its movement as Chance gets out
of the saddle and walks to the side of the road.

98.   MEDIUM CLOSE   98.

Chance picks up Nancy's hat from the side of the
road. He surveys it a moment, then looks to the
soft shoulder of the road.

99.   CLOSE SHOT ROAD   99.

We can see the wheel tracks of a steel rimmed wagon
wheel as it had pulled off the road a bit and has
sunk into the soft shoulder, then moves on back to
the hard road and the marking is lost.

100.   CLOSE SHOT CHANCE   100.

His eyes looking down at the wheel tracks, then to
the hat, he holds in his hand. He pushes his own
hat to the back of his head -- puzzled....

                                        FADE TO:

101.   EXT. WESTERN STREET MEDIUM WIDE DAY   101.

Chance rides in, alone. Both horse and rider are
tired and streaked with sweat and dirt from their hard
ride. Nancy's hat can be seen hooked over the saddle
horn. Suddenly, looking off scene towards the boardwalk, Chance pulls in.

102.   MEDIUM CLOSE EZRA   102.

Walking along the boardwalk, muttering to himself as
he moves. He carries a battered suit case in his
hand. He wears a tight fitting checkered suit and
his light slouch cowboy hat. On his shoulder is
perched a small colorful bird - perhaps a lovebird.
He is mumbling, disgruntedly to the bird as he moves.

103.   CLOSE SHOT CHANCE   103.

                      CHANCE
               Where do you think you're
               going?

104.   MEDIUM CLOSE EZRA   104.

He stops - looks o.s. to Chance.

                      EZRA
               Tombstone, El Paso, Dodge City -
               anyplace but here. Me and
               Fooey...
                  (indicates bird)
               .. are gettin' the next stage
               out...

105.   MEDIUM WIDE   105.

Chance surpresses a smile then directs his horse
towards Ezra. Chance gets out of the saddle and
moves to stand in close to him.

106.   MEDIUM TWO SHOT   CHANCE & EZRA   106.

                      CHANCE
               I understand your feelings,
               old timer, but I'm going to
               need you around town for a
               spell.

                      EZRA
               You gonna' stand there and
               tell me you won't let me leave
               town?

                      CHANCE
               That's about the size of it.

                      EZRA
               This town has seen the last
               of me, except for the dust
               me and Fooey make in leavin'.
               You ain't got one charge you
               kin arrest me for -- I ain't
               done nuttin' but get my brains
               slammed around....

                             (CONTINUED)

106.   CONTINUED: 106.

                              CHANCE
                    Either you stay on your own
                    accord.. or....

          Chance points down to Ezra's hip where a big bulge
          under his suit can be easily detected.

                              CHANCE
                    - I'll have to lock you up
                    for carrying a concealed
                    weapons...

          Ezra looks down to his suit, then he pulls it open
          to reveal gun, holster and gun belt of an ancient
          vintage.

                              EZRA
                    Ahhh -- Now Chance...

                              CHANCE
                    I mean it..

                              EZRA
                    It ain't concealed. Just
                    had mi coat over it. Why -
                    this thing is so old it'd blow
                    yer hand off if ya' tried
                    shootin 'it -- It's a hair loom.
                    Been with my family since my great-
                    great grand pappy crossed the
                    Mississippi back in the winter
                    of... Well it was a long time
                    ago -- Jist didn't have room
                    to pack it in my suit case.

                              CHANCE
                            (smiling)
                    You know it - and I know it --
                    but the Judge   dont know it...

                              EZRA
                    Ahhhh - Now dog, gone it...

          Chance takes the suitcase from the man's hand quietly.
          Chance is smiling at the apparent discomfort and
          disappointment in the man's face.

                                           (CONTINUED)

106.   CONTINUED: 106.

                          CHANCE
               Don't fret so, Ezra.. There'll
               be another stage in the morning.
               In the meantime I'll take your
               suitcase over to my office.
               You beat it back to your
               shack an' bring me the
               burial records for the last
               couple of months...

                          EZRA
               Ahhh - dog, gone it.. Come
               on Fooey.

107.   INT. SHERIFF'S OFFICE   MEDIUM CLOSE   DAY   107.

       As Chance moves into the room Steve gets up from
       behind the desk. They talk as Chance puts Ezra's
       suitcase against the wall behind a clothestree and
       Nancy's hat on one of the arms of the clothestree.

                          STEVE
               Buy a new hat....?

                          CHANCE
               Nancy's.. Found it on the
               trail.

       He sits down behind his desk, pushing his hat to the
       back of his head...

                          STEVE
                    (pointing to paper)
               That report will interest
               you...

       Chance reaches to the desk and picks up a written
       report. He goes into deep thought as he studies the
       report. He lets the report flutter back to the desk
       as the door opens to admit Doc. Simpson. Chance and
       Steve both turn to face the man. Doc moves in and sits
       down in a chair near the desk.

                          DOCTOR
               You looked a hundred miles
               away.

                          CHANCE
               I've been thinking about giants.

                                   (CONTINUED)

Gary D. Rhodes   **121**

107.	CONTINUED:	107.

> DOCTOR
> Come, now, Chance...

Chance reaches over and picks up the report again.
He eyes it thoughtfully as he speaks...

> CHANCE
> It'd take a mighty big man
> to make footprints like the
> ones we saw out at the cemetery...
> Here's the report.

> DOCTOR
> (whistles)
> I've heard of medicine show
> giant's with feet that big. But
> we haven't had a show around here
> in five years.

> CHANCE
> Men that big can't stay hidden
> long.

> DOCTOR
> They've done pretty well so far.

> CHANCE
> Maybe we've been going after
> them in the wrong way...
> (to Steve)
> ...Steve - Tom's out at Nancy's
> ranch. I want you to get out
> there and get him back pronto...

> STEVE
> Take me twenty minutes...

> CHANCE
> Make it fifteen...

Steve goes quickly out of the door. The doctor
again turns on Chance.

> DOCTOR
> Sound's like you've got a plan?

> CHANCE
> Just an idea....

> DOCTOR
> Do I figure in?

(CONTINUED)

107. CONTINUED: 107.

                              CHANCE
                 I'm counting on you. It's going
                 to be up to you to tell me if
                 it can be done and how. Ezra
                 will be here directly with his
                 record books. - Now -- all these
                 bodies have been taken from
                 their graves within a few hours
                 after burial -- so here's what
                 I have in mind...

                                              DISSOLVE TO:

109. EXT. ROAD NEAR CEMETERY   MEDIUM LONG SHOT DAY   108.

      Ezra, the bird perched on his shoulder, cussing his
      situation out to the bird, (ad-lib), prods along.
      He carries the ledger under his arm. He kicks at
      the dust along the road. From behind him can be
      seen the Professor driving his hearse. Ezra stops
      and looks towards the vehicle. The hearse is
      pulled to a stop. Ezra moves to the point near the
      driver.

110. ANGLE TWO   PROFESSOR & EZRA   109.

      Professor Smoke secures the reins as he looks down
      to Ezra and Ezra looks up to him.

                              EZRA
                 Afternoon, Professor.

                              PROFESSOR
                 Can I give you a ride, Ezra....

                              EZRA
                 On that thing -- Well -- alright.
                 I was leavin' town when the Sheriff
                 made me go back to that cemetery
                 for my record books. Ya, know --
                 even in daylight I don't like it out
                 there no more.....

111. CLOSE SHOT   PROFESSOR   111.

                              PROFESSOR
                             (reacting)
                 Why do you suppose the Sheriff
                 want's your record book...?

112.   CLOSE SHOT   EZRA   112.

                         EZRA
              Search me. All I want is to
              get this thing over with, so's
              me and Fooey can hit it out for
              the tall timbers....

113.   MEDIUM CLOSE TWO   EZRA & PROFESSOR   113.

                       PROFESSOR
              I don't blame you. I certainly
              wouldn't want to be hit on the
              head a first time, let alone
              the chance of a second time...
              But do climb up....

114.   MEDIUM LONG SHOT   114.

        Ezra, reluctantly eyeing the coach, climbs up onto
        the seat. The hearse starts off....

                                                   FADE TO:

115.   INT. SHERIFF'S OFFICE   MEDIUM CLOSE   DAY   115.

        Chance, the Doctor, Steve and Tom are grouped
        around Chance's desk in the Sheriff's office. All
        have been in a close huddle. Now they pull away.

                       DOCTOR
              It's a long chance and a dangerous
              one.

                       CHANCE
              But, is it worth trying?

                       DOCTOR
              Chance -- A crazy scheme like that
              is bound to be worth something.

                       CHANCE
              You think it's crazy?

                       DOCTOR
              Of course it's crazy. You're playing
              it about ninety-ten to come out alive.

                                        (CONTINUED)

115.   CONTINUED: 115.

                          CHANCE
              Where do you think I got
              my knick-name - Ninety-ten
              is good enough.

                          DOCTOR
              Okay -- You can count on me --
              I'll do my part.

                                      FADE TO:

116.   INT. SALOON   STAGE   MEDIUM WIDE DOLLY TO MED. CLOSE 116.

With the blare of a four piece orchestra in the pit
below the small stage, four dancing chorus girls
high step (can-can) out onto the stage. There is
shouts of expectation from the males in the audience.
The girls skip gaily about for a moment -- then --
with a sudden fanfare the star of the review comes
on stage. She does the suggestion (within good
taste) of a strip tease, with the other four girls
backing her up from the chorus. The CAMERA DOLLYS
into a MEDIUM CLOSE of the girls as she does her act.

117.   MEDIUM CLOSE   BAR   117.

Marty, seemingly quite drunk, stands at the bar,
turned to face the stage. He slugs down his shot
of whiskey. Without looking, he turns to put the
glass on the bar. The Bartender steps in to refill
the glass. He looks to the drunken Marty, and the
look is of deepest worry.

118.   MED. CLOSE   STAGE   118.

The dancers doing their routine.

119.   CLOSE SHOT   MARTY   119.

His eyes on fire as he looks off scene to the girl.
His hand and shot glass enter the scene. He slugs
down the whiskey.

120.   CLOSE SHOT   BARTENDER   120.

Looking öff to Marty. His face grave with worry.

121.   CLOSE SHOT   MARTY   121.

Tense.

122.   CLOSE SHOT   DANCER   122.

The girl's face and head only, sexy, as she dances.

123.   MEDIUM WIDE   123.

         The whole saloon. Marty suddenly throws his glass
         to the floor and heavily, but not fast, makes his
         way across the room towards the stage. He pushes
         over one man and chair that is in his way, and turns
         over an empty table near the stage....

124.   CLOSE SHOT   HOPE   124.

         One of the dance hall hostesses in the audience. She
         is watching Marty's advance.

125.   MEDIUM CLOSE   STAGE   125.

         Marty jumps up on the stage and grabs the lead
         dancer. The other four of the chorus, screaming,
         run off scene...

126.   MEDIUM CLOSE   HOPE   126.

         The hostess runs off scene.

127.   MEDIUM CLOSE   STAGE   127.

         Marty is wrestling with the girl trying to kiss her.
         The Bartender, club in hand, runs in, Marty stiff
         arms him and he lands in the orchestra pit.

128.   MEDIUM CLOSE   OFFICE DOOR   DOLLY TO MEDIUM WIDE   128.

         On a door marked "OFFICE-PRIVATE". Hope runs into
         the scene. She knocks rapidly, looks back over her
         shoulder, then knocks again. The noise of Marty's
         attack is heard in the background. The door opens
         to reveal Melody, a lushious beauty, dressed in the
         costume of a dance hall girl owner.

                              MELODY
                    What is it, Hope?

                              HOPE
                    It's Marty Bullock, Miss Melody.
                    He's acting like he's gone crazy...
                              (she points)

                                          (CONTINUED)

Gary D. Rhodes   **127**

128.   CONTINUED: 128.

                            MELODY
                         (looks off then
                         back to the
                         girl)
                    You get the sheriff. I'll try
                    to calm him...

                            HOPE
                    Yes ma'am...

The girl moves quickly off scene. Melody holds her
position at the door a moment longer then as the
CAMERA PULLS QUICKLY back, ahead of her, she moves
out into the saloon. As she moves past the bar she
reaches over and pours a double shot from a bottle into
a tall glass. She picks this up then moves on towards
the stage. As she steps up onto the stage where Marty
has two men in a headlock, and a couple more laying at
his feet on the stage, and the chorus girls seen
huddled in the background....we...'

129.   MEDIUM CLOSE TWO   MARTY ADN MELODY   129.

She is carelessly holding the glass of whiskey.
Marty, nearly stupified, is holding the two men in
the headlock. As Melody speaks she holds out the
glass to him.

                            MELODY
                    Haven't seen you hittin' it so
                    hard before, Marty...

Marty drops the two men. They lands out cold, on the
stage...He takes the glass from her hand and slugs it
down quickly.

                            MARTY
                    Maybe I ain't felt like hittin'
                    it hard before.....

130.   CLOSE SHOT   MELODY   130.

                            MELODY
                    Maybe you've had enough - You
                    oughta' get on back to your
                    ranch.

131. CLOSE SHOT   MARTY   131.

                         MARTY
               Maybe you oughta' mind your own
               business...I'll get back to the
               ranch when I get ready -- who
               knows when enough is enough? Do
               you know when enough is enough,
               Melody?

132. CLOSE TWO   MARTY & MELODY   132.

                         MELODY
               Just as you say, Marty - but Miss
               Nancy ain't going to like her
               foreman in this shape.

                         MARTY
               Miss Nancy - huh - She ain't at
               the ranch - Them Ghouls got her.
               Maybe she...Ah, what's the use...
               I just feel like bustin' somethin' -
               Might just as well start with this
               dump....

He goes for his gun...

                         CHANCE (O.S.)
               Hold it, Marty.....

Marty lets his hand fall away from the gun, still in
the holster. He turns to face the off scene Sheriff.
Melody backs away. She has also turned to face the
off scene Sheriff...

133. CLOSE SHOT   FIGURE   CHANCE   133.

Chance stands just inside the doorway. His hands
straight down at his sides, but near his guns.

134. MEDIUM WIDE   134.

Marty comes down from the stage and moves towards
the bar. Chance comes in from the opposite direction.
Melody is seen, at the cut, to move out towards them,
from the stage.

135. MEDIUM CLOSE   135.

The men at the bar...

                                   (CONTINUED)

135.   CONTINUED:

                              MARTY
                    Ahh.. Miss Nancy's boy friend.
                    The law himself -- Hello -- Law...

                              CHANCE
                    Hand over that gun belt...

Marty hooks his fingers over his gun belt and narrows
his eyes at Chance. His tone is one of complete
defiance.

                              MARTY
                          (cold - but
                          softly)
                    Suppose you try and take it
                    from me.

                              CHANCE
                    We've been friends a long time,
                    Marty - You don't want trouble
                    now....

                              MARTY
                    Friends......

Viciously he reaches around, grabs Melody by the wrist
and tosses her around him and into the Sheriff's arms.

                              MARTY
                    Why don't you take Melody - She
                    loves you - Why don't you leave
                    Miss Nancy alone...

Chance ushers the girl safely to the side of the bar.

                              CHANCE
                    So that's it...

                              MARTY
                    Yeah---That's it...

                              CHANCE
                    I'm takin' that gun...

Chance moves in swiftly. His head goes to Marty's gun
belt, but Marty is a step ahead of him. He side steps
the Sheriff and brings his hand down in a rabbit
punch on the back of the Sheriff's neck. Chance
sprawls to the floor.

136.   MEDIUM WIDE   136.

Marty roars with laughter. The saloon's occupants
start to move back out of the way.

                          MARTY
               Look at our tough Sheriff now...
               How's the air down there, Sheriff..?
               Maybe Miss Nancy should see her
               hero now...

Marty moves in close to Chance. With a lightening
like movement, Chance grabs the man's foot and trips
him up. Marty sprawls to the floor. Chance gets up.
Marty gets up and charges in - directly into a left
hook from Chance which sends him back against the
bar. Chance moves in. Marty hoists himself up onto
the bar and swings his feet out to catch Chance in
the stomach. Chance flies backward...

137.   MEDIUM CLOSE   137.

Chance lands on a card table. The table over turns
under the sudden weight. Cards, chips and Chance go
to the floor. Marty moves in with a chair raised
for the kill. He brings it down heavily....

138.   CLOSE SHOT   CHANCE   138.

The chair crashes to the spot he rolls quickly away
from....

139.   MEDIUM WIDE   139.

Chance gets to his feet. He readies a haymaker and
lets it fly.

140.   CLOSE SHOT   MARTY   140.

The tremendous blow lands on Marty's chin. He is
stunned.

141.   MEDIUM CLOSE   141.

Chance follows his advantage with a right to the
stomach then a chin blow which puts Marty, battered
and bloody up against the bar...He hangs onto the
bar for dear life and breathes deeply.

142.   CLOSE SHOT   CHANCE   142.

Battered - fist doubled - dazed, but ready to
continue if there is any fight left in his
opponent...

143.   CLOSE SHOT   MARTY   143.

Leaning heavily against the bar. Slowly he turns
to face Chance. He breathes heavily...

                    MARTY
          You win, Sheriff... Guess I'm
          gettin' old.

144.   CLOSE SHOT   CHANCE   144.

                    CHANCE
          Let's have that gun.

145.   CLOSE SHOT   MARTY   145.

                    MARTY
          Sure....

146.   MEDIUM WIDE   146.

Chance starts to move forward, slowly. Marty
takes the gun from its holster and hands the gun
butt forward to Chance - then suddenly Marty pulls
a Stage Coach gun switch and brings the pistol
into firing position. He fires four quick shots
into Chance....

147.   CLOSE FIGURE   CHANCE   147.

He seems to re-act to the bullets -- Gives a
startled expression then slips silently to the
floor.

148.   CLOSE FIGURE   MARTY -   148.

Holding the smoking gun. Suddenly he seems to
realize what he has done. He looks for an exit.

                    TOM (o.s.)
          Hold it...

149.   CLOSE FIGURE   TOM   149.

Tom stands near at hand. His gun is trained on
Marty o.s. The doctor can be seen entering quickly
behind Tom. He is moving across the scene towards
the prone body of Chance.

                    TOM
          Drop the gun and don't move,
          Marty.

150.   CLOSE FIGURE   MARTY   150.

He moves as if to run to the left.

                    STEVE (o.s.)
          That's afar enough...

151.   CLOSE FIGURE   STEVE   151.

Steve stands, hard eyed, with his gun trained on
Marty o.s. Hope moves in to Steve's side, almost
for protection.

                    STEVE
          Just stay like he told you...

152.   MEDIUM CLOSE   PAN   152.

On the doctor and Chance. The doctor makes a
hurried examination of Chance. Then he takes up
Chance's arm to feel for a pulse. He lets the arm
drop limply back to the floor. He lifts an eye lid.
The CAMERA follows the doctor's movements as he
stands up. The doctor turns on the others in the
saloon. His face is grave as he speaks to them.

                    DOCTOR
          Sheriff Hilton is dead.....

153.   MEDIUM WIDE   153.

The doctor stands over Chance's body. Tom and
Steve move quickly in, roughly grab Marty. Marty
screams.

                    MARTY
          I didn't mean it -- He drew
          on me first.

                              (CONTINUED)

153.   CONTINUED: 153.

                              STEVE
                          (murderously)
                    The Sheriff's gun is still in
                    the holster.

          They drag him from the saloon. The doctor turns
          from watching the action to look down at Chance.
          Melody moves in close to him.

154.   CLOSE GROUP   154.

          Melody stands dazed, her back to the bar. The
          doctor looks to some men standing near at hand.

                              DOCTOR
                    Here - you men - take Chance
                    over to the Professor's....

          A couple of strong men move in and lift Chance up,
          they carry him out of the saloon. Melody watches
          the movement. As Doc Simpson is about to leave she
          takes his arm lightly.

                              MELODY
                    Chance..... is.....

                              DOCTOR
                    You always did like him, didn't
                    you, Melody?

                              MELODY
                    Like him - I loved him - But he
                    couldn't see it that way.

          Doc takes her arm reassuringly.

                              DOCTOR
                    I wouldn't take it too hard,
                    Melody. Things just seem to
                    work out - one way or another...

          He turns quickly and exits the saloon.

155.   EXT. STREET   MEDIUM WIDE   DAY   155.

          The doctor comes out of the saloon. Melody is
          seen to come out and stand in the doorway. As
          Doc Simpson crosses the street the Professor and
          his hearse arrive at the Undertaking parlor at the
          same time.

156.   EXT. FUNERAL PARLOR MEDIUM CLOSE   156.

The Professor is getting off the hearse as a Preacher
comes out of the Undertaking parlor. The Professor
halts him.

                        PROFESSOR
                What is it, Parson? -- What
                has happened.

                        PARSON
                The Sheriff is dead...

The crowd mumble loudly. The doctor joins the
Professor and both men start for the door to the
undertaking establishment.

157.   INT. FUNERAL PARLOR MEDIUM CLOSE DAY   157.

A small four walled room with a door leading to the
rear of the establishment. There is a bare wooden
table in the center of the room. Several chairs
and potted plants are situated about the room.
Two fancy coffins are on display near the window.
An organ is set near the wall. Several prayers
in wooden frames hang on the wall along with framed
state license and school diploma. It is into this
atmosphere that the doctor enters. Chance has been
layed out on the table. Two or three men, the ones
who have carried him into the room, stand near,
their hats in their hands out of respect for the
dead. The doctor and Professor Smoke make their
entrance. The Professor's face is one of complete
sadness.....

158.   MEDIUM CLOSE   158.

                        PROFESSOR
                This is indeed a sad day for
                our little town...

                        DOCTOR
                It was always Chance's wish,
                that if something like this
                should happen, he be buried
                immediately. I'm sure he
                would like his friends
                present at his sunset
                burial....

                                        (CONTINUED)

158.   CONTINUED: 158.

                          2ND MAN
                  They'll be there, Doc...

        The men who have carried Chance into the room leave.
        The doctor quickly shuts and bolts the door.

159.   MEDIUM CLOSE FRONT DOOR   159.

        The doctor throws the bolt into place.

                          DOCTOR
                  Now we will have no
                  interruptions.

160.   MEDIUM SHOT   160.

        The Professor is confused. The smiling doctor
        returns to Chance.

                          DOCTOR
                  Alright -- They're gone,
                  Chance...

        Chance opens his eyes and sits up on the
        edge of the table. He is smiling...

                          CHANCE
                  How did I do?

161.   CLOSE SHOT PROFESSOR   161.

                          PROFESSOR
                  It seems -- almost as well
                  as one of my -- er -- regular
                  clients.. But what's this all
                  about....

162.   MEDIUM GROUP   162.

                          DOCTOR
                  You Professor - are the one
                  flaw in our plan -- We forgot
                  you -- Yet you actually would
                  be the most important part of
                  the scheme...

                                           (CONTINUED)

162.   CONTINUED: 162.

                    PROFESSOR
          Pardon me if I seem rude,
          Doctor - But you're talking
          in riddles...

                    CHANCE
          Do you have that gadget, Doc?

                    DOCTOR
          Yes.. right here...

The doctor opens his bag and takes out an oxygen
mask and air bottle. He hands it to Chance who
showed it to the Professor. The Professor takes
it in his hand to examine it.

                    CHANCE
          With this oxygen gadget
          I'll have enough air to
          last several hours.

                    PROFESSOR
          But -- but - - this is all
          very strange -- why do you
          need this oxygen helmet...

                    CHANCE
          At sundown, Professor - you
          will lay me to my final rest
          in full view of all the
          townsfolk...

                    PROFESSOR
          You mean--- bury you -- alive?

                    DOCTOR
          It's Chance's idea that the
          ghouls will appear to dig
          him up. Thus leading him
          to Nancy and what this thing
          is all about.

                    PROFESSOR
          And if the ghouls do not
          appear?

                    CHANCE
          I think they will - but if
          I'm not taken up within a
          couple of hours after you
          put me down - come a runnin'
          and don't forget to bring
          a shovel...

                                        (CONTINUED)

Gary D. Rhodes   137

162.   CONTINUED: 162.

                          DOCTOR
                 I still think the whole plan
                 is too risky.

                          PROFESSOR
                      (gravely)
                 Doctor Simpson is right, you
                 know. Supposing this thing
                 doesn't work?
                      (indicates mask)

                          CHANCE
                 It was designed a couple of
                 years back for trapped
                 miners..No reason for it not
                 to work in a coffin.

163.   CLOSE SHOT PROFESSOR   163.

                          PROFESSOR
                      (cautiously)
                 Do your deputies know of
                 this plan?

164.   CLOSE SHOT CHANCE   164.

                          CHANCE
                      (shakes his head
                      "yes")
                 Both of them - and Marty, my
                 assassin!

165.   MEDIUM GROUP   165.

                          PROFESSOR
                 This has all come rather
                 sudden. There are many things
                 I must do... I suggest you have
                 one of your deputies stay with
                 you, here, for the time being.
                 I will be back in plenty of
                 time for -- your funeral....

                                              DISSOLVE TO:

166.   INT. SHERIFF'S OFFICE   MEDIUM GROUP   DAY   166.

With Tom, Steve and Marty in the room. Marty
stands back near the open door of a cell. Tom
is at the desk and Steve is peering cautiously
out around the corner of the drawn front window
curtains. He turns back to Tom as he speaks...

                    STEVE
          It ain't a healthy look on
          the faces of them folks out
          there.

                    MARTY
          He's right. When we came
          in they gave me the biggest
          cut-throat look I ever saw.

                    STEVE
           A lynchin'?

                    TOM
          It's been done before.

                    MARTY
          An' this jail don't look none
          too safe to me.

                    TOM
          Suppose we cross that bridge
          when we come to it.

                    MARTY
          Maybe it don't mean nuttin'
          to you -- but it does to me.
          It's my neck they're looking
          to stretch. Chance was well
          liked.

                    TOM
          Nobody forced you into this -
          Did you ever think - maybe Miss
          Nancy is in a worse fix than
          you ....

                    MARTY
          Yeah -- guess I'm just
          nervous.

                              (CONTINUED)

56.

166.   CONTINUED: 166.

                    TOM
                 (softer)
            Sure and I don't blame
            you. But we only have to
            hold out until morning.
            Then we can tell the whole
            story.

167.   CLOSE SHOT MARTY   167.

       He looks to a big pocket watch.

                    MARTY
            It's a long time from
            now until mornin'.

168.   MEDIUM GROUP SHOT   168.

                    STEVE
                 (reflectingly)
            A long time.

       He looks out the window towards the crowd outside.

                    MARTY
            Now look here - I like Miss
            Nancy. And Chance as Much as
            any man - but I ain't gonna
            let any lynch crazy mob string
            me up just to play along with
            the gag.

169.   MEDIUM WIDE ANGLE   169.

       The door opens to permit Doctor Simpson to enter.
       He closes and bolts the door behind him. He
       indicates a big cross bar as he speaks his first
       line.

                    DOCTOR
            Better put the cross bar on
            the door. I don't like the
            looks of things out there.
            Tom, you beat it over to
            the funeral parlor. Stick
            it out with Chance.

                                            (CONTINUED)

169.   CONTINUED: 169.

Tom turns and moves to the door. He opens it and
shuts it quickly, Steve moves in as Tom moves, with
the cross bar.

170.   EXT. SHERIFF'S OFFICE MEDIUM WIDE DAY   170.

Tom stands with his back to the door and his
hands on his hips. He faces a crowd of fifteen
or twenty angered people. They are so far a
silent, but restless mob with expressions of a mob
that may not remain silent long. Tom leaves.
the door to move to the edge of the boardwalk.
He faces the mob authoritatively.

                    TOM
          You folks seem to be mad
          about something...

Melody steps up from the center of the mob until
she stands in close to Tom.

                    MELODY
          Speaking for the boys - We
          liked Chance.

                    TOM
          Then do like Chance'd want
          it.. Break it up and go
          home before somebody gets
          hurt...

                    MELODY
          Most of us'd rather stick
          around a spell.

                    TOM
          Do just like you please.-
          but remember one thing - The
          first one that moves toward
          that door will find himself in
          real trouble.

A low murmur goes through the crowd but they neither
back up or move forward. They just stand their ground
murmering low and with the same angered expression on
their faces. Tom steps down from the boardwalk into
the group and shoves his way through their midst as
he heads across the street for the funeral parlor.
Most of the mob turns to watch him.

171.   INT. FUNERAL PARLOR   MEDIUM CLOSE   171.

With Chance seated,as before, on the edge of the
table. He is fiddling with the Oxygen tank. Three
quick knocks comes at the door. He gets up and moves
to it. He lifts the corner of the door shade to look
out then he throws the bolt open and steps back so
the door will shield him from sight. When Tom is
in the room Chance closes the door and bolts it
quickly. Chance moves in Close to Tom. Tom indicates
the outside.

                    TOM
          They ain't got real mean yet...
          but it looks like the start of
          a real lynchin' party.

Suddenly excited, Chance moves to the door. He
lifts the drawn curtain a bit and looks out. A
moment later he replaces the curtain and moves back
to Tom.

                    CHANCE
          Can you handle them?

                    TOM
          I can try.

                    CHANCE
          Hold them as long as you
          can -- then come for me.

                    TOM
          How come you don't just put
          down a dummy coffin then
          we hide out and catch whoever
          digs it up?

                    CHANCE
          We might get the ghouls, but
          we still wouldn't know where
          Nancy is.. This way -- if
          they come for me at all -
          they'll take me to her...
          Actually it's safer this
          way.

                    TOM
          For who...?

                              FADE TO:

172.   INT. PROFESSOR'S ROOM CAVE CLOSE SHOT   172.

Nancy paces back and forth across the room. She
stops and looks up the window again, then begins
to walk. Suddenly the sound of the bolt is
heard as it is released from its hasp. She
stops and turns towards the door.

173.   CLOSE SHOT DOOR   173.

Professor Smoke enters. Smilingly he looks to her,
then closes the door and enters the room.

> PROFESSOR
> I trust you are comfortable,
> my dear.

174.   CLOSE TWO   174.

Nancy moves in close to him.

> NANCY
> When are you going to let me
> out of here.

The Professor shrugs - almost sadly.

> PROFESSOR
> I'm sorry.

> NANCY
> You're -- You're going to
> kill me?

> PROFESSOR
> You are of no use to my work --
> alive..

> NANCY
> When Chance finds out...

175.   CLOSE SHOT   PROFESSOR   175.

> PROFESSOR
> (cutting in)
> Chance --ahh, Yes -- our
> noble Sheriff - I bear news
> of interest to you
> concerning your friend,
> the Sheriff.

176.   CLOSE SHOT NANCY   176.

                        NANCY
              What have you done to him?

177.   CLOSE SHOT PROFESSOR   177.

                          PROFESSOR
                 I..? I have done nothing to
                 him. Your sheriff was --
                 killed -- in a saloon gun battle
                 this afternoon.

178   CLOSE SHOT NANCY   178.

                          NANCY
                 Chance...

179.   CLOSE SHOT PROFESSOR   179.

                          PROFESSOR
                 Yes -- Oddly enough -- he
                 was killed by your own foreman.

180.   CLOSE TWO   180.

        Unbelieving, Nancy snaps her head to look to the
        Professor. Slowly she sinks to the bed. She is
        stunned into speechlessness. Her eyes, wide,
        horrified, look up to the Professor as he again
        speaks.

                          PROFESSOR
                 Even now he is lying in my
                 office in town - waiting for
                 the sunset.

        The Professor turns towards the door. He stops and
        looks back to her. His smile is eerie...

                          PROFESSOR
                 BUT do not fear -- you will see
                 him again -- when I have his
                 coffin brought here tonight --

        He moves out of the scene. The door is heard to
        open and to close, then the bolt is thrown into
        place. Nancy comes to realization. The tears fill
        in her eyes as she brings her hands up to cover her
        face. Slowly she sinks down to the bed..helpless.

181.   INT. LABORATORY   MEDIUM GROUP   181.

With Tanz and Karl standing near the operating
table.

Karl holds a small glass bottle which is filled
with a clear liquid in his hand. He is curiously
studying the liquid.. The Professor enters the
scene... His face suddenly fills with anger as
he snatches the little bottle from the giant's hand.
Even though it he has snatched the bottle, he has
done it with much reverence.

                    PROFESSOR
          You fool - do you want to ruin
          all my work.

He carefully places it on a shelf with many other
bottles and tubes.. He turns to face the giant.

                    PROFESSOR
          Keep your hands from the
          things in this room unless
          I order you to pick up
          something. I have warned
          you of this before.

182.   CLOSE SHOT KARL   182.

A glimmer of defiance in his eyes.

183.   CLOSE SHOT PROFESSOR   183.

His eyes narrow.

                    PROFESSOR
          I see you would like to
          disobey me.   Twice today
          you have shown such signs...
          The drug is wearing off.
          We will fix that immediately.

184.   MEDIUM GROUP   184.

The Professor moves to a tray which is covered with
a towel. He takes the towel away and reveals a
hypndermic needle. He picks it up and with it moves to

                                        (CONTINUED)

184.   CONTINUED: 184.

another shelf where he selects a bottle filled with
a colored liquid. He pushes the point of the needle
through the cork and fills the needle. When this is
done he turns back on Karl. Karl slowly begins to
back up but he stops this movement as he backs up
against the wall. Wall clamps snap into place
around his arms, neck and middle. Tanz, curiously,
steps up. Karl sneers, but the professor only
laughs. He steps into cover the CAMERA as he jabs
the needle into the giant's arm. A moment later,
the needle empty, he steps back. The big giant
looks with contempt to the man.

                    PROFESSOR
          In a moment the contempt will
          be washed from your face...

The Professor looks to the needle in his hand. He
scowls with disgust and throws it to a corner,
across the room.

                    PROFESSOR
          One day I will find the
          solution. Then I shall not
          need such devices to control
          you...

He turns back on the giants. Karl's face has
changed now, for he no longer has a will of his
own. The Professor presses a release switch and
the clamps release. Karl stands trance-like.

                    PROFESSOR
          Now - make ready -- We have
          work to do again this night...

                              FADE TO:

185.   INT. SHERIFF'S OFFICE MEDIUM GROUP SUNDOWN   185.

The Doctor slowly paces the floor. Steve, the

                         (CONTINUED)

185.   CONTINUED: 185.

deputy stands near the window. The Doctor looks
impatiently to the window, then to Marty, who is
seen in the cell. There is a low hubub of voices
from the outside, but none of the words are fully
distinguishable. However, words such as "HANG HIM" -
"MURDERER" - "LAW WILL LET HIM GO" - "DESERVES TO
HANG", come over the scene.

                    MARTY
          How long do I stay in this
          coop?

                    DOCTOR
          For the moment you're safer in
          there.

                    MARTY
          I'm beginnin' to wonder...

                    DOCTOR
          Stop worrying - Everything
          will work out.

                    MARTY
          I'm glad somebody thinks so.

He looks over towards Steve.

                    DOCTOR
          The funeral ought to be soon
          now...

                    STEVE
          Kinda spooky - ain't it?
          Don't think I'd like the
          idea of layin' down in that
          hole even with the thought I'd
          be comin' up again...

                    DOCTOR
          I don't see much trouble for
          him as long as he's down in
          the hole - it's when those
          creatures dig him up that his
          troubles will start...

                    STEVE
          Yeah - By the way.. who's
          gonna be stickin' close to
          the grave?

                    DOCTOR
          That will be Tom's job.

186.   EXT. STREET   MEDIUM LONG SHOT   186.

Same type of shot as Scene 170. With the mob in
front of the Sheriff's office we see the Professor's
hearse draw up in front of the funeral parlor.

187.   EXT. FUNERAL PARLOR   CLOSE SHOT   187.

The Professor gets out of the hearse, stops a
moment to look down towards the mob, then he
moves to the door of the funeral parlor and knocks
three times quickly.

188.   INT. FUNERAL PARLOR   MEDIUM CLOSE   188.

Tom opens the door and permits the Professor to
enter.

                    PROFESSOR
            I'm sorry I'm late. I was
            detained longer than I
            expected.

                    CHANCE
            When does the show start..?

                    PROFESSOR
            I suggest we get started now.

                    CHANCE
            Tom, you get over to the
            office and stand by.
            Doc Simpson will give
            the orders.

                    TOM
            Right...

Tom moves to the door and goes out. When the
door is again closed Chance turns to the
Professor.

                    CHANCE
            I want to thank you for your
            help, Professor.

                    PROFESSOR
            It's a pleasure to be able to
            help!

189.   MEDIUM WIDE 189.

The Professor leads Chance to the far wall where two caskets are on display. Both their tops are closed, however.. The Professor looks to the rear one, then selects the one closer to CAMERA. He pats the top of it lovingly, then opens the lid.

> PROFESSOR
> Stall the use of your oxygen
> mask until the very last
> moment - to insure it lasting
> as long as possible.

> CHANCE
> All right, Professor.

> PROFESSOR
> Now all you have to do is -
> climb inside.

Chance walks up close to the coffin and looks at the snap locks on the outside. Then he looks at the lining on the inside.

> CHANCE
> Well - here goes...

Chance moves to get into the coffin as the Professor leaves the scene, moving back towards the table.

190.   MEDIUM CLOSE 190.

The Professor reaches the table. In the background, Chance can be seen getting in the coffin. He is paying no attention to the Professor. The Oxygen mask and pistol lay on the table. The Professor quickly empties the pistol of bullets, then looks cautiously over his shoulder as he picks up the mask and squeezes one of the rubber hoses which connects with the oxygen bottle, and nose piece. He holds it tightly for a long moment, then he turns to walk back towards Chance.

191.   MEDIUM CLOSE 191.

The Professor walks back into the scene. Chance is sitting in the coffin. The Professor hands him the mask and puts the pistol, himself, into Chance's empty holster.

(CONTINUED)

191.   CONTINUED: 191.

                         PROFESSOR
              May I wish you luck?

                         CHANCE
              Something tells me I'll
              need it!

192.   EXTREME FACE CLOSE UP PROFESSOR   192.

         With his eyes narrow - menacing - with a look of
         almost eager anticipation to close the lid over
         the young lawman.

193.   MEDIUM CLOSE   193.

         Chance is already out of sight in the casket.
         The Professor lowers the lid then quickly snaps
         the catches. When it is done his face breaks
         into a wide grin. He laughs dryly, without
         humor, not loud, but weird and eerie. His voice
         is low as he speaks...

                         PROFESSOR
              Yes - you will need luck --More
              luck than the mind can conceive.

         He is still laughing as he moves across the room to
         the little rear door and exits into the off scene
         room.

                                        FADE TO:

194.   EXT. SHERIFF'S OFFICE MEDIUM CLOSE SUNDOWN   194.

         The doctor, Steve and Tom come out. The doctor
         looks across towards the funeral parlor. The
         others match his gaze.

195. EXT. FUNERAL PARLOR   LONG SHOT   195.

Across the street to the Undertaking parlor where
we see the crowd of townspeople who had previously
been in front of the Sheriff's office. A big black
horse drawn hearse waits in front of the place.

196. EXT. SHERIFF'S OFFICE   CLOSE GROUP DOC TOM & STEVE 196.

The doctor turns from looking across the street to
face Steve...

                    DOCTOR
          Steve, you'd better stay here
          with Marty...

                    STEVE
          Looks like I'm missing out on
          all the action.

                    DOCTOR
          You'll get enough action to
          last a life time before the
          sun rises again...

Steve turns and re-enters the sheriff's office and
closes the door behind him.

                    TOM
          With all them folks at the
          funeral it will give Marty a
          little time anyway...

                    DOCTOR
          The part that bothers me is
          what happens after the funeral.

                              DISSOLVE TO:

197. EXT. FUNERAL PARLOR   MEDIUM LONG SHOT   197.

The funeral parlor door is seen to open and the
six bearers, preceeded by the Parson, brings out the
coffin on their shoulders. They walk directly to the
rear of the horse-drawn hearse.. They slip the coffin
into the vehicle, then shut the door. The Professor
can be seen moving out of the funeral parlor to stand
in the doorway, looking to the action at the hearse.

198.   INT. FUNERAL PARLOR   MEDIUM WIDE   SUNDOWN   198.

         The Professor turns to look, from the outside of
         the door, into the room. The rear door is seen
         to open. Tanz and Karl come into the room. The
         Professor makes a motion to them, then motions
         the coffin which sits in the same place as
         when Chance got into it. The two ghouls move
         to it.

199.   EXT. FUNERAL PARLOR   MEDIUM LONG SHOT   SUNDOWN   199.

         The Professor pulls the door shut. He moves to
         the hearse, climbs into the seat and slowly starts
         to drive off. The parson leads the procession of
         mourners who walk or ride behind the hearse......

200.   EXT. SHERIFF'S OFFICE   MEDIUM CLOSE   SUNDOWN   200.

                              DOCTOR
                    It's about time we got
                    started.

         The doctor and Tom step out of scene.

201.   MEDIUM WIDE ANGLE   201.

         The doctor and Tom get into their saddles. They
         turn their horses around and head out after the
         funeral.

                                        DISSOLVE TO:

202.   EXT. CEMETERY   MEDIUM CLOSE   DEEP   SUNDOWN   202.

         The shadows are falling fast and the scene is
         becoming the dark of night. The funeral crowd
         is around the open grave. The casket has already
         been lowered. A minister, his book open in his
         hand, stands at the head of the grave. His head
         is raised to the heavesn and his hands are folded
         in silent prayer. The others have their heads
         bowed.... The doctor and Tom stand searching the
         faces of the crowd. The Professor is seen to stand,
         silently, apart from the others. His back is to a
         tall tree. Dark and foreboding as he himself is.

203.   CLOSE SHOT   THE PARSON   203.

He looks once more to his book, then closes it.
For a moment he seems to be in silent prayer, then
his lean features look to the off scene mourners.
His small eyes open.

                        PARSON
            Friends...

He pushes his coat back, instinctively, and hooks
it over two guns at his hips.. His face becomes
stern - commanding...

                        PARSON.
                       (cont'd)
            The sun is setting - and is
            as it goes to rest, with it goes
            the soul and spirit of our
            dearly beloved Sheriff. But -
            do not think of him as gone
            forever - In reality...
                    (voice builds)
            he has gone on to a better
            world.....

204.   CLOSE TWO   DOCTOR & TOM   204.

                        PARSON (O.S.)
            One more beautiful - more
            forgiving than this...

The eyes of the two men search the gathered crowd...

205.   CLOSE SHOT   MELODY   205.

Her eyes are stern - she too searches the faces of
the crowd.

                        PARSON (O.S.)
            Chance Hilton was a friend - a
            close friend to all of us -
            some perhaps more than
            others - but nevertheless -
            a friend to the trouble maker
            and to law abiding citizen...

206.   CLOSE SHOT   PROFESSOR   206.

Smiling.

PARSON (O.S.)
Ashes to ashes - dust to dust...

207.   CLOSE SHOT PROFESSOR   207.

PARSON
That which comes from the earth
must then be replaced...

He slowly bows his head in prayer......

208.   CLOSE SHOT   PROFESSOR   208.

He is looking towards the action. He smiles, then
silently and cat-like, he turns away to walk off
scene, away from the action.

209.   EXT. CARETAKER'S SHACK MEDIUM CLOSE   209.

The Professor comes into the scene. The hearse
is prominent in the background. He gets into the
black coupe.

210.   MEDIUM WIDE ANGLE   210.

The Professor puts the vehicle into motion and
drives off.

211.   EXT. CEMETERY MEDIUM WIDE ANGLE   211.

The minister lowers his head to the grave and closes
his book. Then he moves away. The others follow
him out of scene. The doctor and Tom remain in
the scene until a little old man in overalls moves
up with a shovel and begins to shovel on the dirt...
then they turn away.

212.   EXT. EDGE OF CARETAKER'S SHACK CLOSE TWO SHOT   212.

The doctor and Tom move into the scene as if out
of the cemetery. Melody's voice comes over the
scene. The doctor pulls Tom into the shadows of
the shack as they listen.

                    MELODY (O.S.)
              I say he should be strung
              up before any law can get
              him out of it - give him
              as much a chance as he gave
              the sheriff...

213.   MEDIUM GROUPSHOT   213.

of the crowd of townspeople standing around Melody,
who seems to be the spokesman for the mob.

                    MELODY (cont'd)
              .. Any man that would shoot
              another man down in cold blood
              don't deserve no more than a
              rope - Let's take him outta
              that jail and see that he
              gets what's comin' to him....

214.   CLOSE TWO   DOCTOR & TOM   214.

The men speak in a whisper.

                    DOCTOR
              Come on - we've got to
              get back to town -
              quick!...

                    TOM
              What about Chance?

                    DOCTOR
              He'll be all right for
              awhile...Marty won't...

The doctor pulls Tom after him and they run
around towards the rear of the shack.

215.   MEDIUM WIDE ANGLE   215.

The doctor and Tom can be seen getting into
the saddle. The mob are cheering to something
Melody has said. The two men race off...

The mob turns quickly towards the noise.
Several have to jump out of the way as Doc
and Tom race through their midst....

216.   CLOSE SHOT MELODY   216.

Excitedly - pointing.

                        MELODY
            They'll get Marty if we don't
            move fast!

217.   MEDIUM WIDE ANGLE   217.

The mob race for their various modes of
transportation.

They race out of the cemetery, heedless of
the harm they can do to each other in their
careless haste.

A townsman jumps onto a moving wagon, pushes
a little man driving aside, and whips the
horses into full gallop with a long black snake
whip.

It is a mad scramble of moving vehicles that
leave the cemetery and head for the road and
town.

                                    DISSOLVE TO:

218.   EXT. TOWN STREET   MEDIUM WIDE ANGLE   NIGHT   218.

The Doc and Tom race into town and come to a sliding
stop in front of the Sheriff's office. The doctor
and Tom quickly get out of the saddle and race
towards the Sheriff's Office...

219.   INT. SHERIFF'S OFFICE   MEDIUM WIDE   NIGHT   219.

The doctor and Tom enter on the run. Steve jumps
out of his chair and stands waiting for orders. The
doctor races for the desk and picks up the key ring
He moves quickly to Marty's cell and opens it, then
throws the door open.

                         DOCTOR
            Come on - we haven't much time.

Marty grabs his hat and he with the others race
toward the door and out.

220.   EXT. SHERIFF'S OFFICE   MEDIUM CLOSE   220.

The four men race out and come to a sudden stop on
the board walk as they look towards the other end
of town.

221.   EXT. STREET   LONG SHOT   221.

To see the mad scramble of vehicles, horses and
people as they race into the edge of town and are
heading for the Sheriff's office, quick double
time.

222.   EXT. SHERIFF'S OFFICE   CLOSE GROUP SHOT   222.

                         DOCTOR
             Back inside - we're too late to
             make a run for it...

The men move quickly back into the sheriff's office.

223.   INT. SHERIFF'S OFFICE   MEDIUM WIDE ANGLE   223.

The doctor throws the bolt into place then puts the
heavy cross bar across the door itself.

                                            (CONTINUED)

223.   CONTINUED: 223.

                          STEVE
               What do we do now...?

                          DOCTOR
               Fight...if necessary...

The vehicles are heard to be screeching to skidding
stops outside. The voices of the mob raise in a
blood thirsty din...There is a pounding at the door.
The bartender's voice can be heard as he encourages
the violence of the mob..."OPEN UP IN THERE" - "YOU
CAN'T HOLD OUT ON US..." - "WE WANT THAT DIRTY
MURDERER..." "GET A BATTERING RAM...."

                          MARTY
               They'll bust the door in.

                          STEVE
               The first one to put his foot
               through that door will get a
               bullet.

                          DOCTOR
               I'll try to stall them...Marty
               you get back in the cell. Lock
               him in, Steve.

                          MARTY
               Let me get my gun first.

                          DOCTOR
               You don't need a gun.

                          MARTY
               Sez who?

                          DOCTOR
               Lock him in, Steve...

Marty reluctantly moves toward the cell and Steve
snaps the lock in place, then moves back to join the
doctor and Tom...The doctor moves towards the door.

                          TOM
               You don't want to go out there.

                          DOCTOR
               I've got to try and stop them.

                                    (CONTINUED)

223.   CONTINUED: 223.

                         TOM
               Now look Doc...Bein' a hero is
               one thing, but facin' a lynchin'
               mob with it's mind set on blood
               is another. I've been in these
               things before. There's no arguin'
               with 'em. Talk through the win-
               dow if you want - but don't go
               out there - they'd never give you
               a chance. They want Marty's
               blood and it don't matter none if
               a little of yours or mine or
               Steve's flows right along with
               his.

                         DOCTOR
               Maybe you're right.

                         TOM
               I know I am.

          The doctor moves towards the window. He throws up
          the shade.

224,   CLOSE SHOT   DOCTOR   224.

                         DOCTOR
               You folks out there...Leave this
               thing to the law....!

225.   EXT. SHERIFF'S OFFICE   MEDIUM CLOSE   225.

          On Melody with the mob behind.

                         MELODY
               You're a nice guy, Doc - we don't
               want to see you hurt. But we
               ain't movin' from here, 'till we
               get that killer.

226.   INT. SHERIFF'S OFFICE MEDIUM CLOSE   226.

                         DOCTOR
               I tell you you're making a
               mistake.

227.   EXT. SHERIFF'S OFFICE   MEDIUM CLOSE   227.

                         MELODY
               He made the mistake...

228. INT. SHERIFF'S OFFICE   MEDIUM CLOSE   228.

A rock crashes through the window near the doctor.
The doctor ducks out of the way.

                         DOCTOR
                There's no reasoning with
                them.

Steve draws his pistol and moves towards the window.

                         STEVE
                I'll show you how to reason
                with them!

Tom moves in and stops him.

                         TOM
                That ain't the way - not yet...

Tom walks to the window...

                         TOM
                Melody - I'm lockin' you up for
                disturbin' the peace...

229. EXT. SHERIFF'S OFFICE   MEDIUM CLOSE   229.

MELODY LAUGHS.

                         MELODY
                Why don't you open the door
                and try....?

230. MEDIUM WIDE ANGLE   230.

Four men break through the crowd carrying a heavy
battering ram.

                         MELODY
                This is your last chance to
                open that door before it's
                busted in!

                         TOM (O.S.)
                I'll shoot the first man that
                comes in....

                         MELODY
                Being a woman - I guess that
                makes me safe...

The four men move up to the door. Several other men take
hold of the heavy pole and they begin to pound on the door
with it.

231.   INT. SHERIFF'S OFFICE MEDIUM WIDE NIGHT   231.

The door shakes from the heavy blows.

> TOM
> The fools.

> MARTY
> Hey --- Get me outta here!

> STEVE
> What do you suppose we should
> do?

> DOCTOR
> There's only one thing we can
> do. Tell them the truth.

> TOM
> Chance ain't been down long
> enough.

> MARTY
> Chance'll just have to think up
> another plan. I ain't done
> nothin' to be hanged for.

> DOCTOR
> He's right...We can't jeopardize
> his life or the life of any of
> those out there.

The door has begun to splinter from the steady pounding of the battering ram...The mob's cries are violent.
The Doctor moves towards the windows...

> DOCTOR
> Melody...Listen to me!...

232.   EXT. SHERIFF'S OFFICE   MEDIUM CLOSE   TOWNSMEN   232.

With Melody in the foreground and a townsman in the
background who picks up a rock and hurls it towards
the sheriff's office window.

233.   INT. SHERIFF'S OFFICE   MEDIUM CLOSE   233.

The rock crashes through the window. The doctor
grabs his head and silently sinks to the floor.

234. MEDIUM WIDE   234.

The battering ram breaks the door in. The mob pushes
the broken pieces of the door out of the way as they
barge into the room. Tom and Steve along with Marty
yell protests but their voices are drowned out by the
violent cries of revenge from the mob. Melody moves
to the desk and picks up the ring of cell keys. She
takes them to the cell and unlocks it. Several of
the townspeople charge into the cell and drag the
screaming Marty out...

                    MARTY
                  (Screaming)
          The Sheriff ain't dead - Chance
          ain't dead - You gotta believe
          me...Dig him up - It's only a
          scheme of his to catch the ghouls!

The violent mob raises their voices to drown out Marty.
Tom and Steve are quickly knocked unconscious and they
are put out of action as the mob, clawing, pushing
and punching at Marty, drag him from the cell, into
the office and out of the broken door to the street.

235. EXT. SHERIFF'S OFFICE   MEDIUM WIDE   235.

Marty is dragged out of the Sheriff's office and
into the street with the rest of the mob. They
start him down the street.

236. EXT. STREET   MEDIUM FULL SHOT   236.

Of the mob dragging Marty through the street towards
the edge of town to a big oak tree with a low limb.
One of the townsmen breaks out of ranks and goes
across the street to a horse. He unties it, gets
into the saddle and races the horse down the street
to the tree. He stops just under the low limb. The
mob, slower in movement than the rider, continues on.

237. INT. SHERIFF'S OFFICE   MEDIUM CLOSE   237.

The doctor is on the floor. Slowly he regains consciousness. His hand goes to the injured head where
the blood flows freely. He staggers to a sitting
position. The the rememberance of the past come to
him. He gets to his feet, unsteadily, looks around
at the broken and battered office. He sees Steve and
Tom both layed out on the floor. He moves to Steve,
tries to bring him around. The man is completely

                                        (CONTINUED)

237.   CONTINUED: 237.

unconscious. The doctor moves to Tom. He shakes
him. Tom comes around quickly...As Tom sitting up,
the doctor reaches into his pocket and uncaps a
smelling salts...He sticks it under Steve's nose.
The man comes too.

                    DOCTOR
            We've no time to lose.

The two men get to their feet and try to get their
bearings. The doctor races across the room, grabs
a pistol from the wall cabinet, then turns out
through the broken door.

238.   EXT. SHERIFF'S OFFICE   MEDIUM SHOT   238.

The doctor comes out into the night. He pauses long
enough to see the direction the mob has gone, then
he races, unsteadily, after them.

239.   EXT. HANG TREE   MEDIUM WIDE   NIGHT   239.

The rope is over the limb. Marty is forced to get
into the saddle. The mob yells for his blood.
Melody is in complete charge of the action.

240.   EXT. STREET   HANG TREE   CLOSE FIGURE   240.

The doctor runs in and stops. He lifts the pistol
and fires over the mobs head.

241.   EXT. HANG TREE MEDIUM WIDE   241.

The mob turns towards the shot. They quiet down
quickly. Doc walks into the scene. His eyes are
cold. His hand and gun steady. He levels it on
Melody.

                    DOCTOR
            Melody, you've got to stop
            them. What you're doing is
            all wrong.

                    MELODY
            Keep outta this, Doc...

                              (CONTINUED)

241. CONTINUED: 241.

                          DOCTOR
              Just one move out of any of you
              and.....
                     (to Melody)
              ...I'll shoot you first.

     Tom and Steve, their guns drawn, move into the scene.

242. CLOSE FIGURE SHOT TOM   242.

     Indicates his two guns, which he has trained on the
     mob. His eyes are as cold as those of the doctor.

                          TOM
              We mean business....

243. CLOSE SHOT MARTY   243.

     Perspiring badly. His nerves are at the cracking
     point.

                          MARTY
              Tell them Chance ain't dead....

244. CLOSE SHOT MELODY   244.

                          MELODY
              Sure, Doc. Tell us -- Tell me!!!
              Tell me I didn't see Chance cut
              down in cold blood....

245. CLOSE SHOT DOCTOR   245.

                          DOCTOR
              That's just it, Melody... You
              thought you did -- but you didn't...
              Chance is alive - it was all a
              trick to catch the grave robbers.

246. CLOSE GROUP   246.

                          MELODY
              You're the one trying to pull a
              trick -- Don't believe him, boys...
              He's just out to save...
                     (to Marty)
              ...his hide -- I know what I saw...
              A lot of you saw the same as I did.

247.   CLOSE SHOT   MARTY   247.

                         MARTY
                        (frantic)
                It's the truth...He's tellin'
                you the truth...

248.   CLOSE SHOT   MELODY   248.

                         MELODY
                      (spitting out
                       her words)
                Shut up!

249.   MEDIUM CLOSE   MARTY   249.

        Melody's fire brings back some of Marty's nerve. He
        snaps at her.

                         MARTY
                When this is all over I'm goin'a
                paddle you good.....

250.   MEDIUM CLOSE SHOT   GROUP   250.

                         MELODY
                The only thing you'll be doin'
                is shovelin' coal or playin' a
                harp -- - and you never was
                musical--
                      (turns on doc)
                ...Okay, Doc...We'll go back to
                the cemetery and dig up Chance's
                grave....

                         TOM
                You'll ruin the whole thing.

                         MELODY
                We're gonna keep Marty right
                close - and when I show you up -
                Maybe it ain't gonna be necessary
                to bring him back from the bone
                yard.....

251.   MEDIUM WIDE ANGLE   251.

        The mob puts up a howl of protest at the thought of
        losing out on the hanging sport. Melody puts up her
        hands to quiet them.

                                          (CONTINUED)

251.   CONTINUED: 251.

                              MELODY
                    Quiet down - You'll get your
                    hangin' -- There are trees in
                    the cemetery as well as there
                    are around here.

252.   CLOSE SHOT GROUP DOC, TOM & STEVE   252.

        They stand, guns in hand, defiant, ready for any
        slight off color move.

                              TOM
                    I'm personally going to see
                    that you pay for this, Melody...

253.   CLOSE SHOT   MELODY   253.

                              MELODY
                    You better watch your words or
                    maybe it won't be necessary to
                    bring you back from the bone
                    yard either.....

254.   MEDIUM WIDE ANGLE   254.

        Melody turns to the mob and Marty.

                              MELDOY
                    Bring that killer along...

        Marty is dragged from the horse and forced back along
        the street.
        As the mob is heading for their vehicles and modes of
        transportation, the Preacher, still putting on his
        coat runs down the lone street to join the mob.

                              PARSON
                          (to Melody)
                    I heard what you're up to...

                              MELODY
        So what...

                              PARSON
                    It's sacreligious...You can be
                    like those ghouls...You just don't
                    go into cemeteries and dig up graves...
                    You just don't...

                                        (CONTINUED)

254.   CONTINUED: 254.

> MELODY
> Out of our way, Parson... We've
> got work to do...
>
> PARSON
> Fire and Brimstone on you...for
> this...
>
> DOCTOR
> It's alright, Parson. Every-
> thing will be alright.
>
> PARSON
> One must not desecrate hallowed
> ground.
>
> MARTY
> (yelling)
> Tell him off, Doc...Get me out
> of this...
>
> PARSON
> If you are not guilty there must
> be other ways of proving it.
>
> MELODY
> Stop you're chatter... This is
> the easiest way...Take him on boys...

255.   EXT. WESTERN STREET   MEDIUM WIDE ANGLE   NIGHT   255.

The various vehicles, horses and foot traffic once
more take off in crazy angles out of town, back
towards the cemetery. Doc, Tom and Steve stay with
the group until the reach their horses, they get
into the saddle quickly and race off with them.

                                        DISSOLVE TO:

256.   EXT. CEMETERY   MEDIUM CLOSE   NIGHT   256.

Showing some of the mob, along with Doc, Tom and
Steve and Melody who are-featured in the shot. The
men have their guns away. Two men, peeled
down to the waist, dig in the grave we have seen
before, supposedly holding Chance's body.

257. MEDIUM CLOSE   257.

Marty is being held captive by two strong men,
men as big as he himself is. His face is tense
as he watches the off scene action. There are
several people near him, but none except his two
guards are close enough to be of much effect
should he suddenly make a break for freedom. All
those in the scene have their eyes glued on the off
scene grave action.

258. MEDIUM GROUP   258.

Melody narrows her eyes as she looks towards the
grave. The sound of the shovels hitting the wood
or metal of the casket is hit. Melody looks from
the grave to the doctor. She holds a sneer on her
face.

                    DOCTOR
          Chance took a big risk in this.
          He isn't going to like what
          you folks are doing....

                    MELODY
          Open it up...

The eyes of the principals move towards the casket
in the hole. One of the men, digging, gets out
of the grave as the others move in to his work.

259. MEDIUM CLOSE INTO HOLE   259.

The man works at the coffin clasps...

260. CLOSE GROUP OUT OF GRAVE   260.

The CAMERA is low in the grave, looking up to
Melody, Doc and Tom.

                    MELODY
          Well - get it open - get it
          open - we ain't got all
          night!!!

It is apparent this grave opening is unnerving her
slightly. The creek of the opening of the coffin
is heard. The faces of all in the shot suffer a
definite change.

261.   CLOSE SHOT MARTY   261.

He is tense - not being in a spot to look into the
grave.

262.   CLOSE SHOT TOM & STEVE   262.

They are looking into the grave - look to each
other unbelievingly.

263.   MEDIUM CLOSE DOCTOR   263.

He reaches down, his hand out of scene, then he
draws his hand back. On his finger is perched fooey,
the bird Ezra has always carried on his shoulder. The
bird jumps around gaily, at his new found freedom...

264.   CLOSE SHOT MELODY   264.

                    MELODY
                 (disbelief - almost
                  a gasp)
           It's ---It's old Ezra....

265.   MEDIUM CLOSE GROUP OUT OF GRAVE   265.

The doctor bends in close - looking into the
grave. For a moment he is silent...

                    DOCTOR
           He's been shot in the back...

                    MELODY
           Then --then what happened to
           Chance?

266.   MEDIUM CLOSE   266.

Marty suddenly takes advantage of the fact that
his guards have relaxed their vigilance and are
intent at the off scene action. Marty swings his
arms clear - hits one man a left to the mouth and
drops him. The other, also caught off balance is
hit a quick right to the stomach which caves him in.
The crowd near him puts up a howl and starts after
him as he races out of the scene.

267.   CLOSE SHOT   MELODY   267.

                          MELODY
                 Don't let him get away.

She charges after him.

268.   EXT. CARETAKER'S SHACK   MEDIUM WIDE   268.

Marty races out of the cemetery - jumps onto a
horse and makes a fast get away.

269.   EXT. CEMETERY   MEDIUM GROUP   NIGHT   269.

The voices of those in pursuit of Marty are heard,
then the horses hooves and sounds of wagons come
over the scene. Doc stands up from beside the
grave. He faces Tom and Steve. His face holds a
puzzled look.

                          TOM
                 But...what happened to Chance?

                          DOCTOR
                 Unless I miss my guess there's
                 only one man who can give us
                 the answer to that...

The men make their way out of the cemetery.

                                        DISSOLVE TO:

270.   EXT. FUNERAL PARLOR   MEDIUM WIDE   NIGHT   270.

Doc, Tom and Steve ride in, dismount and quickly
enter the undertaking parlor.

271.   INT. FUNERAL PARLOR   MEDIUM WIDE   NIGHT   271.

The place is empty. Steve moves to the rear door
and throws it open. He looks inside, then comes
back to the others.

                          STEVE
                 Nobody back there, either.

                          TOM
                 What do you make of it, Doc?

He shakes his head.

                                        FADE TO:

272.   INT. LABORATORY   CASTLE   CLOSE SHOT   272.

On the big casket as it lays, still tightly
closed, on the operating table...the sound of
the organ can be mutely heard over the scene.
One of the big doors opens as Tanz enters through
it. He looks to the coffin then moves to the
bolted door behind which Nancy is held captive.
He opens the door and enters the room.

273.   INT. PROFESSOR'S ROOM   MEDIUM WIDE   273.

When Nancy sees the giant framed in the doorway,
she backs up against the wall...The giant only looks
to her a moment then moves to the Professor's desk
and takes up a big ledger. He carries it to the
door and goes out.

274.   INT. LABORATORY   MEDIUM WIDE   274.

The giant pulls the door shut but forgets to lock
the bolt. He places the big ledger on a small
instrument table near the casket then leaves by
way of the door through which he had entered.

275.   INT. PROFESSOR'S ROOM   MEDIUM CLOSE   DOLLY   275.

With Nancy standing against the wall at the far
side of the room. She cocks her head as if listening for some sound which does not come. Slowly
she comes away from the wall...The CAMERA DOLLYS
BACK as she makes her way to the door. Slowly she
grips the handle and pulls it open. She looks out
into the laboratory...

276.   INT. LABORATORY MEDIUM WIDE   276.

Cautiously she steps out into the laboratory.
She looks around, then moves slowly across the
room.

277.   CLOSE SHOT   CASKET   277.

A soft thumping can be heard from within, as if
someone is trying to get out...

278.   CLOSE SHOT NANCY   278.

She stops dead in her tracks. Her eyes, wide in
horror, shift towards the sound.

279.   MEDIUM CLOSE NANCY   279.

Slowly, Nancy makes her way across the room to
the casket. She is completely frightened, but
some force within her causes her movement. She
stops at the casket. The thumping has become
faint...irregular...

280.   CLOSE SHOT NANCY   280.

Her hand slowly raises to the first snap. Then
there is a loud thump from within the coffin.
Her hand drops back to her side. She jumps back...
for a moment she remains back away from the coffin
then slowly she again approaches it and quickly
unsnaps the first lock. She continues
unsnapping the locks until they are finished.
Then she steps back.

281.   MEDIUM CLOSE   281.

With Nancy in the foreground and the coffin in
the immediate background. The lid slowly raises
until it stands on end under its own power.
All we have seen is Chance's arm and pistol as
it pushes back the top - until the top is
completely open. Nancy stands transfixed -
horrified. Chance, exhausted with the need
for air, sits up in the coffin....

282.   CLOSE SHOT NANCY   282.

Her eyes wide with horror as they change to
one of complete resignation...

                        NANCY
        Chance...

The organ music, although faint in the distance, is
wierd and eerie through all of these scenes previous
and comes to a loud crescendo as Nancy's eyes
flutter and close. She slips silently to the floor
in a deep faint.

                              DISSOLVE TO:

283.   INT. SHERIFF'S OFFICE   MEDIUM CLOSE   NIGHT   283.

With the Doctor, Tom and Steve seated at and
around the desk. Their faces are grave.

                         TOM
              What about Marty?

                         DOCTOR
              My guess is he's in a better
              spot right now than Chance is...

The doctor and the men turn to look towards the
little form of Skimpy as he comes in.

                         SKIMPY
              What's all the excitement
              around here-a-bouts...?

                         TOM
              Thought you were prospectin'
              up in the buttes...

                         SKIMPY
              Did --but Ain't gonna
              stay with them ghosts a'flittin'
              around up by the haunted mine...

The doctor becomes suddenly very interested.

                         TOM
              You been at the bottle again...?

                         DOCTOR
              Wait a minute, Tom. What's this,
              about ghosts?

                         SKIMPY
              Don't rightly know, Doc...
              Didn't really see none - but
              lots of hootin' and hollerin' -
              and screamin' - and all the
              time the organ is playin' --
              Up at the old haunted mine...

The Doctor jumps to his feet. He slams his fist
into his open palm.

                         DOCTOR
              Why didn't we think of it.
              The haunted mine would be
              just the place they would pick.
              It's the only answer.

                              (CONTINUED)

283. CONTINUED: 283.

Tom and Steve are on their feet standing beside the
doctor now. Tom suddenly reaches into a
drawer, takes out a deputy badge and brings
a rifle down from the wall. He thrusts the
rifle into Skimpy's hands and pins the badge
quickly to his shirt.

                    TOM
          Here - You're a deputy now...

                    SKIMPY
          Me - A lawman - What will
          my ancestors think --I don't
          get any of this...?

                    DOCTOR
          There's no time for talk now --
          We'll tell you all about it
          on the way...

They push the man towards the door.

284. EXT. SHERIFF'S OFFICE MEDIUM WIDE NIGHT   284.

The four men run out of the Sheriff's office, climb
into the saddle and take off at top speed.

                              DISSOLVE TO:

285. INT. LABORATORY MEDIUM CLOSE TWO   285.

Chance is bending over the fallen girl. He
craddles her head in his arms as he shakes her
lightly. The girl's eyes flutter open. She
gives a quick start, then sighs with relief.

                    NANCY
          Chance -- Oh, chance -- It
          really is you -- He told me
          you were dead...

                    CHANCE
          Guess he thought I would be.

He helps the girl to her feet.

                    CHANCE
          Where are we?

                              (CONTINUED)

285.   CONTINUED: 285.

                         NANCY
               The haunted mine. That's
               Professor Smoke playing the
               organ. But he's protected by
               two giants. One of them was
               just here -- He may come back.

                         CHANCE
               I'm a little dizzy. I've got
               to clear my head. That oxygen
               thing went bad...Thought I was a
               gonner for awhile. Tell me what
               you know....

286.   INT. ORGAN ROOM   MEDIUM CLOSE   286.

        On the back of Professor Smoke as he plays. Tanz
        moves in close to him... The Professor, without
        stopping his music, turns slightly to face him.

                         PROFESSOR
               It is time to make our -----
               patient ready...

        He turns back to the organ, a broad smile breaks
        over his features as the giant moves out of the
        scene.

287.   INT. LABORATORY   MEDIUM CLOSE   287.

        Chance walks back towards the casket then turns to
        face Nancy who slowly walks up to him.

                         CHANCE
               Has he told you why he takes
               the bodys.

                         NANCY
               Only that he uses them in some
               kind of experiments - giants
               or something...

        A bolt is heard to be thrown open. Chance and
        Nancy both swing towards the laboratory door....

288.   CLOSE SHOT   DOOR   288.

        The hulking figure of Tanz stands framed in the
        doorway. The corners of his mouth go back in a
        snarl.

289.   CLOSE TWO   NANCY & CHANCE   289.

Nancy shrinks back. Chance moves as he eases her
back.

                         CHANCE
                        (softly)
              Get back against the wall.

Nancy eases away from him, backing towards the far
wall. Chance pulls his gun from his holster. His
eyes are on those of the giant across the room from
him.

290.   CLOSE SHOT   DOLLY   TANZ   290.

Tanz lifts his bone crushing arms and with a deep
throated snarl he moves slowly in towards Chance.
The CAMERA DOLLIES with him in this movement.

291.   CLOSE SHOT   CHANCE   291.

Chance brings up his gun, aims and presses the
trigger. Nothing -- It is empty. He snaps the
trigger several more times and the same. He tosses
the gun away and braces himself back against the
casket. (It will be herewith noted that Tanz uses
strictly a wrestler's technique through out the
fight and Chance does more dodging than striking
actual blows.) Chance's eyes are glued on his
monster opponant.

292.   THE REMAINDER OF THIS VERY POWERFUL FIGHT WILL BE   292.
         LEFT TO THE DESCRESSION OF THE DIRECTOR USING THE
         SCENES 292 292A - 292B - etc. FOR ALL NECESSARY FIGHT
         SHOTS * - During the fight however either Chance
         or Tanz is knocked up against the lever which con-
         trols the covering of the bottomless pit. A close
         shot of the floor as it opens will be necessary.
         Shots of first Chance then Tanz nearly falling into
         the gaping hole is necessary....

293.   MEDIUM CLOSE SHOT TANZ & CHANCE   293.

Chance is failing fast. Tanz moves in for the kill.

                                        (CONTINUED)

293.   CONTINUED: 293.

Chance swings around and pushes the shelf affair
containing the bottles and equipment which the
Professor uses in his experiments. The shelf
falls forward. Tanz steps aside to duck the
crashing, crushing force and in so doing he has
side stepped himself into the bottomless pit.
His scream in falling is that of a frightened wild
animal. Chance staggers back as the
scream dies out in the distance....

294.   MEDIUM CLOSE   294.

Chance, his clothes torn, bleeding and bruised,
sits heavily on one of the laboratory seats. Nancy
comes up to him. There are no words spoken as
Chance forces a smile and takes her arm reassuringly.
She dabs at a cut on his forehead with a clean white
handkerchief from her pocket. Chance takes several
deep breaths. Through all the previous scenes in
the lab, the music of the organ has been heard
faintly. Chance points to a door.

                    CHANCE
          Where does that lead to?

                    NANCY
          The organ room.

                    CHANCE
          Let's go.

295.   MEDIUM WIDE ANGLE   295.

Shaken, but his strength coming back, Chance
moves towards the door. Nancy takes hold of
his arm. Chance opens the door cautiously, then
they go through it.

                              DISSOLVE TO:

296.   INT. ORGAN ROOM MEDIUM CLOSE DOOR   296.

The door to the organ room is opened, slowly,
soundlessly. Chance and Nancy enter. Both hold
their eyes straight on the Professors off scene back.
The music of the organ is very loud and extremely
weird.

297.   MEDIUM LONG SHOT   297.

        To the far end of the room where the Professor,
        unsuspectingly, plays the organ. He seems lost
        in the eerie refrains he plays. He moves his head
        in tune to the music.

298.   MEDIUM CLOSE DOLLY   298.

        On Chance and Nancy as they move into the room
        and down the long distance towards the Professor;
        when they are very close to him they stop.

299.   CLOSE SHOT PROFESSOR   299.

        On the Professor's back as he plays the organ.
        He still does not realize the presence of
        anyone.

300.   CLOSE TWO SHOT   CHANCE & NANCY   300.

        They are watching the Professor. Nancy's eyes
        show only hatred for the man. Chance has
        become the officer of the law he is.

                         CHANCE
                Turn around, Professor Smoke.

301.   CLOSE SHOT PROFESSOR   301.

        His hands suddenly stop their movement over the
        key board. He freezes momentarily with one note
        being sounded long and mournful... Then even
        this note dies out... He does not turn on them as
        he speaks.

                         PROFESSOR
                I am un-armed...

302.   CLOSE TWO SHOT   CHANCE & NANCY   302.

                         - CHANCE
                So am I... You saw to that.

303.   CLOSE SHOT   PROFESSOR   303.

The words sink in...He smiles...

                    PROFESSOR
            Ahh - Yes - Your empty
            pistol.

He turns to face them very slowly.

304.   MEDIUM CLOSE   CHANCE & NANCY   304.

With Chance and Nancy in the foreground, their
attention completely taken up with the Professor.
The Professor has smiled because in the background,
moving slowly, silently towards Chance and Nancy,
is the hulking figure of the eight foot monster,
Karl...

305.   CLOSE SHOT PROFESSOR   305.

He is completely at ease now - knowing that all
again is about to be put right.

                    PROFESSOR
            You are indeed an interestingly
            lucky young man, Sheriff Hilton.
            Did...Did you - kill my big
            associate, Tanz....?

306.   CLOSE TWO SHOT   CHANCE & NANCY   306.

Behind them can be seen that Karl has come in very
close. He stops - awaiting orders.

                    CHANCE
                  (evading)
            Would you like to tell me
            what it's all about now - or
            wait for the trial?

307.   CLOSE SHOT   PROFESSOR   307.

                    PROFESSOR
                  (feigning)
            Trial? --- What trial?

The Professor nods his head towards Karl.

308. MEDIUM GROUP SHOT   308.

Karl puts his hand lightly on Chance's shoulder.
Chance, his fist ready, springs back, but then he
holds his punch-- realizing he is beaten before he
starts in this case. Nancy stifles a slight scream
as her hand goes to her mouth. The giant, Karl,
towers over both of them. The Professor moves into
the shot. Chance turns to him.

                    CHANCE
          Guess you know best -- what
          trial?

                    PROFESSOR
          I don't mind you knowing
          my reasons for what I have
          done. You won't be telling
          anyone.

309. CLOSE SHOT PROFESSOR   309.

                    PROFESSOR
          It was for the fluid contained
          in their brains. All accidental
          deaths - but with good sound
          brains --

310. CLOSE TWO SHOT CHANCE & NANCY   310.

                    PROFESSOR (O.S.)
          Years ago in another place I
          perfected the use of glands.
          By transplanting them to a
          living being I was able to
          make that being two - three
          even four times as big and as
          strong as a normal healthy person.
          Think of how this would benefit
          all of humanity. It would make a
          mockery of illness....

311. CLOSE SHOT NANCY   311.

                    NANCY
          He's mad.

312.   CLOSE SHOT   PROFESSOR   312.

PROFESSOR
Mad? - Tanz whom you somehow
subdued - and Karl who now gazes
upon you. Is this the work of a
mad man? But one little thing
has always stood in my way of
complete success....

313.   CLOSE SHOT KARL   313.

PROFESSOR (o.s.)
I have no control over my two
subjects without the use of
drugs which I slip into their
arms once every forty-eight
hours....

314.   CLOSE SHOT   PROFESSOR   314.

PROFESSOR
Strange isn't it? - To perfect
one such as he and still not be
complete master....

315.   CLOSE GROUP SHOT   315.

CHANCE
How long do you think you can
get away with this sort of thing?

PROFESSOR
I've been -- getting away with
it --- a good many years. Of
course it will not be convenient
for me to return to our little
town - but there are other towns -
and the people will be constructed
the same - - But now -- enough
has been said.

The Professor turns full on Karl. He nods his head.
The giant grips Chance and spins him around. Chance
is powerless in the big hands. Nancy steps back
horrified...Then - at this point comes the sounds of
many off scene gun shots and the shouting of men.

316.   CLOSE SHOT   PROFESSOR   316.

His head snaps toward the mine entrance.

317.   CLOSE GROUP   317.

The giant and Chance turn to look to the mine
entrance where the double doors remain open.
Nancy in the background also looks.

318.   WIDE ANGLE   318.

The Professor gets quickly down from the organ
bench and walks to the mine entrance. He looks
out.

319.   EXT. MINE   LONG SHOT   EARLY MORNING   319.

From the Professor's point of view. Marty riding
hell-bent-for-leather towards the mine entrance.
Directly behind him rides the posse. Their guns
blazing. Melody rides the lead horse. She is
shouting the loudest and tries to shoot the
straightest.

320.   CLOSE RIDING SHOT   MARTY   320.

Riding as fast as his horse will go. He looks
back over his shoulder as he rides, then looks
ahead again and tries to speed the horse to
even greater speed.

321.   INT. ORGAN ROOM   CLOSE SHOT   321.

The Professor is standing by the big double doors
looking out through the mine shaft. He is worried.

322.   CLOSE SHOT   322.

The giant still holds Chance in the powerful grip.
It would seem he is awaiting orders for further
movement.

323.   EXT. MINE ENTRANCE - WIDE ANGLE   NIGHT   323.

Marty rides up to the mine entrance and dismounts on a dead run. He races into the entrance.

324.   CLOSE SHOT   MELODY AND MOB RIDING   324.

325. INT. MINE   LONG SHOT   325.

Marty races along the mine. He sees the open
double doors. He races to them.

326. INT. ORGAN ROOM   WIDE ANGLE   326.

Marty comes into the room and immediately, without looking anywhere else, slams the big bolts
into place as the door is closed. Then he leans
with his back against the door as if suffering
from extremem nervous exhaustion...Slowly his head
comes up...Surprise...

327. LONG SHOT   327.

From Marty's point of view. Chance is held in the
locked arms of the giant. Nancy cringes back
against the wall. The Professor stands near the
organ. The noise of the possee getting close to
the entrance of the mine is heard now. They begin
to pound at the big double doors leading to the
organ room.

                    MELODY (o.s.)
        , Break the door in -- Somebody
          get me a couple' sticks of
          dynamite outta' my saddle bags.

The mob roars its approval. Professor Smoke moves
up beside Nancy to grab her arms firmly. Marty moves
to far wall away from the door.

328. CLOSE GROUP   FEATURING CHANCE & KARL   328.

Chance is held by the giant. It is apparent he is
in deep thought. He looks to the big arms around
him.

329. INT. MINE   DOORS   MEDIUM GROUP   329.

The man runs in with a bundle of dynamite. He
tosses it to Melody. -

                    MELODY
            That's enough to blow this
            whole place to Kingdom come...

She breaks the bundle and puts a couple of sticks
near the base of the door. She tosses the rest
wildly back to the man.....

Gary D. Rhodes   **183**

330. CLOSE SHOT   MELODY   330.

She is at the base of the door placing the firing
cap into the dynamite.

331. INT. ORGAN ROOM   CLOSE SHOT   PROFESSOR   331.

The sound of the angered mob is heard through the
door. The Professor is perspiring badly. His eyes
dart nervously about. He holds Nancy in a vice
like grip.

                    CHANCE (o.s.)
          You're finished, Smoke - You'd
          better give up while you can.

332. CLOSE SHOT   CHANCE   332.

                    CHANCE
          That mob won't give you a chance.

333. MEDIUM CLOSE   CHANCE & KARL   333.

Chance suddenly throws up his arms, catching the
giant off guard. He is free. The giant comes
after him immediately. Chance stops, turns to
face him.

334. MEDIUM CLOSE   MARTY   334.

Marty makes a running dive directly into the
CAMERA.

335. MEDIUM CLOSE   335.

Marty has grabbed the giant by the legs. The
giant goes down. Chance races in. The giant
grows vicious. He kicks Marty back away from
him. Chance dives on him. The giant pushes
Chance into the CAMERA.

336. CLOSE SHOT   336.

Chance flies back against the wall. His head
makes a dull thud - he sinks to the floor unconscious.

337. MEDIUM CLOSE   337.

The giant picks Marty up, throws him hard to the
floor.

338. INT. MINE   DOORS   MEDIUM CLOSE   338.

Melody lights the dynamite fuse - a short fuse,
then she and the others get out of the danger
area.

339. INT. ORGAN ROOM   MEDIUM CLOSE   339.

The noise of the mob is violent. The Professor
turns on Karl. He points to the door.

                    PROFESSOR
          Stop them...

340. REVERSE ANGLE   LONG SHOT   340.

Karl turns to face the door and walk to it. His
great strides make him cover the space in a short
time. The door suddenly blows up in his face as
he reaches it.

341. CLOSE SHOT   PROFESSOR & NANCY   341.

Shock sets in on the Professor's face. He turns

342. WIDER ANGLE   342.

The Professor pulls Nancy after him. He makes
his way to the side of the organ, hits a key, the
organ swings out and the Professor with Nancy as
his captive go out through this secret doorway,
just as the mob surges through the ruptured doorway. Marty, half stunned, is trying to get to his
feet. Chance, his hand to his head gets up. Melody,
without having seen the sheriff goes immediately
to Marty. Several men drag him to his feet.

                    MELODY
          This time you're not getting
          away.

Several of the mob have turned with wide eyed
amazement to watch Chance. Melody notices this
move. She turns. Her eyes open wide.

                    MELODY
          But -- Sheriff -- I thought --

                    CHANCE
               (looking around)
          Where's Nancy -- Professor Smoke.

343.   EXT. MINE   MEDIUM WIDE ANGLE   EARLY DAYLIGHT   343.

The Professor, dragging Nancy comes out of a
crevace near the mine entrance. He reaches his
hearse and tries to drag Nancy onto the vehicle
with him. She fights. It is too much for him.
He throws her to the ground and climbs aboard,
alone.

344.   INT. MINE ORGAN ROOM MEDIUM GROUP SHOT   344.

The sound of the horses hooves and wagon in movement
comes over the scene. All eyes turn towards the
door Chance springs off and races to the
ruptured doorway and through it.

345.   EXT. MINE MEDIUM WIDE ANGLE EARLY DAYLIGHT   345.

With Nancy struggling to her feet. Chance comes
out around the wall, fast...He stops and helps her
as the others join them.

                        NANCY
               He's getting away!!!

Chance jumps to his feet and makes a running pony
express mount to the nearest horse. He races off
down the road.

346.   EXT. MOUNTAIN ROAD MEDIUM LONG SHOT EARY DAY   346.

The hearse is speeding at a terrific speed -
it races down the winding dirt mountain road...

347.   MEDIUM WIDE ANGLE   347.

Chance races his horse down the mountain road.
Suddenly he cuts off and pushes his horse forward
up a mountain pass....

348.   MEDIUM LONG TO CLOSE   348.

The hearse speeds in from the background, to and
past the CAMERA. Dust kicks up as it screeches
past.

349.   MEDIUM LONG TO CLOSE   349.

Chance races his horse along the mountain pass in
from the background, to and past the foreground
CAMERA. The dust and dirt kick up into the CAMERA
eye.

350.   MEDIUM CLOSE   350.

The Professor's hearse speeds over a cliff road.
The cliff is on the right side of the winding one
lane road. It is heading down the steep grade.

351.   MEDIUM CLOSE   351.

Chance riding at terrific speed suddenly cuts his
horse off to the right and starts down an
incline.

352.   WIDE ANGLE   352.

A fork in the road. The cliff is on the right.
A fork comes in from the left. The Professor's
hearse passes it at terrific speed. Chance rides
in from the fork almost immediately the hearse
passes...

353.   REVERSE ANGLE MEDIUM CLOSE   353.

Doc, Steve, Tom and Skimpy, riding close together
are racing up the incline.

354.   REVERSE ANGLE MEDIUM CLOSE   354.

The Professor's hearse. His eyes hard on the road,
determined in his escape.

355.   REVERSE ANGLE CLOSE   355.

Close on Doctor Simpson as he rides. Suddenly
his eyes go wide.

356.   WIDE ANGLE   356.

The hearse is about to collide with the riders.

357. CLOSE SHOT   PROFESSOR   357.

  He throws up his arms and screams...

358. WIDE ANGLE   LONG SHOT   358.

  Looking up from the bottom of the cliff as the
  Professor's hearse crashes off the road and falls
  end over end down towards the CAMERA.

359. MEDIUM WIDE ANGLE   ROAD   359.

  The doctor, Steve, Tom and Skimpy pull their horses
  from the terror they feel, Chance rides into the
  scene. They move to the edge of the cliff.

360. MEDIUM GROUP   360.

  Looking down over the cliff.

                                        DISSOLVE TO:

361. EXT. MINE WIDE ANGLE DAY   361.

  Marty and Melody stand with Nancy at the head of
  the mob of townspeople. The sheriff and
  the others ride in and dismount. Marty runs
  up to Chance.

362. MEDIUM GROUP SHOT   362.

  As Marty speaks, Melody and Nancy step into the
  scene, as do Doc, Tom, Steve and Skimpy.

                    MARTY
          Chance - am I glad to see you.
          Now tell these crazy people you
          ain't dead. Tell them I didn't
          shoot you.

                    CHANCE
                 (to Melody)
          Do I look dead...?

                    MELODY
          I don't get this...

                                        (CONTINUED)

362.   CONTINUED: 362.

Tom and Marty move in to stand close beside her.

                        TOM
                Told you - you were heading
                for trouble...

                        MARTY
                And I told you what I was going
                to do...

                        MELODY
                Ah, now, Marty -- You wouldn't
                do that to me -- Would you?

363.   CLOSE TWO MELODY & MARTY   363.

                        MARTY
                You bet your sweet hangin'
                rope I will...

He looks menacing...

                        MELODY
                Now - Marty -- take it
                easy...

He moves towards her. With a little squeal she
turns and runs off -- Marty takes off after her.

364.   WIDER ANGLE   364.

Melody reaches her horse, swings into the saddle
and races out -- Marty gets to his horse and takes
off after her....

                        TOM
                Bet he catches her -- and
                second bet -- He don't
                whomp her...

The doctor turns as Chance starts his line.

                        CHANCE
                      (to mob)
                Alright - the rest of you -
                move on back to town....

                                        (CONTINUED)

364.   CONTINUED: 364.

                    DOCTOR
          Reckon you better take a
          collection between you to
          pay for the jail damage...

                    TOM
          Move on before I lock the
          whole mess of you up...

They move out quickly heading for their horses, etc.

365.   CLOSE GROUP CHANCE DOC TOM STEVE & NANCY   365.

Chance turns back to his friends.

                    DOCTOR
          Going back to town, Chance?

                    CHANCE
          I'll be along later.

                    DOCTOR
          How about you, Miss Nancy -
          You going with us?

                    NANCY
          I think I'll stay with Chance,
          if you don't mind...

                    TOM
          Looks like you'll have to
          settle for Steve and Me,
          Doc...

Doc, Tom and Steve get into the saddle and ride
off. They wave back at Nancy and Chance. Skimpy
walks in close. He leads his horse...

                    SKIMPY
          All that talk about giants --
          Thought everybody was drunk.

                    CHANCE
                    (smiling)
          You were the one who was
          probably drunk...

                              (CONTINUED)

365.   CONTINUED: 365.

                              SKIMPY
                    Ahh - Now, Chance. You
                    know I give you my promise -
                    I wouldn't no more touch a
                    drop of that stuff than I
                    would try an 'ketch a rattle-
                    snake by the tail with my bare
                    hands.

Skimpy raises up his leg to put his foot in the
stirrup. The bulge of a bottle is seen at his hip.
Chance takes out his gun and hits the pocket. The
man remains frozen as if in mid air as the liquid
from the broken glass flows out of his pants.. He
puts his foot down.

366.   CLOSE SHOT SKIMPY FIGURE SHOT   366.

Skimpy turns to face Chance and Nancy. His hands
go to the damaged area...

                              SKIMPY
                    Ah - no dog gone...

He turns, picks up the reins of his horse and leads
him slowly off.....

367.   CLOSE TWO CHANCE & NANCY   367.

They laugh heartily - Chance puts his arm around
the girl's waist and she snuggles in close to
him....

                                        FADE TO:

                         THE   END

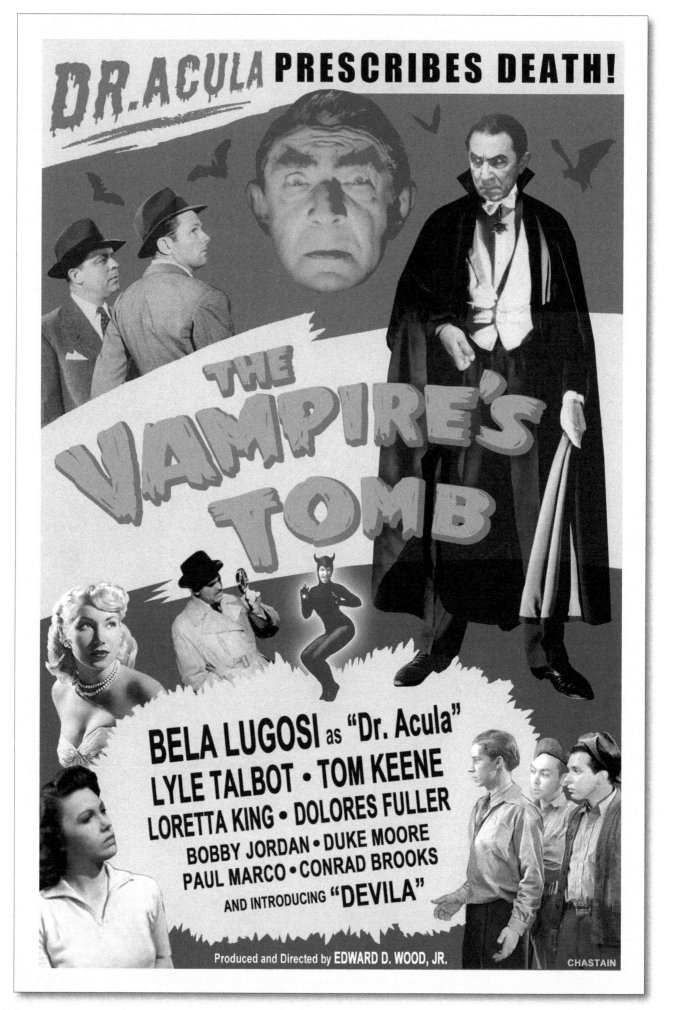

An imagined movie poster for the unproduced Lugosi film *The Vampire's Tomb*, as created for this book by George Chastain in 2016.

"The Vampire's Tomb"

By

Edward D. Wood, Jr.

Editor's Notes: *The copy of this script dates to at least 1954. However, this title page is a recreation.*

On August 26, 1954, Wood revised pages 21, 22, 23, 40, and 65, typing them on colored paper. As a result, the quality of reproduction on those pages is less than perfect.

Gary D. Rhodes

"THE VAMPIRE'S TOMB"

Dr. Acula............................ *BELA LUGOSI*

Lucille (The Vampire)............. *DEVILA*

Lake Lyon........................... *RICHARD POWERS*

Barbara.............................. *LORETTA KING*

Judson Ruppert.................... *BOBBIE JORDAN*

Boris Ruppert...................... *LYLE TALBOT*

Diana Cordoni..................... *DOLORES FULLER*

Frank Cordoni..................... *FRANK MACONELLI*

Flinch Ruppert....................

Paula (The Maid)................

Emma (The Housekeeper)........

Sheriff.............................

1st Deputy Sheriff.............

2nd Deputy Sheriff............

EdWood

PO-61560

JAMES MOORE
MONA MCKINNON
HAZEL FRANKLIN
BUD OSBORNE
RON DAVIS
CLANCY MALONE

Registered - 1951

Screen Writers' Guild

"THE VAMPIRE'S TOMB"

A1.   EXT. TOMB & CEMETERY - MEDIUM CLOSE - PAN TO WIDE
      ANGLE - MOVING BEHIND CREDIT TITLES - NIGHT

      The scene opens on Dr. Acula, his cape held high up
      over his face, a dark foreboding figure. Slowly the
      cape is lowered until the eyes appear. The CREDIT
      TITLES appear --(BELA LUGOSI in)-- He turns to look
      to the right.....The CAMERA moves showing the small
      wind lashed cemetery. The CAMERA stops on a vault
      which looms brightly against the dark of the night.
      The CREDIT TITLE ("THE VAMPIRE'S TOMB") appears and
      the rest of the credit titles appear, behind which
      we see the thick door squeeks open as the figure of
      a once lovely girl dressed in the long flowing robes
      of the dead moves slowly out into the night. The
      CAMERA follows her movement through the wind lashed
      cemetery ---- until the credit titles are finished.
      (The music is deep and haunting.)

                                        DISSOLVE TO:

1.   EXT. OLD MANSION - MEDIUM LONG SHOT - NIGHT

      A once proud mansion now old and gloomy, near ruin.
      The grass surrounding the semi-circle driveway is high
      and burned brown by the long hours of the scorching
      sun's heat without proper care. The drive is directly
      in front of the large wooden front door of the two
      story mansion. A private cemetery can be seen off to
      the far left and a long winding lake beyond that.
      There are trees, vines and brush intermingled among the
      grave stones of the cemetery. The night is very dark
      with heavy rain clouds in the sky. However the mansion
      is streaked in light as lightening suddenly flashes
      across the sky followed by deep rolling, crashing
      thunder claps. It is at this time, during one of the
      lightening flashes, that a giant bat flies into view -
      hovers in the sky a moment -- then heads in a streak
      towards the old house.

                                        DISSOLVE TO:

2.   EXT. MANSION - LIBRARY FRENCH WINDOWS - MEDIUM CLOSE -
      NIGHT

      Through the thin curtains on the French windows, look-

                                        CONTINUED

2.   CONTINUED

ing into the library, can be seen two men, both in
their early forties and a woman some years younger,
perhaps in her early thirties. She wears a slinky
satin pajama outfit. It is apparent they are talking,
but we cannot hear their words through the closed
windows. A flash of lightening, lights up the area.
The vampire, we have seen before, glides into the scene.
She stops and spies on those in the room through the
curtained French windows.

3.   INT. LIBRARY - MANSION - MEDIUM GROUP - NIGHT

The sound of the brewing storm outside is apparent even
within the room. Thunder rolls across the sky to a
resounding climax. Diana Cordoni stands nervously at
the liquor cabinet mixing a drink. Her brother, Judson
stands with his back to a lighted fire place. Flinch,
the second brother is seated in a chair with a glass of
whiskey and soda in his hand. He is apparently the
only calm one in the room. He kills off his drink and
holds onto the empty glass for the moment.

                    FLINCH
          I don't see anything to worry about.
          Barbara and Lake came here only for
          the will reading -- We expected
          them -- After all she is Lucille's
          neice. There is no reason for them
          to become suspicious.

                    JUDSON
          Let's not be so cock sure!

                    DIANA
          I'd feel a lot better if Boris and
          Frank would get here --- Get that
          thing read and over with.

                    FLINCH
          What's the rush - We all know
          what it says....

                    DIANA
          But it doesn't become official until
          Boris reads it here -- I'm getting
          jittery -- I don't like this waiting -
          or this weather - or this mausoleum
          we laughingly call a house -- I hate
          it - I've hated it since the first
          time I layed eyes on it -- I want to
          get back to Hollywood and the bright
          lights on the Sunset Strip.....

4.   CLOSE SHOT - FLINCH

                         FLINCH
               After tomorrow you'll be able to
               buy Hollywood, lock, stock and
               barrel....Just take it easy.....
               There is nothing to panic about.

5.   CLOSE SHOT - JUDSON

                         JUDSON
               Everything was so well planned.

6.   MEDIUM GROUP SHOT

                         FLINCH
               There always are complications when
               this much money is at stake. Mark
               my words -- complications are just
               beginning.

                         JUDSON
               What are you driving at?

                         FLINCH
               Complications.

                         JUDSON
               So....?

                         FLINCH
               Are you satisfied with your share
               of Lucille's estate?

       Judson looks -- unsure of himself -- or of an answer.

                         FLINCH
               You see -- You are not -- And you,
               Diana? -- Are you also satisfied
               with your share?

                         DIANA
               I'll let you know when I get my
               hands on the cash.

7.   CLOSE SHOT - FLINCH

                         FLINCH
               Every angle of Lucille's departure
               from this life has been so care-
               fully planned - and executed -- Now
               we find loose ends.....

8.   CLOSE SHOT - DIANA

                    DIANA
          You're referring to Barbara and
          Lake......

Flinch puts his empty glass down on the floor beside
his chair.

                    FLINCH
          I'm referring to us -- as indiv-
          iduals out for our own selfish
          gain.....

                    JUDSON
          You're talking in riddles.

                    FLINCH
          Then I'll be more concise. Most
          people wouldn't be happy with a
          share of the money. They'd want
          it all.

                    JUDSON
          Maybe we should put the same
          question to you. Maybe you're
          not satisfied with your share.

Flinch picks up his empty glass from beside the chair.
He moves to the liquor cabinet as he talks. He refills
the glass - kills it off quickly - then lays the empty
glass on the cabinet top.

                    FLINCH
          I have no intentions of being the
          richest man in the cemetery.
                    (taps his
                    heart
                    lightly)
          .....You tell me I have a weak ticker.
          I might not live the night out, or I
          may live to be a hundred - Who knows --
          But my share of Lucille's estate will
          keep me in fine style no matter how
          much time I do have left --- Yes --
          I'd say, I am satisfied with my share.

                    DIANA
          Don't you think this vein of
          talk is silly?

                    FLINCH
          Is it?

                              CONTINUED

8.   CONTINUED

                              DIANA
                    It certainly is. Each of us did
                    our share in Lucille's death.
                    None of us could have done it
                    alone.

                              FLINCH
                    True....

                              DIANA
                    Then let's stop this foolishness.

                              FLINCH
                    It's far from foolish -- You're
                    right -- each of us did his share
                    to accomplish the end -- Now --
                    Each of us becomes a hazzard to
                    the others --- Do you think Emma
                    will accept anything less than a
                    full share? She'll want the same
                    as the rest of us.

9.   CLOSE SHOT - JUDSON

                              JUDSON
                    Over my dead body.

10.   CLOSE SHOT - FLINCH

                              FLINCH
                         (smiling)
                    Exactly.......

11.   CLOSE SHOT - JUDSON

       He re-acts quickly.

12.   MEDIUM GROUP

       Judson and Diana look at each other, then turn back to
       Flinch. He leans back against the whiskey cabinet. He
       folds his arms as his eyes look directly at them.

                              FLINCH
                    I wonder which of us will be --
                    the one who will outsmart all the
                    others --- It should prove an
                    interesting test to our nerves.

13.   EXT. FRENCH WINDOWS - LIBRARY - MEDIUM CLOSE - NIGHT

The thunder and lightening persist. The girl vampire
moves away from the window, gliding off into the
shadows along the side of the house.

14.   INT. LIBRARY - MANSION - MEDIUM WIDE - NIGHT

Flinch stands in the position as before, facing Judson
and Diana.

                    FLINCH
            Think it over -- It's something
            to think about.

Flinch turns and walks to the library French windows.
Judson and Diana have turned to watch his movement.
Flinch opens the window. He breaths deeply of the
fresh night air. He turns his head back to look at
them.

                    FLINCH
            Rain's going to start again ---
            But even with the storm - tonight's
            kind of special. Sort of a million
            dollar feeling in the air....

He turns to look off into the night and up at the dark
clouds above.....

                    FLINCH
            That neice of Lucille's is beautiful.
            Too bad she's gotta' pass away so
            young.....

A loud clap of thunder rocks the scene as Flinch smiles
and leaves the room, pulling the French windows closed
after him. Judson and Diana look to each other.....

                                    DISSOLVE TO:

15.   INT. OLD MANSION - BARBARA'S BEDROOM - MEDIUM CLOSE -
        DOLLY TO MEDIUM WIDE ANGLE - NIGHT

On the beautiful Barbara as she lies in her soft lux-
urious bed. She wears a flimsy low-cut night gown. She
sleeps soundly, heedless of the night or anything around
her. The screech of a bat is heard again from somewhere

                                    CONTINUED

15.   CONTINUED

out in the night --- but close to the house now. It
is a screech which could well make the dead shiver.
Barbara's lovely head of dark hair is spilled picture-
squely against the bright whiteness of the pillow on
which she lies. A slight shiver suddenly shakes her
body and in her sleep she pulls the bed clothing up
higher under her arms....The CAMERA pulls back to a
WIDER ANGLE....to take in fully the bed upon which she
sleeps and includes the slightly opened French windows
which lead out on the grass beyond. A slight wind
stirs the curtains -- but -- slowly the French windows
are opened wider and - directly in the center appears
the figure of the vampire which we have seen before ---
her eyes are bright, sparkling as if kindled by some
tormenting fire crom deep within her. Almost dream-
like the figure lowers its arms to its sides, then
glides across the room to the bed to stand over the
unsuspecting, sleeping beauty. The figure at no time
moves quickly or suddenly during this sequence.

16.   CLOSE FIGURE SHOT

The vampire moves into the shot, then stops to look down
at the girl. A weird smile crosses the vampire's
features as she slowly bends down towards Barbara.

17.   CLOSE SHOT

On Barbara's bare neck. Her head is turned away. The
head of the vampire moves into the scene, her lips
moving close to the bare neck. Suddenly Barbara's eyes
open -- her head snaps to look towards the pending
horror.

18.   EXTREME HEAD CLOSE UP - VAMPIRE

Who at one time must have been a lovely woman, but now
is weird and death like. Her eyes blaze in the darkness -- her lips too blood red, her white teeth cruel
and sharp. A lustful smile has captured her face.

19.   EXTREME HEAD CLOSE UP - BARBARA

Her face filling even more with the terror at the sight
above her. Her mouth opens in a blood curdling scream,
then she falls back in a faint.

20. MEDIUM WIDE ANGLE

The vampire stands up straight; a cruel look of being
cheated crosses her face. Barbara lies half out of the
bed, her arms hanging limply, her head unnaturally
slack. The vampire looks towards the naked, unprotected
throat and again begins her movement towards it....
Then....There is a violent banging at the door, and the
worried calls from an off scene young man.

                    LAKE (o.s.)
           Barbara.....Barbara.....What's
           wrong in there.......Open this
           door.......

The vampire snaps up straight again and looks to the
door then, turns quickly and moves to the open French
windowds, and with her long gown flowing out behind her,
she disappears out into the darkness of the night....

There is a hard thud as the shoulders of the man hits
the door from that side which is off scene -- then the
sharp splintering sound as the wood begins to pull apart
under the impact. The man gives the door one more
great shove and it pulls the lock apart. Lake, a handsome young man wearing night clothes and a robe, rushes
into the room. He pauses but a moment, then, on seeing
the girl laying half out of the bed, rushes towards her.
A moment later the elderly housekeeper runs in....

21. CLOSE GROUP SHOT

With Lake's aid, Barbara is lifted back into bed. Lake
begins to massage her hand as he turns to Emma.

                    LAKE
           Brandy --- Quickly ---

Emma steps quickly out of the scene to an off scene
cabinet to pour the brandy, as Lake rubs the girl's
wrists, getting the blood circulation started again.
After a moment Barbara's eyes begin to flutter as
consciousness returns to her. Emma moves into the
scene with the brandy. Lake takes the glass from her
hand and lifts it to the girl's mouth. He forces a
bit of the liquid between her lips. Barbara splutters,
then sits bolt upright on the bed. Her eyes glaring
towards the French windows. She has made such a sudden
movement she has nearly knocked the remainder of the
brandy from Lake's hand. For a moment it appears she
might again scream -- but she eases up slightly as Lake
moves in close to her.

                              CONTINUED

21.   CONTINUED

                              LAKE
                   Barbara --- What was it....?
                   What happened?

                              BARBARA
                            (searching for
                              her voice)
                   She was here...Just - just now.
                   Here....

                              LAKE
                   You were having a nightmare,
                   darling...

                              BARBARA
                   It wasn't a nightmare -- She was
                   leaning over me -- She was real --
                   Her lips were close to my neck....

22.   CLOSE SHOT - DOOR WITH BROKEN LOCK

        Judson and Diana run into the room.

                              JUDSON
                   What's all this racket?

        Judson sees the action. His face frowns in grave worry.

                              JUDSON
                   Barbara -- What happened?

        He crosses the room.....Diana moves in to follow.

23.   CLOSE GROUP SHOT

        Judson and Diana move in close to them.

                              BARBARA
                   Ohh, Uncle Judson --- She was
                   here -- in this room -- I saw
                   her -- It was horrible -- Her
                   eyes were like burning coals --
                   Her mouth......

                              CONTINUED

23.   CONTINUED

She hides her eyes in her hands, trying to shut out the
horrible sight she still seems to be witnessing. Lake
sinks down beside her to take her hand in his. Diana
and Judson look to each other quickly, then back to
Barbara.

                    JUDSON
          What in the world are you talking
          about....?   Who was here...?

                    BARBARA
          Aunt.....Aunt Lucille....

Lake's mouth drops open.....Emma crosses herself, then
all stare at the frightened girl.

                    DIANA
          The child must be out of her mind.

                    JUDSON
               (assuringly)
          You were dreaming.

                    BARBARA
               (pleading)
          Someone has to believe me. I
          was awake -- It was Aunt Lucille --
          She was closer to me than you are
          now. She was.....

                    JUDSON
               (cutting in)
          It's impossible, Barbara. You
          know your Aunt Lucille has been
          dead and buried nearly two months.

A man's blood curdling scream issues over the scene ---
So suddenly and unexpectedly that the occupants of the
bedroom jump with fright. Barbara's hand goes to her
mouth to stifle a scream of her own. The man's scream
seems to have come from somewhere out on the mansion
grounds. The scream noticably affects Diana....Emma
moves in to try to comfort Barbara. Lake and Judson
have immediately jumped to their feet and turn to the
open French windows. Lake shoots a command to Emma
and Diana.

                    LAKE
          Stay with Barbara.....

                              CONTINUED

23.   CONTINUED

Lake and Judson rush out through the French windows to
the grounds beyond....

24.   EXT. FRENCH WINDOWS - (BARBARA'S BEDROOM) - MANSION
GROUNDS - MEDIUM CLOSE - NIGHT

The two men come out onto the darkened grass of the
estate through the French windows. They pause to look
around --- The scream comes again but this time choaked
and weak. Lake turns frantically to Judson.

                    JUDSON
          That came from the cemetery!

Judson in the lead, with Lake directly behind, turns
and races off towards the cemetery.

25.   EXT. CEMETERY - MEDIUM CLOSE - NIGHT

Judson and Lake run in and stop. Lake looks off one way
and Judson the other....Judson suddenly does a double
take. His features fill with terror as his eyes are
rivited on something off scene.

26.   LONG SHOT - INTO CEMETERY

The vampire glides off among the headstones.

27.   MEDIUM CLOSE - JUDSON & LAKE

Judson stares straight ahead - words frozen in his
mouth - his eyes wide....Lake turns - notices something
wrong with Judson -- Lake looks to where Judson is
looking.

28.   LONG SHOT

Same as Scene #26 with the exception the vampire is no
longer in sight.

29.   MEDIUM CLOSE - JUDSON & LAKE

Lake, frowning, turns to the frightened Judson.

                              CONTINUED

Gary D. Rhodes   205

29.   CONTINUED

                        LAKE
                What was it, Judson? You look
                like you've seen a ghost....

The spell is broken. Judson moves his eyes to Lake.
He licks his dry lips....His eyes still appear as if
they had seen a ghost.

                        JUDSON
                        (slowly)
                May.....Maybe I did.....

Lake is about to make a remark to this when his roving
eye falls on something. He points off scene.

                        LAKE
                Look - over there, by the cliff...

Judson turns quickly, perspiration breaking out on his
face, to look where Lake is pointing.

30.   LONG SHOT - TO CLIFF EDGE

On the brink of cliff a man's hat can be seen.

31.   MEDIUM CLOSE

Lake and Judson run out of scene towards the off scene
cliff's edge.

32.   MEDIUM CLOSE

Lake and Judson move in. Judson picks up hat.

                        JUDSON
                It belongs to Flinch!

It will be noted the ground and brush at the edge of
the cliff near where the hat is found, is torn up.

                        LAKE
                No man could survive a fall
                down there.

                                CONTINUED

32.   CONTINUED

        Judson, looking about the area, spies something. He
        goes to it and picks it up. It is a man's shoe.

                            LAKE
                Flinch's?

                            JUDSON
                Yes.

                            LAKE
                What do you make of it?

                            JUDSON
                I don't know, Lake. I just don't
                know -- Let's get on back to the
                house.

                                        FADE TO:

33.   EXT. TOMB - CEMETERY - MEDIUM CLOSE - NIGHT

        Lucille, the vampire, glides across the small cemetery
        grounds to the vault. The door stands open....She moves
        inside. The vault door slowly creeks shut behind her.
        A streak of lightening crosses the sky followed by a
        loud clap of thunder as the rain begins to fall heavily
        upon the scene.....

                                        FADE TO:

34.   EXT. FRONT OF MANSION - MEDIUM CLOSE - STORM - NIGHT

        The lightening is furious as it races across the sky.
        The rain falls hard as a sedan pulls up to the columned
        doorway to the mansion. The thunder rolls heavily over
        head and with each clap of thunder the rain becomes that
        much heavier......

35.   CLOSE SHOT - THROUGH CAR FRONT DOOR WINDOW

        On two men. Boris Ruppert an attorney, and Frank
        Cordoni an undertaker. Boris sits behind the steering
        wheel.

                            BORIS
                You go ahead, Frank. I'll put
                the car in the garage.....

36.   MEDIUM CLOSE

Frank pushes open his door, bows his head against the
rain, slams the door, then runs up to the big door and
begins to knock on the door by using the iron knocker.
Boris backs the car in the direction from which he had
come.

37.   EXT. GARAGE - MEDIUM CLOSE - STORM - NIGHT

The rain makes a violent rattling sound on the metal of
the car as it backs into the scene, changes gears and
moves into the garage.

38.   INT. GARAGE - MEDIUM CLOSE - DOLLY - NIGHT

The sound of the storm is heavy as Boris brakes the car
when it is in place.....He opens the door and gets out.
(The music must build for suspense.) When he slams the
door his eyes suddenly dart about him as if some unheard
sound -- some unseen figure -- is lurking in the shadows.
A clap of thunder rolls to a crash. Boris looks skyward,
smiles, shrugs his shoulders, bows his head as if to
move out into the rain --- then moves on out of the scene
past the CAMERA. The CAMERA dollys out to a MEDIUM
CLOSE on the darkest corner of the garage....(Music rises
to sting). A dark figure lurks there. This is Dr.
Acula with cape up over his face. Slowly the cape is
lowered until just the eyes are visible - staring coldly
-- with hatred. The cape remains in this position.

                                        FADE TO:

39.   INT. BARBARA'S BEDROOM - WIDE ANGLE - NIGHT

The storm is heard raging outside. Barbara lays back on
a stack of pillows. Her eyes are closed in deep sleep.
Emma, now fully dressed is seated on a chair beside the
bed. She gets up as Judson enters.

                    JUDSON
          Did you give her the sleeping
          tablets?

                    EMMA
          Yes, sir....

40.   MEDIUM CLOSE

Judson moves in close to Barbara. He feels of her
pulse then turns to Emma who indicates Barbara as she
speaks.

                    EMMA
          Does her arrival change anything?

                    JUDSON
          Not really - but we have to be
          more careful -- She must not be-
          come suspicious of anything.

                    EMMA
          Perhaps I had better stay close
          to her.

                    JUDSON
          It would be best.

                    EMMA
          I'll sleep in this chair. If she
          so much as rolls over I'll hear
          her. - I'm a light sleeper. What
          of this maid, Paula, she brought
          with her?

                    JUDSON
          What about her?

                    EMMA
          She's taken complete liberty of
          the house.

                    JUDSON
          Well...?

                    EMMA
          She tells me she worked for both
          Lucille and Barbara in the past --
          before you married Lucille...

                    JUDSON
          That's right - She went with
          Barbara when Barbara left -- You
          were hired to take her place.

                              CONTINUED

40.   CONTINUED

                    EMMA
          That may all be well and good,
          but I get nervous.

                    JUDSON
          Nerves are a dangerous thing in
          our kind of business...But if it
          will make you feel easier - You
          may restrict her movements.

                    EMMA
          I'll do that - first thing in
          the morning.....

Judson turns and walks to the door. He pauses and turns
to face Emma as she speaks again.

                    EMMA
          About Mr. Flinch....I'm sorry.

                    JUDSON
          Yes. It's a blow to all of us.
          We couldn't attempt to locate
          him tonight in this weather.....
          Lucille's father must have been
          a mad man to build a house on a
          cliff.....Watch her closely.

                    EMMA
          I will.....

Judson leaves the room quickly, closing the door behind
him. Emma looks to the sleeping girl once more, then
sinks down in an easy chair beside the bed.

41.   CLOSE SHOT - EMMA

In the chair. Her head is looking towards the off
scene Barbara.....

                    EMMA
              (her eyes hard)
          I've waited a good many years
          for a chance like this....No,
          my dear, you or no one else is
          going to ruin it for me....

                                        DISSOLVE TO:

42.   INT. HALL - MANSION - STAIRWAY - MEDIUM CLOSE - NIGHT

Judson is moving towards the library. Paula, the pretty
maid comes out of a room and moves towards the stairs.
She sees Judson, turns to him.

PAULA
Mr. Boris and Mr. Frank have
arrived, sir.

JUDSON
Good! -- Where are they?

PAULA
In the library, sir.

JUDSON
Thank you....

Judson stands poised, thoughtfully a moment, as the maid
moves up the stairs and out of the scene, then he too
moves on towards the library door. The door opens before he can put his hand on the door knob. Lake comes
out into the hall. He smiles a greeting to Judson,
then closes the door behind him.

LAKE
What do you suppose brought on
such a night - mare?

JUDSON
Many things could have caused it.
Barbara and her Aunt were very
close -- then her death -- Barbara
took it very hard. Now the reading
of the will in the house she and
Lucille had so long shared. Barbara
will be alright - she will probably
have forgotten tonights dream by
morning. Most of us do.

LAKE
I'll drop by her room to see how
she is.....

JUDSON
I don't think it would be wise to
disturb her just now, Lake! I
gave her a sleeping tablet. She
was in a pretty nervous state.

CONTINUED

42.   CONTINUED

> LAKE
> Well - if you're sure she's
> alright - I'll go on to my
> room.

> JUDSON
> Barbara is a strong, healthy
> girl.

> LAKE
> Good night, Judson - and thanks
> for everything.

> JUDSON
> There is nothing to thank me for --
> I'm as interested in what my neice
> is up to as you are !!!!

Lake moves out of the scene and up the stairs. Judson
watches him go before he moves to enter the library.

43.   INT. LIBRARY - MEDIUM WIDE - NIGHT - STORM

A silence seems to prevail over the group until Judson
enters and closes the door behind him. Diana is at the
liquor cabinet pouring a drink for herself. Boris and
Frank are seated in chairs. Boris gets immediately to
his feet. He goes quickly to Judson.

> BORIS
> What's going on?

44.   CLOSE TWO - JUDSON & BORIS

> JUDSON
> Flinch is dead.

> BORIS
> That much I know - Who killed
> him?

> JUDSON
> No one said he was murdered.

> BORIS
> According to Diana it happened
> under very strange circumstances.

> CONTINUED

44.   CONTINUED

                            JUDSON
            I suppose you might put it that
            way.

                            BORIS
            There's no other way of putting it.
            What happens to his share of
            Lucille's money?

                            JUDSON
            We split it among us.

                            BORIS
            Very convenient.....And if
            another of us happens to pass
            away -- The individual pot
            grows that much greater for
            whoever is left.....So what do
            we do now?

                            JUDSON
            We cover up - Just as before.

                            BORIS
            How long do you think we can go
            on covering these things?

                            JUDSON
            Just as long as necessary. After
            all - what else do we need.

45.   CLOSE SHOT - BORIS

                            JUDSON (o.s.)
            You're an attorney - You dully
            register the incident with the
            law....

46.   CLOSE SHOT - FRANK

                            JUDSON (o.s.)
            Frank -- an undertaker. He dis-
            poses of the remains rather
            quickly and efficiently....

47.   CLOSE SHOT - JUDSON

                    JUDSON
              .....and I, the doctor, sign the
              death certificate.....

48.   MEDIUM GROUP

                    JUDSON
              ....What could be more satisfactory.

                    BORIS
              I'm beginning to think we're all
              out of our minds....

                    JUDSON
              We just happen to be a self
              sufficient family. Who is to
              dispute our words. It worked
              out perfectly with Lucille.

                    BORIS
              Up to a point.

                    JUDSON
                 (exhausted)
              Now what have you got to gripe
              about?

                    BORIS
              Barbara, Lake and the maid.

                    DIANA
              They can disappear...

                    BORIS
              ....Lucille also has a sister --
              Helen....

                    JUDSON
              Who hasn't been seen or heard of
              in years...

                    BORIS
              Lucille left ninety percent of
              her money to this unheard of
              sister and to Barbara.....

                    JUDSON
              ....A mistake I'm sure you were
              able to correct in the will....

                         CONTINUED

48.   CONTINUED

                    BORIS
          Sure - I corrected it -- in our
          favor -- I'm getting in deeper
          and deeper.

                    JUDSON
          Sure you are -- a million and a
          quarter deeper -- but why worry
          -- As I said before -- Who is to
          doubt our word? Lucille died of
          a heart attack - I know - I
          examined her - and I signed the
          death certificate.

                    BORIS
          ...and what did Flinch die of?

                    JUDSON
          Flinch went over the cliff -- We
          can't be sure until his body is
          recovered -- Probably a heart
          attack.

                    BORIS
          I wouldn't give odds on it. So
          what brought on this so sudden
          heart attack?

                    JUDSON
          It wasn't sudden - You know he
          had a bad heart, and those mid-
          night walks of his weren't doing
          him any good.....
                    (breaks - turns
                    to Frank)
          .....Hello, Frank - Didn't mean
          to ignore you -- Good to see you
          again.....

49.   WIDE ANGLE

          Judson crosses the room quickly to shake Frank's hand as
          Frank has gotten to his feet.

                    FRANK
                    (smiling)
          With my wife in Hollywood and me
          in town - the will reading seemed
          to me to be an excellent opportunity
          to see her again in person instead
          of just on the silver screen - her
          profession.....

                                        CONTINUED

49.   CONTINUED

Diana salutes him with her glass of whiskey.

> DIANA
> Someday, darling, I'd like to see
> you in one of your wooden boxes --
> Your profession....

> BORIS
> (grumbling)
> Heart attack !!! - Pretty convenient
> if you ask me.....I don't like the
> look of it, Judson -- and I don't
> mind telling you further....

> FRANK
> (cutting in)
> Suppose we let Judson finish
> what he has to say?

50.   CLOSE SHOT - DIANA

> DIANA
> Now there's a man with brains -
> Why didn't you think of that,
> Boris.....?

51.   CLOSE SHOT - BORIS

> BORIS
> Oh, be quiet, Diana. You drink
> too much.....

52.   CLOSE GROUP

> DIANA
> Sure I do - Only I admit it - Other
> people drink too much and don't
> admit it...

> BORIS
> Someday I'd like to meet you when
> you're sober.

> DIANA
> I'd be very dull - ask my husband --
> Frank -- don't you think I'd be
> very dull.....?

CONTINUED

52.   CONTINUED

                    FRANK
          Dull, did you say? That's an
          understatement. Being an under-
          taker I find a corpse very good
          company.

                    DIANA
          I should have known -- Dead
          stiffs stick together.

                    JUDSON
          Please, Diana.....

                    DIANA
          Please, Diana.....Please, Diana.....
          All of you treat me as if I were a
          spoiled brat -- I'm tired of it --
          Why doesn't someone, just once, tell
          me to go jump in the lake...

                    BORIS
              (sarcastically
               cutting in)
          .....We like you, Diana.

Boris and Diana glare at each other.

53.   INT. BARBARA'S BEDROOM - MEDIUM CLOSE - DOLLY - NIGHT

Barbara sleeps soundlessly. Emma, seated as before in
a large easy chair beside the bed, is nodding -- then
her head falls down on her chest as sleep finally
overtakes her.

54.   EXT. CEMETERY - MEDIUM CLOSE - STORM - NIGHT

The storm rages violently.....Beneath a big tree in the
deep shadows of the trees and tombstones stands a tall
darker shadow.....It is again Dr. Acula. Slowly he
lowers the cape to permit once again only his eyes to
show. His eyes are intense - hypnotic.....

55.   INT. BARBARA'S BEDROOM - MEDIUM CLOSE - DOLLY

Dr. Acula's eyes carry over to this scene which shows
Barbara's head on the pillow. Her eyes open. Dr. Acula's

                              CONTINUED

Gary D. Rhodes   217

55. CONTINUED

eyes dissolve out. Barbara slowly raises up in bed.
The CAMERA moves back to take in all of the room. Emma
is sound asleep. Barbara slowly opens her eyes. She
sits up slowly, moves her feet off the bed and gets up.
Soundlessly she crosses the room to the French windows.
She opens them. The wind blows the curtains inward.
Emma stirs, but does not awaken.....Barbara starts out.
Into the night. Suddenly Emma wakes with a start. She
looks to the bed. It is empty. She looks to the
window, where the brightness of Barbara's night-dress
can still be seen moving out into the night towards the
cemetery. Emma rushes to the window and screams hister-
ically......

56. INT. LIBRARY - WIDE ANGLE - NIGHT

The rush is towards the door as Emma's scream carries
over. But Judson has glanced towards the French windows.

                    JUDSON
          Out there.....

He points. The others look to the French windows.
Judson races for the French windows, throws them open
and runs out into the night while Boris, Frank, Diana
remain in the room at the edge of the window and the
room.

57. INT. BARBARA'S BEDROOM - WIDE ANGLE - NIGHT

Emma screaming in the doorway. Lake comes through the
connecting door between his and Barbara's bedrooms. He
wears a shirt, opens at the collar and trousers, having
changed earlier from his night clothes. He runs across
Barbara's bedroom and out the French windows, past Emma,

58. EXT. CEMETERY - MEDIUM CLOSE - NIGHT - STORM

Judson coming from one direction and Lake from the other
meet. They stop, look around -- then race towards the
CAMERA.

59. MEDIUM WIDE ANGLE - NIGHT - STORM

Barbara is walking towards the CAMERA as Judson and Lake

                              CONTINUED

59.   CONTINUED

run in from the background and stop her forward movement. Barbara faints almost immediately Lake has put
his arm around her. She sags to his strength. He picks
her up and carries her back towards the house with
Judson following closely behind....

60.   MEDIUM CLOSE

Dr. Acula as we have seen him before under the trees,
His cape held high so as only his eyes are visible.

                                    DISSOLVE TO:

61.   INT. BARBARA'S BEDROOM - WIDE ANGLE - NIGHT

Barbara in a change of clothes topped with a fluffy
marabau bed jacket is again in bed. Boris, Frank, Lake,
Judson, Diana and Emma are in attendance. Lake sits on
one side of Barbara on the bed and Judson on the other.
Barbara sips a brandy.

                    JUDSON
            Do you feel up to telling us
            about it now?

62.   MEDIUM CLOSE GROUP

Barbara tries to compose herself. Tries to speak without the signs of nervousness when all her nerves are
tingling from the fright and indicision she feels.

                    BARBARA
            It was as though she was calling
            to me from the very tomb itself -
            Hollow - As if coming from a long
            way off.....

                    BORIS
            Isn't this a bit melodramatic?

                    JUDSON
            I wish it were simple dramatics.

                    BORIS
            You talk, but you say nothing....

                                    CONTINUED

62.   CONTINUED

                    JUDSON
          We'll go into that later. What
          happened, then, Barbara?

                    BARBARA
          I woke up.....Emma was asleep --
          In that chair....
                    (points)
          I knew I shouldn't go out in this
          weather dressed as I was -- but I
          couldn't keep from going either --
          It was as though an unseen hand had
          taken hold of mine and led me on
          and I was powerless against it.
          Next thing I knew you and Lake
          were beside me. The power that
          had led me on, stopped, and I
          guess I fainted after that....

Judson stands up. He is thoughtful for a long moment
then he smiles re-assuringly to the girl.

                    JUDSON
          Now the doctor prescribes rest.

                    BARBARA
          I'd rather go down stairs with you.

                    JUDSON
          I'd rather you stay right here
          young lady.

                    BARBARA
          Well - alright - but no sleeping
          pills this time.

                    JUDSON
                    (smiling)
          I guess we can dispense with a
          sleeping pill - as long as you
          stay put.....

                    BARBARA
          I will - I promise.

Judson and the others turn to leave. Judson turns back
on Lake.

63.   WIDE ANGLE

With Judson at the door. The others have gone out.

                                        CONTINUED

63.   CONTINUED

                          JUDSON
              You'll stay here, Lake?

                          LAKE
              If you wouldn't mind.

                          JUDSON
              This time I recommend it.

He leaves.....closing the door behind him.

64.   CLOSE TWO SHOT

Lake turns back to Barbara and smiles comfortingly.

                          LAKE
              You'd better try for some sleep...

                          BARBARA
                    (softly)
              Yes.....

She lays back. Lake straightens the covers around her.
She takes his hand in hers. Lake sits down on the edge
of the bed beside her.

                          BARBARA
                    (thoughtfully)
              Aunt Lucille and I were the best
              of friends. If she has returned
              from the grave I'm sure she could
              mean me no harm....

                          LAKE
              Darling --
                    (cautiously)
              -- I wouldn't talk too much
              about your Aunt Lucille -- If
              I were you...

                          BARBARA
              You don't believe me either...

                          LAKE
              You and your Aunt were very close.
              You were getting over your remorse
              at her loss - You were doing so
              well - Now -- the reading of the
              will tomorrow -- It could do strange
              things to your sub-conscious mind...

                          CONTINUED

64.   CONTINUED

                         BARBARA
               Do you really think it's that,
               Lake?

                         LAKE
               Yes -- I do...

                         BARBARA
               But how could I feel so awake?
               How could I realize things?
               How could I see her so plainly?
               How....?

                         LAKE
                    (cutting in)
               Hey....That's too many How's....
               Supposing we just let things
               ride the way they are until
               morning.....Love me....?

                         BARBARA
                    (softly)
               You know I do....

        He kisses her tenderly...

65.   WIDE ANGLE

        Lake gets up from the edge of the bed and crosses the
        room to open the French windows.

                         LAKE
               I'll just close these in case
               you decide to take another
               stroll in the cemetery.

        He smiles and begins to close the French windows....

                                        DISSOLVE TO:

66.   INT. LIBRARY - MEDIUM WIDE - NIGHT - STORM

        The storm rages outside. Boris paces the floor. Diana
        is again at the liquor cabinet. Frank sits quietly in
        a large easy chair listening attentively. Judson stands
        with his back to the fireplace facing the others.

                                        CONTINUED

66.   CONTINUED

                        BORIS
            I think you've taken leave of
            your senses.

                        JUDSON
            We must be sure.

67.   CLOSE SHOT - FRANK

                        FRANK
            Judson may be right, Boris. The
            girl's words in combination with
            the mysterious death of Flinch
            certainly has me on edge. Then
            add to that Judson's own words of
            seeing something that looked like
            Lucille.

68.   CLOSE SHOT - BORIS

                        BORIS
                    (excitedly cutting
                     him off)
            This is the twentieth century -
            Dead bodies don't rise up out of
            their coffins and walk around ala
            Edgar Allen Poe stories -- We are
            supposedly four so called intell-
            igent adults. But we're talking
            like a bunch of five year old
            children locked in a dark closet.
            I want to go on record as saying
            I don't approve....

69.   CLOSE SHOT - DIANA

                        DIANA
            Why don't you keep your jury
            speeches for the court room....
            Judson - if there is any doubt...
            I think we should follow your
            suggestion.

70.   CLOSE SHOT - FRANK

                        FRANK
                    (amazed)
                Why, my dear - That is the most
                intelligent remark I've ever
                heard you say -- You are showing
                signes of suspended animation.

71.   MEDIUM GROUP

                        DIANA
                Can't you see you haven't struck
                oil -- Now stop boreing...

        Boris throws up his hands in dispare - hopelessly.

                        BORIS
                Suspended animation - boreing --
                I'm in a house of lunitics...

        Judson approaches the bell cord and pulls it, then
        returns to the center of the room.

                        JUDSON
                I take it we are in agreement?

                        BORIS
                Not me - I know she's dead!
                Remember - I was there when the
                poison was administered....

                        JUDSON
                You don't have to come. You can
                stay here with Diana.

                        BORIS
                Not on your life. I wouldn't
                miss the look on your faces, when
                you open Lucille's coffin, for
                anything in the world.

        The pretty little maid enters. She looks to Judson.

                        PAULA
                You rang, sir?

                                        CONTINUED

71.   CONTINUED

                        JUDSON
            Yes! We are going out for a
            bit. See that Miss Barbara
            is not disturbed - also that
            she doesn't go out.

                        PAULA
            Yes, sir.

She turns immediately and leaves the room.

                        DISSOLVE TO:

72.   EXT. TOMB - MEDIUM WIDE ANGLE - NIGHT

Judson, Boris and Frank make their way into the scene
and stop near the vault door. The rain has grown intense and the thunder continues to roll and the lightening to flash.

                        BORIS
            At least we could have waited
            until daylight.

Judson goes to the door, extracting a key from his
pocket as he moves. He is about to insert the key into
the lock when he sees the lock is broken.

                        JUDSON
            Look here.

                        BORIS
            What is it?

                        FRANK
            The lock is broken.

                        BORIS
            What....?

Boris rushes forward to take the lock in his own hands
for a quick examination. When his examination is
finished Boris lets it fall back on the hanging chain
attachment.

                        CONTINUED

72.   CONTINUED

                        BORIS
                Let's get on with what we came
                out in this mess for. I'm tired
                and wet and I don't intend to
                spend the rest of the night
                tramping through this cemetery.

Judson pushes open the door and followed by the others,
he enters the vault.

73.   INT. TOMB - WIDE ANGLE - NIGHT

Before the others enter, Judson takes a match from his
pocket and lights a lantern which hangs near the entrance doorway.....The lantern lights up the gloomy
interior. Directly in the center of the room is a bier
upon which rests a coffin. New and highly polished.
Around the inside, near the walls, in specially built
compartments can be seen many other coffins....older
ones, some of an extremely antique vintage. Each bears
the gold plated first name of the occupants on the lid.
All the coffins are musty, dirty, mouldy. The walls
themselves are lined with cob webs and the grime of
many, many years.

74.   MEDIUM CLOSE

Judson moves out of the scene towards the off scene
casket. Boris looks to the perspiring Frank.

75.   LONG SHOT - TO MEDIUM CLOSE

With Lucille's casket in the foreground. The lid
is closed and the bright letters spell out....

                    " L U C I L L E "

....Boris and Frank start across the room after Judson
who now stands beside the coffin. They move slowly
towards the casket, their eyes riveted on the foreboding object of death's sleep. Judson stands staring
down at the object. Boris looks impatiently to Judson.

                        BORIS
                Well - open it - open it -
                Get it over with...

                                        CONTINUED

75.   CONTINUED

Judson looks to Frank, a feeling of helplessness to his
features. His hands tighten on the lid as he slowly
lifts it up until it blots out the screen.

76.   CLOSE SHOT - INTO COFFIN

The lid is opening. Within, lying on the soft white
satin, is the sexy form of the girl vampire. Her
shrouds are black and tattered. Her hair is dis-
hevelled and her lips are as bright red as before. She
sleeps peacefully as in death. Her hands are crossed
over her breasts. There is no sign of breathing --
of life......

77.   CLOSE SHOT - FRANK

He takes a deep breath - wets his dry lips.

78.   CLOSE SHOT - BORIS

Noticably relieved.

                    BORIS
          There - Just as I've said all along.
          How could it be otherwise? She's
          as dead now as the day we put her
          in there --- I'll admit, however,
          it's a remarkable job of preservation
          you did, Frank.

                    DR. ACULA (o.s.)
          Do not be hasty in chosing the
          quick from the dead.....

Boris's head snaps towards the off scene open tomb
doorway.

79.   CLOSE GROUP - FRANK - JUDSON & BORIS

All are looking to the off scene open tomb door.

80.   FIGURE CHOSE SHOT - DR. ACULA

He stands in the doorway, his long black cape hanging

                                        CONTINUED

80.   CONTINUED

loosely down his back (ala Dracula). He is tall, distinguished looking. His greying hair is neatly and
smoothly brushed back from a sharp widow's peak over
his lean forehead. He moves through the doorway and
stops just inside.

                    DR. ACULA
          Permit me to introduce myself,
          I am Dr. Acula.

He moves in closer to the group. He looks into the
CAMERA as he moves.

81.   MEDIUM GROUP

Dr. Acula moves into the group. He looks into the
coffin, then turns to the others. A smile crosses his
features. A weird smile which could well be mistaken
for friendliness.

                    DR. ACULA
          It seems my sudden appearance has
          startled you. The muddy roads
          trapped my automobile - Coming
          through the cemetery to your house
          I observed you here, and since I
          am a student of life after death
          perhaps I could be of some aid.

                    JUDSON
          Errr...Errr...Yes, Errr....This
          is Mr. Boris Ruppert and Mr. Frank
          Cordoni.....
                    (turns towards
                    casket)
          .....These are the remains of
          my wife, Lucille....She seems to
          have....

                    DR. ACULA
          Yes.....I overheard.....

He turns to take a close look at the coffin and its
contents. He makes a quick examination. His face is
grave as he again turns to the others.

                                        CONTINUED

81.   CONTINUED

                              DR. ACULA
                    In this quick diagnosis - I would
                    say -- in a sense -- she lives --
                    Yet in a sense -- she does not --
                    She is one of the undead -- A
                    vampire....

82.   CLOSE SHOT - BORIS

                              BORIS
                         (beyond reason)
                    Ohh, good, John, Jacob and Harry.
                    Vampires...What next? Vampires
                    exist only in the minds of crazy
                    writers, small children and old
                    wives tales....

83.   TWO SHOT - BORIS & DR. ACULA

                              DR. ACULA
                    That is like saying, there is
                    no -- Satan.....

        Dr. Acula motions the coffin but his words seem to infer
        much more.....

                              DR. ACULA
                    ....The proof is before your eyes.

84.   CLOSE SHOT - BORIS

        Looking into the coffin. For the moment he is trying
        to believe.....

                              BORIS
                    I see it --- I don't believe it -
                    And neither will anyone else.

85.   MEDIUM CLOSE

        Featuring Dr. Acula as he indicates the off scene,
        hidden body in the casket.

                                        CONTINUED

85.   CONTINUED

                                    DR. ACULA
                        The torn dress -- and the hem --
                        It is muddy and wet --- It has
                        recently been worn in weather
                        such as this.....
                              (indicates out-
                               side....)
                        Notice the bright redness to the
                        lips....It appears this young
                        lady has returned to our world
                        a vampire.....

                                    BORIS
                        I'll go along with the gag...
                        What about Flinch? - Was he
                        murdered by a vampire?

                                    JUDSON
                        No....

                                    DR. ACULA
                        Who-so-ever is bitten by the
                        vampire, himself becomes a
                        vampire....

                                    JUDSON
                        I know the legend....
                              (seriously)

86.   CLOSE SHOT - FRANK

                                    FRANK
                        All facts considered, I think
                        we should keep this business as
                        quiet as possible.

87.   CLOSE SHOT - JUDSON

           Shoots a glance from Frank to Boris then back to Dr.
           Acula. He fishes for words.

                                    JUDSON
                        Dr. Acula - I hesitate to ask --
                        But since you heard us talking --
                        I am forced to ask you, for the
                        moment....to.....

88c   CLOSE SHOT - DR. ACULA

                         DR. ACULA
                    (cutting in)
              ......to be silent........
                    (he smiles
                     assuringly)
              ......of course. The incident will
              be closed as soon as the vampire's
              life is sealed forever.

89.   CLOSE TWO - BORIS & DR. ACULA

                         BORIS
              And how do you propose to do that?
              According to your theory - If she
              walked once, she can walk again
              and....Now I'm starting to talk like
              you. I don't believe it and I won't.

                         DR. ACULA
              The strength of the vampire comes
              from the fact no one will believe
              in him.

        Boris storms off soono towards tho ontranco of tho tomb.

90.   MEDIUM GROUP

        Catching Boris as he moves to the doorway and stands
        there.

                         DR. ACULA
                    If I may be permitted.....

        Judson looks to him, a questioning look on his face.
        Then seeing the re-assuring look to Dr. Acula, he nods
        his permission. Dr. Acula turns to Frank.

                         DR. ACULA
              Mr. Cordoni - Would you be so kind
              as to bring me a stake cut from a
              green branch? It must be sharp at
              one end.

        Frank looks to Dr. Acula a long moment, then he moves
        out.

                         JUDSON
                    (weakly)
              Is there no other way?

                                        CONTINUED

Gary D. Rhodes   231

90.   CONTINUED

                              DR. ACULA
                    One.

                              JUDSON
                         (hopefully)
                    What is it?

                              DR. ACULA
                    If the head is removed from the
                    body. I don't think you would
                    want that.

                              JUDSON
                         (hopelessly)
                    Of course not....Enough was done
                    at the autopsy....

91.   CLOSE SHOT - DR. ACULA

        A sudden dangerously mean look crosses his features.

                              DR. ACULA
                         (seriously)
                    Yes --- the autopsy.

92.   MEDIUM WIDE

        Frank moves back into the scene holding a rock and a
        stake. He has heard Dr. Acula's last speech.

                              FRANK
                    What do you know about that?

                              DR. ACULA
                    You performed it?

                              FRANK
                    Judson and I together - Yes --
                    What of it?

                              DR. ACULA
                         (changing
                          tempo)
                    They are always so -- unkind ---
                    But now it grows near the vampire's
                    second awakening. We must hurry.

                                        CONTINUED

92.   CONTINUED

With Boris at the tomb door. He is becoming more and
more irritated at the progression.

                    BORIS
          By all means -- Get your play
          things together -- play your
          little game -- and let's get
          back to the house....

Frank hands the stake and the rock to Dr. Acula. Dr.
Acula in turn hands them to Judson, who looks to them
with horror.

                    JUDSON
          I - I - I couldn't do it....

                    DR. ACULA
          Yes -- It is understandable.

Judson shakes his head in agreement. The others move
in close. Dr. Acula looks to them strangely.

                    DR. ACULA
                    (pointodly)
          It will not be a pleasant sight.

Judson looks to Dr. Acula then to the others. Finding
no wisdom in their features he turns and leaves the
tomb. Frank follows quickly after, then Boris goes out
closing the door after him.

93.   CLOSE SHOT - DR. ACULA

He looks to the door then turns to look to the coffin,
both of which are off scene.

94.   CLOSE SHOT - INTO COFFIN

Showing the lovely vampire within as Dr. Acula looks in
from off scene. The stake comes into the scene and is
placed over the vampire's heart.....

95.   MEDIUM CLOSE

Dr. Acula holds the stake as if he is going to pierce
the vampire's heart another moment, then he tosses the
stick and rock away.....The vampire slowly sits up in
the coffin.

                              DISSOLVE TO:

96.   EXT. TOMB - CLOSE GROUP - NIGHT - STORM

The three men are huddled in close to the tomb door -
out of the light sprinkling of rain.

                    BORIS
          Have you gone completely out of
          your mind. That man is a total
          stranger -- How do we know who
          he is or where he came from? I
          don't like the idea of him being
          alone in there with her body.

                    JUDSON
          What was I suppose to do - Send
          him on his way after all he heard.
          Leave his future to me! He may
          become useful in case of trouble.
          Besides -- Dr. Acula has prepared
          his own death certificate -- It
          only remains for me to pick the
          time and place for signing it...

                    BORIS
          This whole thing is a lot of
          poppycock.....

                    JUDSON
          I still say - it was Lucille
          I saw.....

                    BORIS
          You saw pink elephants....

                    FRANK
          I feel safer with Dr. Acula doing
          just what he's doing.....

Boris turns full on the nervous prespiring man.

                    BORIS
          You, Frank Gordoni, the family
          undertaker - the man who is
          married to my sister - nervous?
          You above all should be at ease
          in these surroundings.....

                    FRANK
          I'm not nervous - I'm just bubbling
          over with perspiring enthusiasm.

Boris glares at him - then turns his attention on Judson.

                                        CONTINUED

96.   CONTINUED

                    BORIS
          Vampires...huh - if you ask me
          that Dr. Acula guy looks more
          like a vampire than Lucille's
          body does.

The tomb door squeeks open. Dr. Acula comes out. He
closes the door securely behind him.

                    DR. ACULA
          It is done.

                    JUDSON
          Will you join us, Dr. Acula?

                    DR. ACULA
          Delighted.

They start off scene towards the darkened cemetery.

97.   EXT. CEMETERY - WIDE ANGLE - STORM - NIGHT

With the wind pushing Dr. Acula's cape up behind him,
giving him the appearance of a great bat. He looks
tall and foreboding as he comes to a stop and stands
looking at the others. He indicates the wind.

98.   CLOSE GROUP

                    DR. ACULA
          The wind sounds like souls crying
          for release from prisons below the
          ground. It is on nights like this
          the dead have been known to rise.

                    BORIS
               (cynically)
          For a moment I thought you were
          a man of science.

                    DR. ACULA
          I am a man of science.

                    BORIS
          Then how can you say such things?

                    DR. ACULA
          Perhaps because I am a man of
          science.

98.   CONTINUED

There is a violent clap of thunder and a streak of
lightening that shoots across the sky almost simultan-
iously. Judson looks to the sky with a slight shudder;
he pulls his coat collar up tighter around his neck.

99.   OUT.

100.   CLOSE GROUP

Dr. Acula, a man of great learning - greater than would
seem possible. He looks to the sky.

                    DR. ACULA
              There is much even men of science
              do not understand.

                    FRANK
              I've never been afraid of dead
                  bodies....But these walking dead
              are a new experience to me ---
              I don't like it one bit.

                    BORIS
              Do you think any of us are enjoy-
              ing it?

101.   MEDIUM WIDE ANGLE - STORM - NIGHT

The group pushes on through wind and darkness - again
their heads are bent low against the driving wind and
rain. Suddenly above the sound of the wind and the
occassional clap of thunder comes the sound of another
presence....Something making its way through the brush
near them. Judson, in the lead, holds up his hand and
they stop. The foreboding cemetery with all its grue-
some darkness surrounds them - vines and weeds. A bolt
of lightening lights the way for a fraction of a second.

102.   CLOSE GROUP

As they listen.

                    JUDSON
              Someone is in the brush.

                                        CONTINUED

102.   CONTINUED

                              FRANK
                  Is it possible she walks again?

                              BORIS
                  Ah - that's a rich one --- Didn't
                  you hear the latest. Dr. Acula
                  finished our late sister-in-law's
                  ghost with a stake through her
                  heart....

Dr. Acula's eyes become narrow. They cut short the
man's laugh.

                              DR. ACULA
                  We do not <u>know</u> it is the vampire.

                              JUDSON
                  There's one way of finding out!

103.   MEDIUM CLOSE

         Judson in the lead, the group snake cautiously through
         the thick brush and trees and grave stones towards where
         they think the sound had come from.

104.   CLOSE FIGURE SHOT - DR. ACULA

         He moves to a tree with a low hanging, very thin branch.
         He is in the rear of the slow moving party. He takes
         the branch in his hand and permits it to move with him
         to almost its cracking point then he lets the branch go.
         It whips back against the tree with a whip like crack
         that echoes through the rain swept night.

105.   MEDIUM CLOSE

         The others turn back to see him, and what has made the
         sound. The branch still has a movement to it. Dr.
         Acula looks rather embarrassed. The sound of the night
         closes in - but the sound of someone else moving through
         the brush has stopped....All is quiet with the exception
         of the wind and an occassional thunder roll. Judson
         quickly turns back to where the sound had come from.
         His face frowns as he turns back to face the group. Dr.
         Acula makes an attempt at smiling.

                                            CONTINUED

105.   CONTINUED

> DR. ACULA
> The branch....It was across my
> path - hidden in the darkness.

> BORIS
> Well --- What ever it was, it's
> gone now.

> DR. ACULA
> (slowly)
> Yes....

Judson moves in close beside Dr. Acula. His hand gives
a reassuring grip on Dr. Acula's arm at the end of
Judson's speech.

> JUDSON
> It could have happened to any-
> one....

As his hand touches Dr. Acula's cape, he pulls it away
suddenly as if he has grabbed onto a hot poker. The
others turn towards Judson.

> FRANK
> What is it?

> JUDSON
> I don't know -- I touched Dr.
> Acula's cape -- it felt like
> fire shooting through my hand.

Dr. Acula smiles.

> FRANK
> Static electricity. As when
> you walk on a rug then touch
> something.

> BORIS
> But this is no rug. It is earth -
> and very wet earth at that...

> DR. ACULA
> Water is a great conductor of
> electricity.

CONTINUED

105.   CONTINUED

Boris moves in close to Dr. Acula. Slowly boris's hand
raises to touch the Dr.'s cape. Dr. Acula draws back
sharply, his eyes burn; narrow as they seem to look
deep into the man's soul.

                    DR. ACULA
          I would not search for problems
          which do not exist.

Boris drops his hand quickly.

106.   CLOSE SHOT - JUDSON

The frown leaves his face.

                    JUDSON
          We're spending so much time on
          things of little importance. Who
          ever it was walking around out
          here is gone by now. We might as
          well go on back to the house.

107.   MEDIUM CLOSE

The group, with the exception of Dr. Acula, walks off
scene. He watches after them a moment, then steps off
the path and into the brush....In the brush he reaches
out and pulls a thick clump of brush apart.

108.   CLOSE SHOT - INTO BRUSH

Dr. Acula's hand reaches into the brush and pulls it
away to reveal -- the vampire -- her eyes blazing....

109.   CLOSE SHOT - DR. ACULA

He smiles, calmly - knowingly.....

110.   MEDIUM CLOSE

The blazing eyes of the vampire cool. Slowly she turns
and walks out of the scene. Dr. Acula lets the brush
fall back into place. Then he turns and heads off
scene towards the others.

111.   MEDIUM GROUP

Dr. Acula joins them. As he moves up close, Judson
turns but no one has realized he has been away from
the group. The rain begins again.

                    JUDSON
          That blasted rain again.....

Judson looks strangely at the man but does not further
his statement....

                                        FADE TO:

112.   INT. HALL - MEDIUM CLOSE - NIGHT

Emma opens the door to permit Judson, Frank, Boris and
Dr. Acula to enter. Emma gives a look of terror for
the moment to the new arrival, Dr. Acula. As they
speak they shake the moisture from their clothing,
Frank turns to speak to Emma.

                    FRANK
          Is Miss Diana still in the
          library....?

                    EMMA
          No, sir. -- She asked Paula to
          help her pack.

                    FRANK
          Pack, why?

                    EMMA
          She said she doesn't feel safe
          here any longer. She wants to
          be ready to leave as soon as
          the will is read tomorrow.

Frank shrugs, as the others take off their coats and
hats, put them on coat racks, then move towards the
library....

                                        DISSOLVE TO:

113.   EXT. CEMETERY - WIDE ANGLE - LONG SHOT - NIGHT

The vampire moves dreamlike among the headstones towards the old house off scene.

DISSOLVE TO:

114.   INT. BARBARA'S BEDROOM - LONG SHOT - NIGHT

With Barbara and the bed in the foreground and the
French windows in the background. The dark form of the
vampire appears on the far side of the window. Slowly
the window opens. The vampire comes in. She makes her
way across the room towards the sleeping Barbara. She
stands looking down at her for a long moment then moves
off to the bedroom door, opens it and goes out. Lake
can be seen sleeping in a chair near the window.

115.   INT. HALL - MEDIUM CLOSE - NIGHT

The vampire slowly, and silently closes the door to
Barbara's bedroom and enters the hall. The CAMERA
follows her as she moves to the stairs and climbs them.
Just as she reaches the top step Emma comes out of a
door across from the library. She moves to the stairs
and starts up.

116.   INT. HALL - STAIRS - MEDIUM CLOSE

Looking down the stairs as Emma comes up. Suddenly
near the top she looks up. Her eyes go wide in some
unseen horror. Her voice is almost a whisper....

                    EMMA
          But...but....It's can't be...
          You can't be...You're...You're
          dead.....

She now realizes she is about to die.

                    EMMA
          No --- No --- Please - not me!

A knife flies through the air and catches Emma in the
heart. She topples over backwards and down the steps
without uttering a sound.

117.   MEDIUM CLOSE - DOORWAY

Where the vampire stands - Suddenly an ear piercing
scream issues across the scene. The vampire looks
towards the one who is screaming off scene.

118.   MEDIUM CLOSE - 2nd DOORWAY

Paula who has come out of Diana's room is screaming --
Frantically she is pointing towards the off scene
vampire as she screams....

119.   MEDIUM CLOSE SHOT - DOORWAY

The vampire goes quickly into the room closing the door
behind her.

120.   WIDE ANGLE - FEATURING LIBRARY DOOR

Boris, Judson and Frank come tearing out of the library.
Dr. Acula comes out last. He stands in the library door
way while the others run to Emma. Lake and Barbara come
out of Barbara's room. Paula, with Diana coming in
close behind her, comes to the top of the landing. She
points back down the hall off scene.

                        PAULA
            In there! --- Lucille! --
            She went in there !!!

Lake takes off up the stairs. Judson and Boris race up
after him, while Frank moves to Emma's body.

121.   MEDIUM CLOSE

On Dr. Acula who remains at the doorway, but looking to
the action. Frank looks up from the body.

                        FRANK
            She's dead....

                            FADE TO:

122.   INT. LIBRARY - MANSION - MEDIUM WIDE - NIGHT

Lake and Barbara are alone in the spacious library near
a blazing fire which burns in the fireplace.

                    LAKE
          Nervous?

                    BARBARA
          Very.

                    LAKE
          They'll find her if she's any-
          where in the house.

                    BARBARA
          I hope so.

123.   CLOSE TWO SHOT

                    LAKE
          I don't know what it is yet --
          But something just doesn't
          ring true about all this...

                    BARBARA
          It's awfully hard to believe --
          Aunt Lucille was always so kind
          to everyone. She wouldn't have
          hurt anyone if her life had
          depended upon it. -- I think
          the police should be notified.

                    LAKE
          Just as soon as the roads be-
          come passable.

                    BARBARA
          Lake - Are you sure the road is
          washed out?

                    LAKE
          When it rains like this these
          mountain roads leave much to
          be desired.....

                              CONTINUED

Gary D. Rhodes   243

123.   CONTINUED

> LAKE (cont'd)
> Barbara....How come the telephone
> was taken out of this house.

> BARBARA
> Uncle Judson had it taken out
> just after he married Aunt
> Lucille -- I thought you knew.

> LAKE
> I've often wondered - but I
> never did know...

> BARBARA
> Something about not wanting to
> be bothered by telephones when
> he came home from the office.
> She loved Uncle Judson very much --
> She'd have done anything for him.

They are quiet a moment, then Barbara turns quickly on
Lake again.

> BARBARA
> Darling....?

> LAKE
> (smiling)
> I don't like the sound of that --
> "Darling".

> BARBARA
> Let's take a chance on the road.
> Let's get out of this place.
> Now - Tonight. I have a feeling
> that......

Lake has reached into his pocket and brought out an
automatic as she talks. Barbara stops in the middle
of her speech and stares at the gun.

> BARBARA
> Where did you get that?

> LAKE
> (softly)
> I took it out of my bag -- Just
> in case....

> DR. ACULA (o.s.)
> What good do you think a gun is?

Lake and Barbara turn towards the off scene voice.

124.   MEDIUM CLOSE FIGURE - DR. ACULA

Dr. Acula has entered the room. The door is closed
behind him. He holds the same weird smile on his face.
He moves to cross the room and the CAMERA moves in
front of him until he stands near Lake and Barbara.

                    DR. ACULA
          It is no protection against a
          vampire....

125.   MEDIUM GROUP SHOT

Dr. Acula seats himself near Barbara and Lake.

                    DR. ACULA
          ....If anything, it will anger the
          vampire.....

                    LAKE
          This gun gives me a good sense of
          security - Besides I'm not sold on
          this vampire business....

                    DR. ACULA
          Judson - The maid - even your
          Barbara has seen the apparition.

                    LAKE
          The more of this spook talk I
          hear the more I'm convinced there
          must be some logical answer for
          the whole thing.

                    BARBARA
          Well -- You can think what you
          want -- It's your priviledge --
          I know what I saw.......
                    (silent for a
                    moment then to
                    Dr. Acula)
          ....Dr. Acula - Is there no way of
          killing a vampire - Killing it for
          good, I mean -- So there is no
          chance of it ever returning?

                    DR. ACULA
          Yes -- then again -- No ---

                              CONTINUED

125.   CONTINUED

                        LAKE
              That's a pretty wide answer.

                        DR. ACULA
              It is the devil's punishment
              upon those he has reason to
              hate.

                        BARBARA
              Are we to be frightened by this
              ghost the rest of our lives....
              Taking for granted we have <u>very</u>
              <u>much</u> <u>more</u> <u>life</u> to live.

          Off scene we hear a commotion as the others return from
          their search of the house. Dr. Acula, Barbara and Lake
          turn to look towards the door.

126.   MEDIUM WIDE ANGLE

          Boris, Frank and Diana come into the room. Judson
          follows last, closing the door behind him. Diana makes
          immediately for the whiskey cabinet, to pour herself a
          stiff one. Judson shrugs his shoulders as he moves to-
          wards Lake.

                        JUDSON
              Not a sign of her on the second
              floor.

                        FRANK
              I searched the attic - Nothing
              there....

                        LAKE
              Nothing in the basement either.

                        JUDSON
              Where can she be?

127.   MEDIUM CLOSE - FRANK & DIANA

          Frank turns on Diana who is still at the whiskey cabinet.

                        FRANK
              Fix me one of those, will you --
              This time I need one....

                                          CONTINUED

127.   CONTINUED

                              DIANA
              Weakening, Frank?

                              FRANK
              What makes you think I was ever
              strong?

128.   CLOSE TWO - FRANK & DR. ACULA

Frank can be seen in the background near Diana. He
moves in close to Dr. Acula as he speaks.

                              FRANK
              Vampires - Huh - Next thing the
              house will be swarming with
              zombies and werewolves - Perhaps
              even - the devil himself...

Dr. Acula smiles broadly.

                              FRANK
              -- That'd be just about all I
              could take. Sanity is a very
              thin line you know....

129.   CLOSE SHOT - BORIS

                              BORIS
              Well - I'm not looking forward to
              being murdered. -- Murdered -- We
              should be so lucky. I'm getting
              out of this hole -- The stench of
              ancestors in that tomb out there...
                    (he points
                     off scene.)
              ....If they had had sense enough
              to be put under ground, maybe we
              wouldn't be worried about who's
              going to climb out of their coffin
              next....

130.   WIDE ANGLE

Diana moves across the room with two whiskeys. She
hands one of the glasses to Boris and keeps the other
herself.

                              CONTINUED

Gary D. Rhodes   247

130.   CONTINUED

                         DIANA
            Here, darling - I think you need
            this more than he does. I made
            it strong.....It'll do you good.

Boris sullenly takes the glass of whiskey from her hand.

                         BORIS
            Nothing will do me good until
            I know where that displaced
            body is...

                         JUDSON
            Well - There's one more place to
            check again.

                         BORIS
            Then get to it....

131.   CLOSE SHOT - FRANK

                         FRANK
            We've gone over this house from
            top to bottom.

132.   CLOSE SHOT - DR. ACULA

Listening to Judson speak.

                         JUDSON (o.s.)
            It is possible she has returned
            to her tomb.

133.   CLOSE SHOT - BORIS

He leans forward in his chair.

                         BORIS
                       (seriously)
            If she's in the tomb - by all
            means, let her stay there ---
            That's the proper place for one
            in her condition.

134.   CLOSE SHOT - DR. ACULA

                         DR. ACULA
            It has been proven - even if she
            is in the tomb, she will not stay
            there.

135.   CLOSE SHOT - FRANK

                    FRANK
          If she's not in the house - she
          must be outside - at least that's
          logical....

136.   CLOSE SHOT - DR. ACULA

                    DR. ACULA
          You may count on my assistance.

137.   MEDIUM GROUP

                    JUDSON
          Well --- err --- Come if you want.

                    FRANK
          At this point you don't leave
          me behind.

                    JUDSON
          And Lake?

                    LAKE
          Of course, Judson.

                    BORIS
          Leave me out of it. I've had
          enough of these crazy cemetery
          treks....

                    JUDSON
          Then I suggest the rest of us
          have at it....

They move to the library door and go out.....

138.   INT. HALL - WIDE ANGIE - NIGHT

The group comes out and immediately begin to put on
their coats and hats. Judson is the first to start
for the door. Judson moves to the door and opens it,
bends his head low against the prospects of entering
the wind-rain swept night. The others follow quickly
behind him. The soundof the wind is low as the door

                                        CONTINUED

Gary D. Rhodes

138.   CONTINUED

is opened. A bolt of lightening lights up the doorway
and the thunder that follows is loud, more like a bomb
exploding. The last of the group is gone and Barbara
pushes the door shut. For a long moment she and Diana
look to the closed door, then Diana moves off to the
library and enters, closing the door behind her. Footsteps are heard behind Barbara. She turns quickly.
It is Paula, dressed for the outside, and carrying a
small suit case in her right hand. A purse is safely
tucked under her left arm.

139.   CLOSE TWO - PAULA & BARBARA

Paula moves in close to Barbara.

                    BARBARA
          Why, Paula - Where in the world
          are you going?

                    PAULA
          I was very fond of Miss Lucille
          when she was alive -- We used
          to have nice long talks in the
          evenings. Sometimes we used to
          sit together -- She even taught
          me to knit - and I taught her to
          sew....But now --- Dead all those
          weeks -- and her walkin' the
          house again' .... Well I
          just ain't up to it....When I saw
          here standin' there in the hall
          a while ago - an Miss Emma's poor
          crumpled body layin at the bottom
          of the stairs - I coulda' just
          run and never stop --- Only I
          couldn't make my feet work....

                    BARBARA
          You mean you're leaving - to-
          night...

                    PAULA
          I mean just that, Miss Barbara ---
          --- Ohh - I ain't quittin' my job
          or nothin like that -- I like you --
          an I like my job -- I'll just go
          on back to the apartment in town
          and wait for you there...

                              CONTINUED

139.   CONTINUED

> BARBARA
> The roads are impassable - You
> couldn't make it into town, to-
> night -- Don't you think you'd
> better wait until morning?

> PAULA
> The way I see it - I might not
> never see mornin' again.....Me
> and Miss Emma were gettin' real
> chummy like -- and Mr. Flinch
> seemed like a nice sort....Now
> they're gone -- Seems like Miss
> Lucille ispickin' on the wrong
> folks -- No ma'am - If it's all
> the same to you - I'd just as
> soon take my chances on the bad
> road....

There is a slight smile on Barbara's face as she tries
for an answer.

> BARBARA
> It's your choice, and I won't try
> to hold you back. But we've gone
> over the entire house -- Lucille
> isn't anywhere in it. Therefore -
> The only place she could be is....
>   (points to
>   door)
> ....out there....

Paula realizes the point. She blinks a couple of times
then sighs.

> PAULA
> Maybe you're right, Miss Barbara.
> Maybe it would be better if I
> wait around until daylight.

> BARBARA
> Good - Now - We'll both go up-
> stairs together. I don't think
> we'll have any trouble as long
> as there are two of us.....

Both girls start up the stairs....

                                        DISSOLVE TO

140.   INT. LIBRARY - MEDIUM WIDE ANGLE

Boris is nervously pacing the floor. Diana kills off a
drink and prepares to mix another. Boris puffs heavily
at his cigar, then he takes it from his mouth and
viciously throws it to the fire place. He turns to face
Diana.

141.   EXTREME CLOSE UP - BORIS

He stops his pacing and turns to face Diana who is off
scene. The perspiration is thick on his face.

                    BORIS
          I've had enough of it - I'm
          getting out of here.

142.   CLOSE SHOT - DIANA

Turns from the whiskey cabinet to face Boris.

                    DIANA
               (quickly)
          You'd better wait for Judson.

143.   MEDIUM CLOSE

                    BORIS
          You wait -- I've waited long enough.

                    DIANA
          Something may come up where you'd
          be needed.

                    BORIS
          The only one who needs me is me --
          Myself. I like life and I'm not
          about to sit around waiting for
       - some zombie to walk in and take
          it from me....Don't get the idea
          I believe these silly vampire
          stories either...Someone is taking
          advantage of a weird idea and weak
          minds -- Believe me - I'll find out
          who -- In my own way. I've gone
          through too much and taken too many
          chances to be cheated out of my
          share........

                              CONTINUED

143.   CONTINUED

                              DIANA
                    That's a silly idea!

                              BORIS
                    Is it?

He moves quickly out towards the hall.

144.   INT. HALL - MANSION - MEDIUM CLOSE - STORM - NIGHT

Boris comes out and quickly gets into his coat and hat.
He opens the big wooden door.   .   In the
doorway he stops and turns to Diana, as she speaks.

                              DIANA
                    The roads -- You can't make
                    it through.

                              BORIS
                    I'll chance it -- and have
                    better odds than I have here.

He goes out slamming the door behind him.

145.   EXT. OLD MANSION - MEDIUM CLOSE - STORM - NIGHT

Boris has moved to the edge of the stone stairs and
stops. He looks out into the darkness of the rain
driven night. For a moment he casts his eyes back
towards the door and the thought of the warmpth and
light back in the house, but then he digs his hands
deep into his pocket, lowers his head against the
driving force of the rain and steps out into it.

146.   EXT. GROUNDS - MEDIUM WIDE ANGLE

We watch Boris walk the length of the front of the
house, fighting his way against the rain and the wind
a bright streak of lightening streaks across the sky.
A clap of thunder rings out. Then he has passed the
end of the front of the house and moves across a
vacant section to the long garage at the rear.....

147.   EXT. GARAGE - MEDIUM CLOSE

Boris moves to the garage and pulls open one of the
large double doors. He secures it against the wind,
then moves to open the other door. A moment later he
disappears inside the garage.

148.   INT. GARAGE - MEDIUM CLOSE

Boris moves in from the double doors. He walks quickly
to the front door of the car. He opens it and gets inside. He starts the motor.....As it warms up he shifts
the gear into reverse. He is looking ahead through the
windshield. Sweat appears on his face.

149.   CLOSE SHOT

Through the right window on Boris. It will be noted
here his hand still holds the gear shift which is set
in reverse. Boris turns to look into the CAMERA. His
eyes open wide, as he recognizes someone. He does not
loose his composure, but it is apparent he has suddenly
become very nervous.

Smoke fills the screen from the pistol shot. Boris
falls forward on the steering wheel. His hand pushes
the gear shift into first.

150.   WIDE ANGLE

The car shoots forward towards the backwall of the
garage.

151.   EXT. GARAGE REAR & CLIFF - WIDE ANGLE - LONG SHOT -
NIGHT - STORM

The car crashes out of the back of the garage and with
a resounding crash it slams down the cliff side to the
rocks of the lake below.....

                              FADE TO:

152. INT. MANSION - LIBRARY - MEDIUM WIDE ANGLE

The dooropens and Judson, Dr. Acula, Frank and Lake
return. All are silent as they cross the room to join
with the others. Judson walks directly to the liquor
cabinet and begins to mix a drink.

                    JUDSON
          Want one, Lake?

Lake now at Barbara's side, turns to face Judson.

                    LAKE
          Huh? - Oh - No, thanks, Judson.

                    JUDSON
          Dr. Acula?

                    DR. ACULA
          Never touch it, thank you.

Diana moves from a chair to stand beside Judson. She
puts her empty glass on the table for re-filling, even
though she is already quite unsteady on her feet.
Judson looks to her frowning, but fills her glass.

                    DIANA
          I take it you didn't locate
          our little friend?

Judson shakes his head "No". Judson looks around the
room, searching for some one.

                    JUDSON
          What happened to Boris?

153. CLOSE SHOT - DIANA

Slightly drunk.

                    DIANA
          He's gone.

154. CLOSE SHOT - JUDSON

Swings to face her.

                    JUDSON
          The fool!

Gary D. Rhodes

155.   CLOSE SHOT - FRANK

                        FRANK
                He doesn't have a chance on
                those roads.

156.   CLOSE SHOT - JUDSON

                        JUDSON
                Why didn't you hold him here
                until we got back?

157.   CLOSE SHOT - DIANA

        Mixing another drink as she talks.

                        DIANA
                When Boris sets his mind to do
                something - No one persuades
                him differently --- Besides ---
                Boris is not a stupid man. If
                the road is impassable he'll
                return.

158.   CLOSE SHOT - FRANK

                        FRANK
                She's right, Judson. But look -
                why don't we let things rest
                until morning. It's getting
                pretty late - We should all try
                to get some sleep.....

159.   CLOSE SHOT - DIANA

                        DIANA
                If you think I'm leaving this
                fireside tonight, you're crazy.

160.   CLOSE SHOT - FRANK

                        FRANK
                You'll surely find it more
                comfortable in bed than in
                these chairs.

161.   CLOSE SHOT - DIANA

                         DIANA
            I don't care what anyone else
            does - I'm going to my room,
            get my negligee and return
            here to this fire as quickly
            as ⊥ can. I happen to have
            Lucille's old room.

162.   MEDIUM WIDE ANGLE

         However Diana turns for a re-fill, instead of leaving
         the room. Dr. Acula stands and faces the others.

                         DR. ACULA
            Since you have been kind enough
            to offer me the hospitality of
            a room -- I too shall retire.
            There is nothing more we can do --
            It is up to the vampire to make
            the next move.

         He moves swiftly from the room. Frank moves to the
         liquor cabinet near Diana and Judson.

                         FRANK
            I don't usually indulge - but
            I think this occassion calls
            for the unusual.....Make a big
            one for me.

         Judson smiles at him, takes up the bottle and another
         glass. He hands the filled glass to Frank. Frank
         takes it.

163.   CLOSE TWO SHOT - BARBARA & LAKE

         In a close huddle, their chairs pulled up closely to-
         gether, as they talk.

                         BARBARA
            I am more tired than I thought.

                         LAKE
            Want to go to your room?

                         BARBARA
            Yes...But...Let's keep our
            connecting door unlocked.

         He smiles, takes her arm and they cross to exit.

164.   WIDER ANGLE

Judson puts his half finished drink back on the cabinet.
He turns to the others.

                    JUDSON
          Goodnight.

                    FRANK
          Goodnight, Judson -- and look --
          Stop worrying -- We'll figure
          it out.

                    JUDSON
          I think I already have....

He takes Lucille's framed picture from the whiskey
cabinet, looks at it a moment, then turns it face
down on the top of the cabinet and leaves.....Frank
and Diana watch his exit carefully.

                              DISSOLVE TO:

165.   EXT. MANSION GROUNDS & CEMETERY - MEDIUM LONG SHOT -
         STORM - NIGHT

The rain has again stoppedbut the wind rips the leaves
of the trees and the brush on the ground. The figure
of the vampire glides through the cemetery. We see it
move through the brush and among the gravestones as it
moves towards the house. The long hair of the vampire
is tossed about by the force of the wind.

                              DISSOLVE TO:

166.   INT. LIBRARY - MANSION - CLOSE TWO - DIANA & FRANK -
         NIGHT.

Diana ispouring another drink as Frank sips from his.

                    FRANK
          Together we have a fortune.

                    DIANA
          So what?

                              CONTINUED

166.   CONTINUED

> FRANK
>
> Diana - Maybe - When all this
> is over -- Maybe we could try
> again.

> DIANA
>
> Try again - What?

> FRANK
>
> Our lives together - Try again
> to make a go of it....

> DIANA
>
> Sure - We'll make a go of it --
> You go your way and I'll go
> mine....Look - Frank -- You and
> me -- It was a mistake from the
> beginning -- I realized it long
> ago -- When are you going to
> realize it...?

She pours another drink into her glass. Frank looks to
it with a frown.

> FRANK
>
> Don't you think you've had
> enough of that for one night?

Diana turns on him quickly.

> DIANA
>
> Is there enough? -- Look. You're
> only my husband -- Not my keeper.

> FRANK
>
> It's up to you, my love, but you
> might need your wits about you
> before this night is over.

Diana tosses down her drink - It is apparent the girl is
now drunk. She rambles on drunkenly.

CONTINUED

166.   CONTINUED

                              DIANA
          I'll have my wits when and if I
          need them....One thing I don't
          need....That's advice from you.
          Who does she think she is......
          Walkin' around when she's supposed
          to be layed out....Tell you what,
          Frank - If I meet her - I'll tear
          that black hair out by the roots....
          I never liked her anyway - even if
          she did have all that money --- and
          she didn't like me either --- That
          made us even --- Frank - why don't
          you go to bed --- You bore me ---
          All husbands bore me.

                              FRANK
          You're the one that's going to
          bed.

He gingerly lifts the glass from her hand and propels
her protestingly to the library door and out....

                                   DISSOLVE TO:

167.   INT. DIANA'S BEDROOM - WIDE ANGLE - NIGHT

The lights in the room are out as the scene opens. The
door is thrown open as Frank forces Diana still spout-
ing, into the room. Frank snaps on the lights. Half
way across the room Diana stops, hands on her hips, and
turns to face Frank...They look at each other for a long
silent moment....

                              DIANA
          Well.....?

                              FRANK
          Well what?

                              DIANA
          You don't think you're going to
          stay in my room, do you?

                              FRANK
          Don't flatter yourself....

                                   CONTINUED

167.   CONTINUED

He turns quickly and leaves....Diana charges at the
door, and kicks it - she kicks it again and again, then
falls back exhaustedly against it.....Slowly the mad-
dened features turn to a broad grin. She faces the room
defiantly....

                    DIANA
               (silly - drunk)
          Alright little Lucille - Come
          out - Come out - Where ever
          you are......

She runs and goes down beside the bed, lifts the bed
covers.

          Are you under the bed?.....No!

She gets to her feet and goes to the dresser and begins
to pull out drawers....

          In the drawers?......No!

Then she steps back and surveys the room cunningly.....
Then with one finger under her lips and the other up
along her face, she winks one eye....

          Ahh - I know where you are ---
          In the closet....

She runs across the room and puts her hand on the door-
knob.....

168.   CLOSE SHOT - INSIDE CLOSET DOOR

The scene opens on the closed door. The door opens.
Diana's laughing face fills the screen. The smile
quickly fades. Her hand goes to her mouth. She drops
to the floor out of the camera's eye.

                              FADE TO:

169.   INT. LIBRARY - MEDIUM WIDE ANGLE - STORM - NIGHT

Paula, the cute little maid, again in her uniform enters
the library. She goes to the liquor cabinet and starts
to clear the glasses from it. Dr. Acula opens the door
carefully - making no sound. He comes in and moves

                              CONTINUED

169.   CONTINUED

cautiously up behind Paula who hasn't heard him enter.
When in position, Dr. Acula coughs. Paula spins around.
Her hand goes to her mouth as she squeels lightly.

                    DR. ACULA
                (apologetic)
            I frightened you.....

                    PAULA
            You fair scared the daylights
            outta' me..

                    DR. ACULA
            I'm sorry. I wonder if you would
            do something for me?

                    PAULA
            That depends!

                    DR. ACULA
            You liked Miss Lucille, didn't
            you....?

                    PAULA
            When she was alive -- she was a
            real friend.

                    DR. ACULA
            Good!

                    PAULA
            What's that got to do with it?

                    DR. ACULA
            You'd like to see Miss Lucille's
            murderer caught, wouldn't you?

                    PAULA
                (eyes wide in
                 real surprise)
            Murderer.......

                                    DISSOLVE TO:

170.   INT. BARBARA'S BEDROOM - MEDIUM CLOSE

Barbara wears a sheer negligee and night dress as she
is seated on the edge of the bed. She puts on a pair
of fur mules, then moves across the room to a side
connecting door. She knocks.

                      BARBARA
                (calling)
      Lake.....

                      LAKE (o.s.)
      Yes.....

He opens the door and they stand in the doorway as they
galk. Lake is in his pajamas and robe.

                      BARBARA
      Lake - I've been thinking!

                      LAKE
      What about.

171.   CLOSE SHOT - BARBARA

                      BARBARA
      Aunt Lucille's death - the tele-
      phone - a lot of things -- If
      the telephone had been here she
      might have called for help ---
      What do you make of Dr. Acula?

172.   CLOSE TWO SHOT

                      LAKE
      Dr. Acula is a man of great
      learning.

                      BARBARA
      He has such a cold appearance
      about him.

                      LAKE
      I suppose most men of his profession
      have that cold, calculating appear-
      ance. They know so much about things
      strange to us....

                      CONTINUED

172.   CONTINUED

> BARBARA
> A little while ago when he looked
> at me I got cold chills....
>
> LAKE
> Just your immagination.
>
> BARBARA
> It's more than immagination. I
> admit it's hard to explain. But
> it's more than immagination...Was
> it immagination that Uncle Flinch
> died under mysterious circumstances?
> Was it immagination that we found
> Emma with a knife in her heart?
> They're awfully dead if it was....
>
> LAKE
> Just what do you think of your
> relatives?
>
> BARBARA
> How do you mean that?
>
> LAKE
> You and I have been going together
> a long time. I remember when
> Lucille first told you she was
> going to marry Judson. You were
> very much against it.
>
> BARBARA
> I thought he was only after her
> money. But I changed my mind
> when I met him.
>
> LAKE
> (pointedly)
> Yes -- You did.
>
> BARBARA
> What has that got to do with it?
>
> LAKE
> Perhaps you form your opinions of
> people too early -- without really
> knowing them.

CONTINUED

172.   CONTINUED

                              BARBARA
          Dr. Acula?

173.   CLOSE SHOT - LAKE

                              LAKE
                    Dr. Acula! -- Forget it now,
                    darling - Let's get some rest -
                    Tomorrow we'll leave here. Let
                    them worry about their spooks....
                    Everything will look differently
                    when the sun shines again.....

174.   MEDIUM WIDE

          Barbara moves in closer to him and he takes her in his
          arms.

                              BARBARA
                    I suppose you're right, Lake.

          He kisses her lightly, then with a re-assuring pat, he
          propells her back towards her bed.

                              LAKE
                    Of course I am.

          He turns and shuts the door part way as Barbara goes to
          her bed and removes her fur slippers and climbs into
          the bed. She turns off the night light as we......

                                        DISSOLVE TO:

175.   INT. FRANK'S BEDROOM - MEDIUM CLOSE - NIGHT

          On Frank in bed reading a book. He is propped up on a
          stack of pillows. There is a knock at the door. Frank
          drops the book and jumps to a sitting position on the
          edge of the bed. He has become frantically nervous. He
          tries to control himself as he struggles for speech.

                              FRANK
                    Yes....? Who is it?

                                        CONTINUED

175.   CONTINUED

                              PAULA (o.s.)
                    It's me, sir.....Paula....

                              FRANK
                    Ohhh! - Just a moment, please....

176.   MEDIUM WIDE ANGLE

         Frank fumbles into his leather slippers which lie be-
         side the bed, then struggles into a flannel robe which
         lays over the foot of the bed. He ties the robe around
         his middle as he moves to the door. He takes the chain
         from the hook, then turns the key in the lock, takes
         hold of the door knob and pulls the door inward.....

177.   MEDIUM CLOSE

         The door is opening to reveal Paula. She steps into
         the room, putting her finger to her lip for silence as
         she shuts the door behind her. When it is closed she
         turns back on Frank.

                              FRANK
                    Isn't it rather late for.....?

                              PAULA
                       (cutting in)
                    Shush!!! Dr. Acula sent me to
                    get you.

                              FRANK
                    Ohh!!!

                              PAULA
                    He has an idea how to catch the
                    vampire.

                              FRANK
                    Ohh!!!

                              PAULA
                    He needs your help.

                              FRANK
                    Why me?.

                                        CONTINUED

177.   CONTINUED

                    PAULA
        Because, sir, you're an under-
        taker -- It's part of his plan.

                    FRANK
        I see --- Where is Dr. Acula now?

                    PAULA
        In the library, sir.

                    FRANK
        I'll dress right away and get the
        others.

                    PAULA
                (quickly)
        No!!!

                    FRANK
                (puzzled)
        No?

                    PAULA
        There is no use disturbing the
        others - He said they can be
        help for the moment.

                    FRANK
        Ohh - I see - Tell Dr. Acula
        I'll be along directly.

                    PAULA
        Yes, sir....Dr. Acula thought
        you'd feel this way.

She turns from him and opens the door. She looks out
into the hall, then turns back to face Frank once more.

                    PAULA
        You will hurry, sir?

                    FRANK
        I most certainly will....

She steps out into the hall again and is gone. Frank
closes the door and turns the key in the lock. For a
long moment he stands facing the door in deep thought,
then he turns, loosening the belt of his robe as if he
is about to change.....

                    FADE TO:

178.   INT. LIBRARY - MEDIUM WIDE - NIGHT

        Dr. Acula stands alone in the library as Frank enters.
        Frank closes the door as he comes in. Dr. Acula goes
        to him./

                        DR. ACULA
                Ahh - my friend - you dressed
                quickly.

179.   MEDIUM CLOSE TWO

                        FRANK
                The sooner we put Lucille in the
                world of the dead - the real dead --
                the happier everyone will be....

                        DR. ACULA
                    (almost
                        jokingly)
                And safer....eh?

                        FRANK
                What is your plan?

                        DR. ACULA
                I will tell you on the spot

180.   CLOSE SHOT - FRANK

                        FRANK
                What do you mean --- on the spot?

181.   CLOSE SHOT - DR. ACULA

                        DR. ACULA
                Err....Yes....Her tomb.

182.   CLOSE TWO

                        FRANK
                Ohh!!! But - but how do you
                know she's in the tomb?

                                        CONTINUED

182.   CLOSE TWO

                         DR. ACULA
            In a short while it will be day-
            light - She must return to her
            coffin - otherwise she would be
            destroyed by the first rays of
            sunlight.....

                         FRANK
            I see - when do we get started?

                         DR. ACULA
            Immediately.

                         FRANK
            I'll get my coat.

                         DR. ACULA
            Yes - Do - The rain has stopped,
            but it has left a strong chill
            in the air.

183.   MEDIUM WIDE ANGLE

            Frank leaves the room and almost immediately returns
            putting on his coat as he walks. They quickly make
            their way to the French windows.

                         DR. ACULA
            It is best to go the shortest way.

            They move through the French windows.

184.   EXT. LIBRARY FRENCH WINDOWS - MEDIUM CLOSE - NIGHT -
              . WIND.

            They come through the French windows. Frank pauses
            and looks back into the house. Dr. Acula turns to him
            quickly.

185.   CLOSE SHOT - DR. ACULA

                         DR. ACULA
            If we are to finish our work we
            must hurry....The night grows
            short.....

Gary D. Rhodes   269

186.   CLOSE SHOT - FRANK

He is startled back into the present.

                    FRANK
          Ohh!!! - Yes - Of course...

187.   MEDIUM CLOSE

THEY MOVE OUT of the scene towards the cemetery.

                                   DISSOLVE TO:

188.   EXT. CEMETERY - MEDIUM LONG SHOT - NIGHT

The two dark figures move through the maze of headstones, brush and trees. Dr. Aucla's cape whips out
like great bat wings behind him as he moves along. It
would appear like the dark silhouette of a man walking
behind the silhouette of a great bat.

                                   DISSOLVE TO:

189.   INT. BARBARA'S BEDROOM - MEDIUM CLOSE

Lake is seated at the window looking out over the
grounds. He smokes a cigarette. The smoke in the
extremely dark droom is shown lazily slipping up into
the air by the light afforded from the windiw. Suddenly
Lake moves his head forward as if to see more clearly
out into the night. Then he gets to his feet, pushing
his chair away from his legs as he stands up for even
more strained sight into the darkness. In moving the
chair back so suddenly it has made a sharp scraping
sound on the floor.

190.   CLOSE SHOT - BARBARA

In bed as the scraping of the chair has awakened her.
She sits bolt upright. Her quickly searching eyes find
the dark shadow of Lake at the window.

                    BARBARA
          Who's there?

191.   CLOSE SHOT - LAKE

He turns to face her.

LAKE
I'm sorry I woke you - it's
me....Lake.....

192.   CLOSE SHOT - BARBARA

Getting into her negligee and fur mules.

BARBARA
Oh, Lake - You scared the life
out of me - What are you doing
in here?

193.   CLOSE SHOT

LAKE
I didn't want anyone sneaking
in your window again - Thought
I'd stick the night out in this
chair.....Then I saw something
out by the tomb.

194.   WIDE ANGLE

Taking in Barbara as she stands up, slips into her
mules and crosses the room to Lake.

BARBARA
What is it?

195.   CLOSE TWO SHOT

LAKE
I couldn't make it out -- I'm
sure someone is out there.

Barbara looks out of the window, straining her eyes into
the darkness.

BARBARA
I don't see anything.

CONTINUED

195.   CONTINUED

                              LAKE
              Who ever it was is gone now --
              It's all very strange.

                              BARBARA
              Could it have been Lucille?

                              LAKE
              I couldn't tell.

                              BARBARA
              Perhaps it's Boris coming back.

                              LAKE
              He'd be way out of his way in
              coming through the cemetery.

Lake suddeny realizes something he has said. His eyes
go wide....

                              BARBARA
              What happened?

                              LAKE
              I just realized something. According
              to the others, when Dr. Acula showed
              up at the tomb he said his car had
              gotten stuck on the road.

                              BARBARA
              It is only natural with the roads
              in the condition they are.

196.   CLOSE SHOT - LAKE

                              LAKE
              But - he came through the cemetery.
              If his car had been stuck on the
              road as he said, he'd of had to
              go five miles along the lake to
              hit the cemetery and come in the
              way he did -- Five miles out of
              his way....Something tells me the
              pieces are going to start fitting
              together......

197.   WIDE ANGLE

Lake turns away from the window and heads across the
room towards his own bedroom.

                    BARBARA
              Where are you going?

                    LAKE
              To get dressed.

Lake moves towards the bedroom, stripping off his robe
as he moves.....Barbara turns and prepares to take off
her negligee.....

                              DISSOLVE TO:

198.   INT. TOMB - MEDIUM CLOSE - NIGHT

Frank and Dr. Acula stand quite close to Lucille's
closed coffin. Frank is extremely nervous. He wrings
his hands. Dr. Acula smiles at the uneasiness of the
man.....

                    DR. ACULA
              You are nervous?

                    FRANK
              Anyone would be in these cir-
              cumstances. How much longer
              are we to wait?

Dr. Acula turns to the coffin. He rests his hands on
the closed lid as he talks.

                    DR. ACULA
              It will not be long now.

                    FRANK
              You seem to know more than you
              are willing to tell.

                    DR. ACULA
              Perhaps...

Dr. Acula opens the coffin. Frank re-acts.....

199.   CLOSE SHOT - INTO COFFIN

Lucille lays in the coffin as we have seen her before.

200.   CLOSE SHOT - FRANK

His eyes wide - his face pale.

                    FRANK
          But - she's there -- the vampire --
               (change of
                pace)
          What's this all about....?

201.   MEDIUM CLOSE

Dr. Acula looks into the coffin as he speaks.

                    DR. ACULA
          It was arsnic poisoning, wasn't
          it?

                    FRANK
          What are you saying?

Dr. Acula slowly lowers the lid of the coffin back into
place. He turns to face Frank again.

                    DR. ACULA
          Lucille was killed by arsnic
          poisoning - It is quite apparent.

                    FRANK
          She - she - she died of a heart
          attack. Judson signed the death
          certificate.

                    DR. ACULA
          False certificates have been
          signed before....

                    FRANK
          Ahhh, Now wait a minute -- you
          can't pin this on me....

                              CONTINUED

201.   CONTINUED

                              DR. ACULA
                    There's enough proof of guilt to
                    hang you many times. However -
                    once will be enough! But you
                    won't be lonely.

                              FRANK
                    You're bluffing.

                              DR. ACULA
                    Am I?

                              FRANK
                    No - I guess you're not.

Frank suddenly pulls a gun. He backs up a step or two
away from Dr. Acula.

                              FRANK
                    You aren't going to spoil this
                    thing now.

                              DR. ACULA
                    Someone already has.

                              FRANK
                    You can't scare me with any-
                    more of your ghosts.....I'm
                    leaving now -- You have only
                    until I reach that door to
                    live....

Frank backs up a step or two. A shot is fired through
the opened doorway. Frank is spun around by the bullet.
He stumbles back to lean against the coffin. He is
dying. But still holds the gun on the empty door. Dr.
Acula is poised - looking to the big black hole which
is the tomb doorway.

202.   CLOSE SHOT - TOMB DOORWAY

A moment longer empty - then, gun still in hand Flinch
Ruppert, appears in the doorway.

203.   MEDIUM CLOSE

Frank stumbles a step or two forward. He can't believe
his eyes. He tries to bring the gun up. Flinch fires
again. Frank doubles up and with one shot from his gun
into the floor, he sinks down. Dr. Acula looks to
Frank, then back to Flinch.

                    DR. ACULA
          You are?

                    FLINCH
          Flinch Ruppert.

                    DR. ACULA
          I am Dr. Acula.

                    FLINCH
          So I've heard...

Flinch moves into the room. His eyes and gun steady on
Dr. Acula.

                    FLINCH
          Looks like I have the upper
          hand in this affair....

                    DR. ACULA
          You still have two share holders
          to dispose of....

Flinch walks to one of the coffin drawers in the wall.
He slides it out. He looks into the box, then turns
smiling to Dr. Acula and indicates that he should also
look into the box.

                    FLINCH
          Only one, Dr. Acula.

Dr. Acula moves to look into the coffin drawer.....

204.   CLOSE SHOT - INTO COFFIN DRAWER

Diana's body is seen, -- dead.

205.   MEDIUM CLOSE

Flinch shuts the drawer - turns to face Dr. Acula.

                              CONTINUED

205.   CONTINUED

                              DR. ACULA
                    You have been very thorough.

                              FLINCH
                    I had to be...

                              DR. ACULA
                    Then I am right in assuming Boris
                    Ruppert is also dead?

                              FLINCH
                    Boris thought he had all the
                    brains in this family....In
                    the beginning it was all his
                    idea - he selected a suitable
                    subject - Lucille - She was a
                    client of his -- Judson became
                    her husband - He always did have
                    a smooth line with the ladies...
                    She was to be killed and we would
                    all share in her estate.....A
                    great plan - but I out witted them
                    all -- Yes, Dr. Acula - I killed
                    Boris - and the others -- Emma -
                    Diana.....
                         (points to
                         Frank)
                    .....Frank....I always liked
                    Frank - He was opposed to this
                    thing from the beginning....Too
                    bad it had to end this way....
                    My plan was the better one....

                              DR. ACULA
                    We might also apply the word
                    "clever" to your operation....

                              JUDSON (o.s.)
                    I wouldn't use the word too
                    loosely, Dr. Acula....

          Dr. Acula and Flinch look to the tomb doorway.

206.   MEDIUM CLOSE - TOMB DOORWAY

          Judson, gun in hand, stands there.

                                        CONTINUED

206.   CONTINUED

                              JUDSON
                You said, "we wonder which one of
                us would outsmart all the others."
                Yes -- It __has__ proved an interesting
                test to our nerves....

He moves forward into the tomb towards the others off
scene.

207.   MEDIUM GROUP

Judson holds his gun on Flinch and Flinch has his gun
leveled on Judson. Both men are tense - realizing that
neither of them now dare fire first.....

                              JUDSON
                You let us believe you were dead
                so you could move freely to kill
                the others - no one would suspect
                you....I did....While searching
                the house for Lucille I discovered
                another pair of your shoes missing --
                and the one which matched the one
                left on the cliff, replaced in
                your closet......

                              FLINCH
                I had no plans of killing you,
                Judson...

                              JUDSON
                   (smiling)
                Of course not - but I won't
                turn my back, if you don't mind.

                              FLINCH
                But you're my brother -- We split
                fifty-fifty, right down the middle.....

Judson shakes his head "no deal"

                              FLINCH
                Ohh - don't like it that way....
                My gun is on you - You're not
                going anyplace....

                                        CONTINUED

207.   CONTINUED

                    JUDSON
               (indicating his
               own gun)
          Neither are you, my dear brother.
          ...This should also prove an
          interesting test to the nerves.

                    FLINCH
          We're not getting anywhere this
          way -- If you'll put your gun
          down, I'll do the same.

                    JUDSON
          You don't sound like the clever
          man, Dr. Acula thinks you are.
          It would be rather silly for
          either of us to put our gun down.

208.   .   CLOSE SHOT - DR. ACULA

                    DR. ACULA
               (smiling)
          Check Mate....

209.   MEDIUM GROUP

        Both men shoot a quick glance to Dr. Acula, but still
        not fully taking their eyes from each other.

                    FLINCH
          Shut up!

                    DR. ACULA
          Nerves, my dear fellow, nerves....

                    FLINCH
          Shut up, or I'll....

                    DR. ACULA
               (cutting in)
          ....kill me - I think not -- at
          least for the moment. You would
          have to take your gun from its
          present target.....

                    JUDSON
          As Dr. Acula said - "Checkmate"

                              CONTINUED

209.   CONTINUED

                              FLINCH
                    We've got to make a deal.

                              JUDSON
                         (sarcastically)
                    Ohh, brother! You've made your
                    deal.

                              LAKE (o.s.)
                         (calling)
                    Who'se out here!!!   Speak up!!!

                              FLINCH
                    Quick - Close that door before
                    they get here.

          Judson automatically re-acts to the command. He turns
          and slams the door closed. The bolt falls into place.
          Flinch's gun speaks just as the door closes. Judson
          never turns around. He slides down the door to the
          floor and is still.

210.   MEDIUM CLOSE

          Flinch walks in to look down at Judson

                              FLINCH
                    He was the only one who had
                    brains enough to stop me --
                    for the moment.....
                         (turns to
                          Dr. Acula)
                    "Clever" is a very good word.
                    It covers a multitude of sins....

211.   MEDIUM CLOSE - REVERSE ANGLE

          From behind Flinch. Dr. Acula has moved so that he
          stands with his back to the coffin. Flinch is facing
          Dr. Acula.

212.   EXT. TOMB - DOOR - MEDIUM CLOSE - NIGHT

          Lake and Barbara run in. Lake tries the door.

                                             CONTINUED

212.   CONTINUED

                    LAKE
          It's locked.

                    BARBARA
          Are you sure they're in there?

                    LAKE
          Those shots came from here.

213.   INT. TOMB - MEDIUM CLOSE - NIGHT

         Flinch still faces Dr. Acula whose back is to the
         coffin.

                    FLINCH
          Now - you present a problem to
          me -- but even that can be
          straightened out....It seems
          my plan has worked perfectly.

                    DR. ACULA
          Almost - but not quite.

         Slowly the coffin lid behind Dr. Acula, starts to open -
         very slowly....

214.   CLOSE SHOT - FLINCH

         His eyes open in surprise - wonderment - the beginning
         of horror.

215.   CLOSE SHOT - COFFIN

         A long, thin hand with long fingernails comes through
         the partially opened coffin.

216.   CLOSE SHOT - FLINCH

         Horrified.

217.   CLOSE SHOT - COFFIN

         It opens. Lucille sits up. Her eyes turn to glare at
         the camera (off scene Flinch).

218.   MEDIUM WIDE

Lucille is seen to be getting out of the coffin. Flinch
suddenly screams, drops his gun and turns to race for
the tomb door. He frantically tries to get the bolt
open. Then he finally does....

219.   EXT. TOMB - MEDIUM GROUP - NIGHT

The tomb door is thrown open. Flinch races out between Lake and Barbara.

                    DR. ACULA (o.s.)
          Stop him.....

                    LAKE
               (shocked)
          Flinch....

Flinch jabs a fist at Lake. It connects knocking the
surprised Lake down. Lake gets to his feet and races
after Flinch who has run off scene. Dr. Acula appears
at the tomb doorway.

220.   EXT. CEMETERY - MEDIUM CLOSE - NIGHT

Flinch runs in - stops - searches like a frightened
rabbit looking for a hole - then runs out of scene.
Lake runs in and out.

221.   EXT. FRONT OF MANSION - WIDE ANGLE - NIGHT

Flinch runs in and out of scene. Lake runs in and out
of scene in pursuit of Flinch.

222.   EXT. GARAGE - MEDIUM CLOSE - NIGHT

Lake catches up with Flinch at the corner of the garage.
Flinch swings. Lake catches the blow on his arm. Lake
lashes out with a powerful right. It catches Flinch on
the jaw knocking him back into the garage. Lake moves
inside after him.

223.　　INT. GARAGE - MEDIUM CLOSE - NIGHT

Flinch gets up to meet Lake's attack....

　　　　　　　(FIGHT SEQUENCE TO BE
　　　　　　　DIRECTED TO THE DIS-
　　　　　　　CRESTION OF THE
　　　　　　　DIRECTOR)

After a powerful right, Flinch stumbles back into a
pile of old tires. They fall on and about him. He is
knocked off balance. With a wild scream he topples
back through the broken gap in the rear wall of the
garage where Boris's car had gone through.

224.　　EXT. REAR OF GARAGE & CLIFF - NIGHT

Flinch's body is seen to go over the cliff.....

225.　　INT. GARAGE - CLOSE SHOT - NIGHT

Lake is staring down towards the bottom of the off
scene cliff. He is tired from his fight.

　　　　　　　　　　　　　　　　　FADE TO:

226.　　INT. TOMB - WIDE ANGLE - DAY

Several deputy sheriff's in khaki uniforms are at work
in the tomb. Also in evident, in their own group are
Dr. Acula, Lake and Barbara standing near the entrance.
As the scene opens two uniformed deputies have lifted
a covered stretcher which holds Diana's body. Another
uniformed man pushes the empty coffin drawer back into
the wall with the others. As Diana's covered body is
carried out, the Sheriff enters. He goes directly to
Dr. Acula.

　　　　　　　　　SHERIFF
　　　　Heard back in town you were in
　　　　on this -- Can't you private
　　　　detectives ever find a case that
　　　　ain't all cluttered up with
　　　　murdered bodies.....?

227.   CLOSE TWO - LAKE & BARBARA

Surprised, they turn to look at each other.

                    BARBARA
          Private Detective.....?

228.   CLOSE GROUP

The sheriff turns to face them.

                    SHERIFF
          Didn't you folks know....?
               (to Dr. Acula)
          ....Don't tell me I ruined
          your set up....?

Dr. Acula shakes his head "no" then smiles. A deputy
Sheriff comes in. He moves to the Sheriff.

                    1st DEPUTY
          Sheriff?

                    SHERIFF
          What is it, Bill?

                    1st DEPUTY
          The one named Judson is gonna'
          live......

229.   CLOSE TWO - DEPUTY & SHERIFF

                    SHERIFF
          Look's like he'll have to swing
          for all of them -- Where is he?

                    1st DEPUTY
          In the wagon headin' for town.
          Doc. said we had to get him to
          a hospital pronto or he'd never
          reach the hangman.

                    SHERIFF
          Okay -- Get out there and give
          Riley a hand with the dead ones.

                    1st DEPUTY
          Right.

230.   MEDIUM CLOSE GROUP

The 1st Deputy turns and leaves through the tomb door.

> SHERIFF
> Let's have the details, Dr.
> Acula.

> DR. ACULA
> You'll get a full written report --
> a copy of that which I will give
> to my client....However -- my
> client gets the report first.

> SHERIFF
> Just who is this client of yours?

> 2nd DEPUTY (o.s.)
> (shouting)
> Sheriff -- Sheriff -- Look out.
> It's comin' this way....

All turn to look to the tomb door. A 2nd Deputy moves
in quickly. The 2nd Deputy looks to the Sheriff then
points back towards the door.

> SHERIFF
> What is it, Riley?

> RILEY
> It's -- It's a zombie....

> DR. ACULA
> Or, perhaps a vampire....?

Lucille appears at the door. There is a gasp from those
in the room. Dr. Acula moves to her and takes her
lightly by the arm.

> DR. ACULA
> Come in, my dear.....

He leads her across the room towards the others. Barbara
leaves Lake's protecting arm. She moves in close to
Lucille.

231.   CLOSE TWO - BARBARA & VAMPIRE

Barbara looks closely, quizically, at the vampire.

                    BARBARA
          You do resemble, Lucille. But
          now -- up close -- in the day-
          light -- there is something --
          different....

232.   CLOSE SHOT - DR. ACULA

Smiling,

233.   CLOSE TWO - BARBARA & VAMPIRE

                    BARBARA
          Are you -- Are you, Helen?

234.   CLOSE SHOT - VAMPIRE

She reaches up and takes the black wig from her head.
With the wig removed we find a smiling blonde.

235.   CLOSE TWO - DR. ACULA & VAMPIRE

                    DR. ACULA
          Yes - As you now know - this is
          Helen -- Lucille's twin sister.
               (indicates wig)
          ...The wig -- to match the black
          hair of Lucille...

                    HELEN
          Secretly four months ago, Lucille
          and I met - She told me, then, of
          her fears - When she died I knew
          it was murder - but I had no proof.
          I hired Dr. Acula to get that
          proof. Playing the vampire was
          all his idea.

236.   CLOSE SHOT - DR. ACULA

                    DR. ACULA
          From that point it simply became
          the power of suggestion. Lucille's
          coffin was switched for the one
          presently here - and along with
          my electrically charged cape --
          and a good illusion....
                    (indicates
                    Helen)
          ....We were successful.........
          Clever -- am I not...?
                    (smiles)

                                        FADE TO

T H E

                              E N D

COMING SOON
BELA LUGOSI

there are worse things awaiting Man!

FINAL CURTAIN

WRITTEN, PRODUCED, AND DIRECTED BY EDWARD D. WOOD, JR.

CHASTAIN

An imagined movie poster for the unproduced Lugosi film *Final Curtain*, as created for this book by George Chastain in 2016.

Edward D. Wood, Jr.

"FINAL CURTAIN"

3300 Riverside Drive,
Apt 2 E
Burbank,
California

EDWARD D. WOOD, JR.
3300 Riverside Drive,
Apt # 2 E
Burbank, California.

1,511 Words
Short story rights
or Book in group
for "PORTRAITS IN TERROR"

Page One.

" F I N A L   C U R T A I N "

by

Edward D. Wood, Jr.

After hours in the theatre, when cast and crew have gone, long
after the last of the audience has left, a new world appears. That of spirit
and the unseen.

Ever since I had entered this theatre I felt some hidden object was
beckoning me. I must find that object, even though I didn't know what it was.
This night the calling is stronger than ever before. This was to be the night
I had looked forward to with fear, knowing all the time there was nothing I
could do but heed the call. This night when all others had gone.

I leaned against the frame of my dressing room door looking out
across the darkened stage. High in the catwalks a board creaks.

Or perhaps some unseen figure is lurking there?

A guide lamp dies; burned out after many long nights of continous
use.

Has the bulb burned out?

Or has some unseen thing poked a hole through the frosted glass
letting in the infectious air?

A gust of wind pours through an open window. I turn, wide-eyed
with fear.

Is it wind?

Perhaps another spirit entering for a night of pleasure.

A cat screams! Why do I pay attention? The scream is outside ---- I only want to know the sounds inside.

Has it come from within?

Again the screams; like someone in mortal terror; in horrible, unbearable pain. The cries echo and re-echo throughout the theatre ---- or are they echoing in my mind alone.

I clasp my hands over my ears to shut out sound. Even this fails. I must have screamed, my throat feels raw from a sudden violence.

What is this blackness? This blackness where a new world appears? The world of the spirit and the unseen that hide in lofts and dark corners during daylight; the unseen that come from hiding to frolic in the massive auditorium when it is night and they are alone.

They return to die and re-die, live and re-live. I want to experience these spine-tingling sensations. Somewhere outside a bell rings. I move from the comforting lights of my dressing room to stand on the empty stage. I look out over the darkened auditorium. The seats, out front, are as I have seen them night after night while doing my lines on this side of

(Final Curtain - 2)

the footlights. But now, empty, they appear like squatty little fat men standing row on row; like soldiers in formation.

There is a movement in the second balcony - perhaps a seat has fallen on its hinges.....

A creak in the galleries.

Another guide lamp goes out as had its counterpart before.

A chill passes through my body; something races past my feet. A rat? Perhaps!

Suddenly somewhere overhead there is a banging in the pipes. Faint. Startling. Almost impossible. Surely it must have been water caught by something that has finally dislodged itself.

I strain my eyes to pierce even deeper into the darkness but I can see nothing; nothing but the blackness; the outlines of the seats and high ridges that are the balconies hanging like dark thunder clouds over an even darker sky. I cannot tell where space ends and the auditorium walls begin.

Something within draws me from the stage. I want — I must explore further into this deep blackness; to go up those stairs; to see the remaining floors above; to enter into the costume department; the scenery room; the make-up rooms; all the rooms where one may change his appearance to any character nameable, and in many cases — unnameable.

I let my eyes drift until they fall upon the spiral staircase at the right of the stage. I hesitate but a moment, then cautiously

(Final Curtain - 3)

make my way through the darkness to the spiral staircase.

Somewhere above the faint light of the moon drifts through a window giving a bluish tint to the guide rail. I take the guide rail in my hand. It is cold ----- Like the cold of the dead. The moisture from my hand causes the rail to feel clammy, unearthly. It is writhing in my hand like a cold, slimy snake. I jerk my hand away quickly. I stand staring at the metal. After a long moment of silent thought I let my hand return slowly to the railing. This time it does not move.

It couldn't have before....

But.....

I climb slowly. The stairs strain against my weight; louder than I had ever heard them creak before......Or is it again, just my immagination?

Impossible.

The sound is echoing throughout the stage and the darkened auditorium below. I find myself wondering why the creaking is so much louder in the night than during the day. This is another strange mystery that only the night can answer ---- That I must learn.

The second floor.

Dance and rehearsel studio with a long rectangular floor. I stop but a moment, then continue on.

A wind howls outside. I am suddenly cold. The dressing gown I had wrapped about my body feels as thin as if I had nothing at all on.

(Final Curtain - 4)

I should think of other things!

I can't!

How can I think of things, of pleasant things, when I am surrounded by shadows and objects that take shapes in the darkness. Any shape my mind can conceive.

The third floor.

Ten rooms on each side of a long corridor. Twenty rooms. Each with a different setting of costumes, wigs, scenery. The shadowy effect of this passage and its evenly spaced doors provoke a deep impression on my mind, and beads of sweat on my forehead. The knob of the first door feels the same as had the rail on the staircase, but this time I am ready for the clammy sensation. The door opens easily —— without a sound. A window at the back lets the moonlight filter through to permit me to see the silhouette of a woman with long, golden blonde hair. I am startled; unable to move for the moment; then I speak to her.

She doesn't answer!

Again I speak, then realize it is only the dummy of a vampire in her long flowing gown. We had been using it these many weeks in our horror play.

I stand in the doorway staring at this creature. The face beautiful, alive; eyes, wide eyes, staring at me. I walk into the room and let the folds of her silk dress brush against my hand. I lift the flowing sleeve and caress it, then rub the smooth material against my

(Final Curtain - 5)

cheek. Inwardly I know I am smiling, enjoying this new sensation....Can it be some strange love for this earthbound, unearthly creature who can not move or speak?

I let the material fall. For a moment my hand runs over the smooth cheek of this beauty, then I walk back to the doorway where I turn for one last look.

Is she smiling?

Yes!

Her lips are drawn apart and the white teeth shine like phosphorescente. Her arms move; beckoning me return. Return? Return to what?

I slam the door!

I must break this evil spell of the night which seems to have captured my very soul. I couldn't have imagined it. It had been too real. She had smiled. She had motioned for me to return.

I look into each room. I look and hunger to look more. I am not so frightened now. Somewhere off in the darkness I know there is another passage.

How do I know?

I had never seen it.

Never before had I ventured above the second floor.

But I know there is yet another passage and one last room.

I must find that room!

Yes! ——— There it is!

(Final Curtain - 6)

Gary D. Rhodes

I'm almost beside myself with the excitement of it. There is no light in this section of the hall, except that of the moon which again enters through a window. I feel my way along the wall. My pace increases. I move faster, until out of breath. I stand in the doorway, looking across the room to the window. My eyes try to force themselves downward. I want to look to where the moonlight hits upon the floor; but am I ready?

A cloud crosses the face of the moon, and as the shadow falls, my eyes fall with it. Below the window frame is a deeper shadow. I cannot make it out for the moment, but I know it is the object of my search — the reason for my adventure into the darkness this night.

My eyes strain, trying to penetrate this heavy blackness.

As the cloud passes and the moon's rays are again permitted to enter into the room, my eyes light up with sudden eagerness — for at the bottom of the window is the form of a large black coffin.

I walk to it and raise the lid. Slowly — ever so slowly.

In this moment I know that I am going to climb into this cushioned box and permit the lid to close over me — forever ....

T H E

E N D

"FINAL CURTAIN" by
Edward D. Wood, Jr.
Apt #2-E
3300 Riverside Drive,
Burbank, Calif.

(Final Curtain - 7)

Author/Illustrator Dwight Kemper's frontispiece for his novel _The Vampire's Tomb Mystery_, published by Helm in 2011. *(Courtesy of Dwight Kemper)*

Acknowledgments

The authors would like to express gratitude to the following institutions that assisted in the research for this essay: the Billy Rose Theatre Division of the New York Public Library, the Harry Ransom Center at the University of Texas at Austin, the Margaret Herrick Library of the Academy of Motion Picture Arts and Sciences in Beverly Hills, and the Cinematic Arts Library of the University of Southern California in Los Angeles.

The authors would also like to extend sincere thanks to the following individuals who assisted on the research and images for this essay: the late Samuel Z. Arkoff, Matthew E. Banks, Marty "The Astounding B Monster" Baumann, Bob Blackburn, Margaret Borst, Ronald V. Borst, Conrad Brooks, Bob Burns, the late Mark Carducci, Mario Chacon, Bill Chase, Frank Coleman, Ned Comstock, Michael Copner, Richard Daub, Kristin Dewey, Jack Dowler, Theodore Estes, Bambi Everson, Beau Foutz, Fritz Frising, the late Dolores Fuller, Christopher R. Gauthier, Donald F. Glut, the late Alex Gordon, Rudolph Grey, Robert Guffey, Bob Gutowski, Roger Hurlburt, Dwight Kemper, Nancy Kersey, the late Loretta King, Dr. Robert J. Kiss, Michael Kronenberg, Dr. Michael Lee, the late Paul Marco, Michael McCarty, Lisa Mitchell, D'Arcy More, Constantine Nasr, Henry Nicolella, the late Maila Nurmi, Dennis Phelps, Robert Rees, Mary Runser, the late Richard Sheffield, Robert Singer, Marlo Toland, Laura Wagner, David Wentink, Stephen B. Whatley, and Wade Williams.

The authors would like to extend special thanks to Buddy Barnett, who provided copies of the *Ghoul Goes West* and *Vampire's Tomb* scripts reprinted herein, and to Lee R. Harris, who provided the *Final Curtain* treatment herein.

The authors also want to extend their deepest appreciation to George Chastain for creating movie posters for *The Vampire's Tomb*, *The Ghoul Goes West*, and *Final Curtain* especially for this book.

Lastly, the authors wish to acknowledge the help and assistance of the heirs to the Ed Wood estate.

DANGER!... THESE GIRLS ARE HOT!

JAIL BA

Lugosi with Ed Wood
(right) planning projects
that never came to be.

Author Biographies

Gary D. Rhodes, Ph.D., currently serves as Postgraduate Director for Film Studies at the Queen's University in Belfast, Northern Ireland. He is the author of *Lugosi* (McFarland, 1997), *White Zombie: Anatomy of a Horror Film* (McFarland, 2002), *Emerald Illusions: The Irish in Early American Cinema* (IAP, 2012) and *The Perils of Moviegoing in America* (Continuum, 2012). Rhodes is also the writer-director of the documentary films *Lugosi: Hollywood's Dracula* (1997) and *Banned in Oklahoma* (2004). Currently he is at work on a history of the American horror film to 1915, as well as a biography of William Fox.

One of the "leading scholars in the horror field" (*The New York Times*), **Tom Weaver** is a Sleepy Hollow, New York-based researcher. Since 1982 he has interviewed nearly 600 actors, writers, producers, directors, *et al.* for a variety of nationally distributed magazines. His 30 books include *Universal Horrors*, an examination of the studio's classic chillers of the 1930s and 1940s. Weaver has written liner notes and production histories for hundreds of laser discs, DVDs and Blu-rays and provided dozens of DVD audio commentaries, mostly for horror and sci-fi movies. He was inducted into the Rondos' Monster Kid Hall of Fame on March 30, 2011.

Robert Cremer was born in Chicago, but has spent a good part of his life as journalist and writer in other parts of the world – as a freelancer in East Asia, syndicated columnist for *The Hollywood Reporter*, and Senior Lecturer at the University of Bayreuth in Bavaria for creative writing. He is the author of *Lugosi: The Man Behind the Cape* (Henry Regnery, 1976). His latest project is a German-language work deciphering the hidden meaning in the lyrics to blues songs.

Lee R. Harris is a Hollywood historian who co-produced and hosted the Ed Wood documentary *Flying Saucers Over Hollywood: The Plan 9 Companion* (1992). His work has appeared in *Cult Movies* and *Bam* magazines, and as a voice actor can be heard in over 30 feature films (including *Men in Black* in 1997), and cartoons and commercials. Lee lives in Burbank, California, with his wife Jana and still tracks down Ed Wood's Hollywood.

JUL 2021

CPSIA information can be obtained
at www.ICGtesting.com
Printed in the USA
LVHW061534150621
690287LV00007B/336